WALKS INTO HISTORY
SURREY

David Weller

COUNTRYSIDE BOOKS
NEWBURY BERKSHIRE

First published 2008
© David Weller, 2008

COUNTRYSIDE BOOKS
3 Catherine Road
Newbury, Berkshire

To view our complete range of books,
please visit us at
www.countrysidebooks.co.uk

ISBN 978 1 84674 065 7

Maps, photographs and illustrations
by the author (unless otherwise stated)

Designed by Peter Davies
Produced through MRM Associates Ltd., Reading
Typeset by CJWT Solutions, St Helens
Printed in Thailand

*All material for the manufacture of this book
was sourced from sustainable forests*

Contents

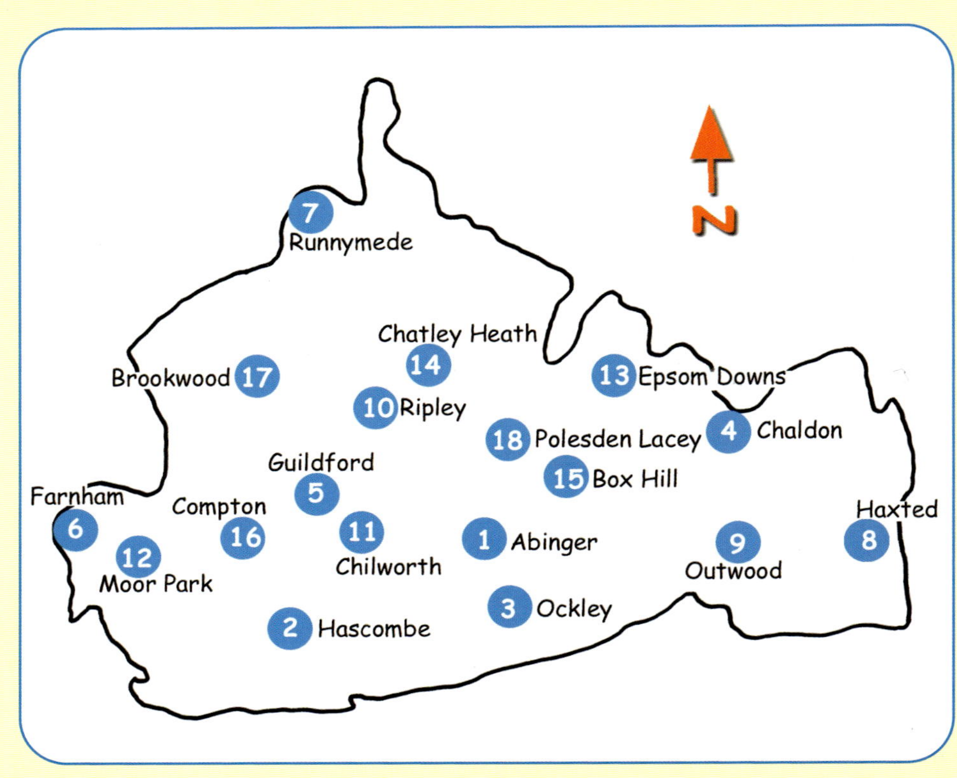

AREA MAP SHOWING LOCATION OF THE WALKS

PUBLISHER'S NOTE

We hope that you obtain considerable enjoyment from this book; great care has been taken in its preparation. Although at the time of publication all routes followed public rights of way or permitted paths, diversion orders can be made and permissions withdrawn.

We cannot, of course, be held responsible for such diversion orders and any inaccuracies in the text which result from these or any other changes to the routes nor any damage which might result from walkers trespassing on private property. We are anxious though that all details covering the walks are kept up to date and would therefore welcome information from readers which would be relevant to future editions.

The simple sketch maps that accompany the walks in this book are based on notes made by the author whilst checking out the routes on the ground. They are designed to show you how to reach the start, to point out the main features of the overall circuit and they contain a progression of numbers that relate to the paragraphs of the text.

However, for the benefit of a proper map, we do recommend that you purchase the relevant Ordnance Survey sheet covering your walk. The Ordnance Survey maps are widely available, especially through booksellers and local newsagents.

INTRODUCTION

Much of early Surrey was covered by an impenetrable Wealden forest, which led to Britain's ancient history largely bypassing the county. The Romans first cut through the forest with an impressive road that linked Chichester and their port of Fishbourne to London, although it was left to the Saxons to name this beautiful area south of the river Thames as *Suthrige*, thereby bringing into being the county that we know today.

Surrey's interior remained largely dormant for almost 800 years until it was finally opened up by the building of turnpike roads and the invention of the railway, but great change was to come. In 1888 an area bordering the Thames stretching from Deptford to Wandsworth was ceded to London with the loss of Southwark, Lambeth, Bermondsey, Battersea, Brixton, Camberwell, Dulwich and Clapham, while in 1965 Richmond, Kew, Kingston, Wimbledon, Sutton, Mitcham, Merton, Morden and Croydon were also overcome by the capital. Other than Middlesex, I know of no other county that has undergone so much change in modern times!

What is left of Surrey after having these towns wrenched from its clasp is, very fortunately, a great joy to explore, an asset on which these enthralling walks capitalise as they lead you through its fascinating history, both ancient and modern. I have begun this collection with a circuit that takes in the Mesolithic period and ended it with a route with an Edwardian flavour, while in between lies a variety of delightful walks covering subjects as diverse as castles, canals, the Magna Carta, watermills, windmills, gunpowder, horse racing and the arts.

Each route is circular, and clear directions are given of how to find the beginning of the walk and where to park, with a recommendation for a suitable place for refreshments along the way. My maps are drawn to scale and numbers refer to each paragraph of the walk directions, although they are no substitute for the Ordnance Survey map that I also recommend as these give a better oversight of the surrounding area.

Please respect the sites that you visit, always remember the country code and above all, have a great time walking through Surrey's captivating history and exquisite countryside.

David Weller

THE MESOLITHIC MEN OF ABINGER

Length: 6¼ miles

The 11th-century motte at Abinger

HOW TO GET THERE: Abinger Roughs is easiest found by turning north at a crossroads on the A25 beside Crossways Farm, 3¾ miles west of Dorking. Follow the narrow road to meet the car park on the left in ¼ mile.

PARKING: Abinger Roughs National Trust car park.

MAP: OS Landranger 187 (GR 110479).

INTRODUCTION

This undulating circuit is fairly energetic but is eminently suitable for a family walk. After beginning in the pristine woodlands that lie below the North Downs, the way soon meets ancient Paddington Farm and follows a cart track through its fields to the top of the valley, where the views are outstanding. The circuit then continues through the hamlet of Sutton Abinger where it follows a sunken lane that leads to the ancient village of Abinger and its village green, the turning point of the walk. More farm tracks and field paths with panoramic views follow as the way heads for the pretty village of Abinger Hammer. After a short climb from the village the circuit soon rejoins the woodland to complete this superb walk.

HISTORICAL BACKGROUND

During 1948, Major Beddington Behrens, then owner of Abinger Manor, began finding worked flints in the ten-acre field that lies behind the manor house. All were discovered on the surface after ploughing and, being an enthusiastic but amateur archaeologist, he thoughtfully kept notes on what he found, indicating that they were mainly concentrated on one small area. By 1950, realising that the

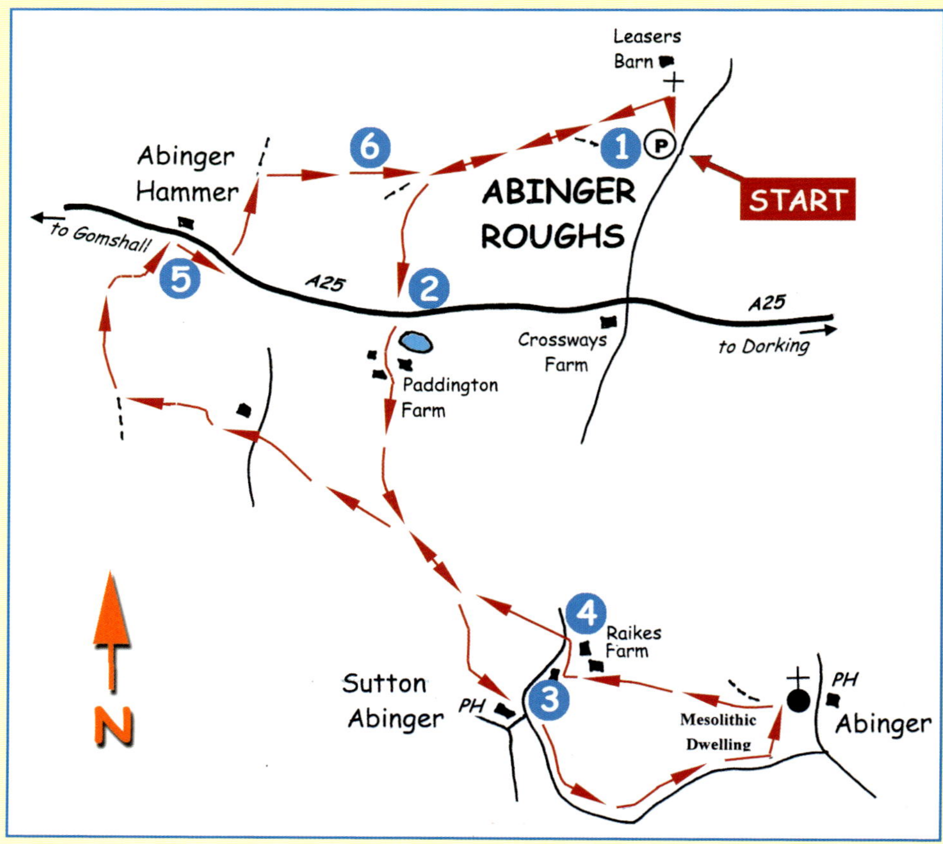

project was becoming too large and important for an amateur, he asked the Surrey Archaeological Society if they would investigate his finds.

Important they certainly proved to be for, unlike other finds of Mesolithic habitation around Surrey, these indicated far more than the temporary hunting camps found previously. Mesolithic man lived in the middle period of the Stone Age, between 8,500 BC and 4,000 BC, at a time when man fashioned flint and bone tools with great skill. He was a successful hunter gatherer living in small, generally nomadic groups, existing on wild boar, deer, fruits, fish and fungi.

Trial excavations at Abinger were begun, led by no lesser person than the renowned anthropologist and archaeologist Dr L. S. B. Leakey, and trenches were dug with enthusiasm. Results were initially disappointing, however, as at first it seemed that many centuries of deep ploughing had disturbed the sub-soil. Not to be put off, the archaeologists continued with further trenches and stone implements began to be found in increasing numbers until, finally, on the eleventh day, eureka! Right in the middle of the greatest concentration of flint tools, they made the discovery of a pit dwelling.

With careful and painstakingly slow excavation they found well-preserved evidence of post holes and a small hearth, while tool implements made from very small flints, known as microliths, proved that it was inhabited by people of the Horsham Culture who had developed this type of microlith called the Horsham Point around 5,000 BC. The depth of the pit was around one metre and with posts supporting layers of branches and foliage above ground, it was believed to have had a head height of 2.5 metres. The pit dwelling was ideally sited as it lay in the sheltered lea of a hill and just a short walk from a spring. Putting all the facts together, archaeologists believe that it is unlikely to be the only Mesolithic pit dwelling in the field, which must make Abinger rate as the oldest permanently inhabited village in Britain. (The pit dwelling is on private property with no public access.)

THE WALK

① With your back to the road, follow a well-worn path near the far end of the car park that leaves to the right. Go up a low incline, pass a picnic table and continue downhill to a large granite cross.

The monument marks the spot where Samuel Wilberforce met his untimely end while out riding in 1873 when his horse stumbled on a rabbit hole and threw him fatally to the ground. He was the Bishop of Winchester but his followers knew him as 'Soapy Sam'; his father was that great man William Wilberforce who did so much to abolish slavery.

Soapy Sam acquired the nickname from his skill of slipperiness during arguments that the Anglican Church was going through at the time; never seemingly coming down on one side or the other. One great debate that he did take sides on, though, regarded his, and the Church's, outrage at Charles Darwin's ideas on evolution. His greatest opponent was Thomas Huxley and before an audience of 700 they slugged it out. To undermine Huxley's case, Wilberforce asked whether Huxley was descended from an ape on his grandfather's side or his grandmother's side. The retort came back from Huxley that he was not ashamed of his ancestry, but that 'he would be ashamed to be connected with a man who used great gifts to obscure the truth'. The suggestion that he would rather have an ape as an ancestor than a bishop caused uproar among the audience. Neither man won the argument that day but the event became a turning point for those who promoted Darwin's theory.

Go left at the cross and continue on a well-worn track that leads through majestic woodland. After climbing a rise the track passes through a clearing and at the far side you should fork left to meet a gate in 60 yards. Pass through the gate, and a second at the far side of a meadow and continue downhill between banks to reach the A25 main road.

2   Cross the A25 and press on along a farm drive signed as a bridleway where you pass between a fishing lake and Paddington Mill, now a bijou residence. Continue on the drive between the barns of Paddington Farm and turn left and right beside the old farmhouse, remaining on the signed bridleway. The bridleway now begins a steady climb between pretty hedgerows and meets a directional post at the top. Continue ahead to another post in 120 yards and then go left for 30 yards before turning right along the left edge of a large field. At the field end, continue ahead between banks and go left at a gateway on a track to meet with a lane. Turn right here to meet the Volunteer pub in 50 yards.

The name Paddington translates to the 'Valley of Pada'; a Saxon landlord.

3   The route turns left on a lane opposite the Volunteer and immediately passes the gates of Water Lane House. Keep to this sunken lane that is so characteristic of Surrey and later pass the entrance to Abinger Manor where a glance over the field leftwards shows the wooden building under which the Mesolithic pit dwelling is preserved. After 80 yards, turn left onto Abinger's village green and continue alongside the cemetery to meet the lych gate. The Abinger Arms is to your right while the village stocks are ahead of you.

The ancient village name of Abinger derives from the Saxon 'farm of Abba's people'. The more recent village of Abinger Hammer grew up around the medieval iron industry and the hammer pond.
*   The 13th-century church, having suffered from the heavy hands of Victorian 'restorers', was badly damaged by a flying bomb during the Second World War and by fire in 1964.*

The route passes through the pretty village of Abinger Hammer

Go left here alongside the church and soon exit on a fenced path that passes close to the ancient motte in the grounds of Abinger Manor on your left.

This motte is evidence of occupation during the 11th century and excavations found post holes, proving that the man-made hill was topped by a wooden stockade.

At a cattle grid, ignore a path forking right and go ahead along the top of the ridge where in the field to your left the covering of the Mesolithic pit dwelling comes into view. When a farm track bends right towards buildings, keep ahead on a track between hedgerows. Follow this track when it later bends sharply right and pass between the buildings of Raikes Farm to meet with a lane.

4   Cross the lane, enter the field opposite and in 15 yards, bear diagonally right across the centre of the field and pass through the tree line at the far side. Here you rejoin a small section of the outward route. Go ahead and turn right in 30 yards to meet a directional post in 120 yards. Now leave your earlier path by forking left on a footpath through fields where you follow the line of overhead cables. Keep to the path and when it meets a lane, continue ahead on a narrow path opposite that skirts a large garden. At a stile, go ahead over a field keeping to the left of a line of trees. Turn right along the field edge and at a directional post in 180 yards go left here to join a sunken bridleway, which you follow rightwards to its end by the gate of Brook Cottage. Turn right along a drive to meet the A25.

REFRESHMENTS

Around the halfway point the route passes the Volunteer (tel. 01306 730798) and the Abinger Arms (tel. 01306 730145), both good pubs for food, while at Abinger Hammer the Abinger Tea Rooms are highly recommended.

5   The way now continues rightwards alongside the A25 and enters Abinger Hammer. Here the route is left on a lane between the Abinger Arms and the unique village clock, but you may wish to explore the village green a few yards ahead of you, and perhaps visit the popular Abinger Tea Rooms. Continue up the lane beside the village clock and at the crest of the rise turn right on a signed bridleway.

6   The way continues ahead along a wide track that soon meets with the outward route. From here all you have to remember is to keep left at a fork and turn right when the Wilberforce memorial is reached.

THE IRON AGE MEN OF HASCOMBE

Length: 4¾ miles

The ramparts of the Iron Age hill fort

HOW TO GET THERE: Hascombe is on the B2130 3½ miles south-east of Godalming.

PARKING: When travelling from the Godalming direction, Mare Lane is on the right and signposted to the village hall. Park at the roadside.

MAP: OS Landranger 186 (GR 997398).

INTRODUCTION

This superb walk, it should be said, is a little energetic but not too taxing. Beginning in the lovely village of Hascombe the circuit follows a bridleway alongside rolling fields and through majestic woodland to reach wonderful

Scotsland Farm. Here the route joins a broad track that offers fantastic views over this remote part of Surrey and brings you to Hascombe Hill. After a short climb, the way continues along the top of the hill where the path circumnavigates the ramparts of the ancient hill fort. From these giddy heights, a downhill path brings you to the oldest part of Hascombe village where seats around the scenic pond make it a great place to picnic.

HISTORICAL BACKGROUND

The Iron Age is the last of the three-age system used for classifying prehistoric societies, the Stone Age being the first and the Bronze Age the second. In Britain the Iron Age began at around 700 BC and continued until Roman occupation in AD 43. For defence these early peoples often constructed hill forts; the first seem

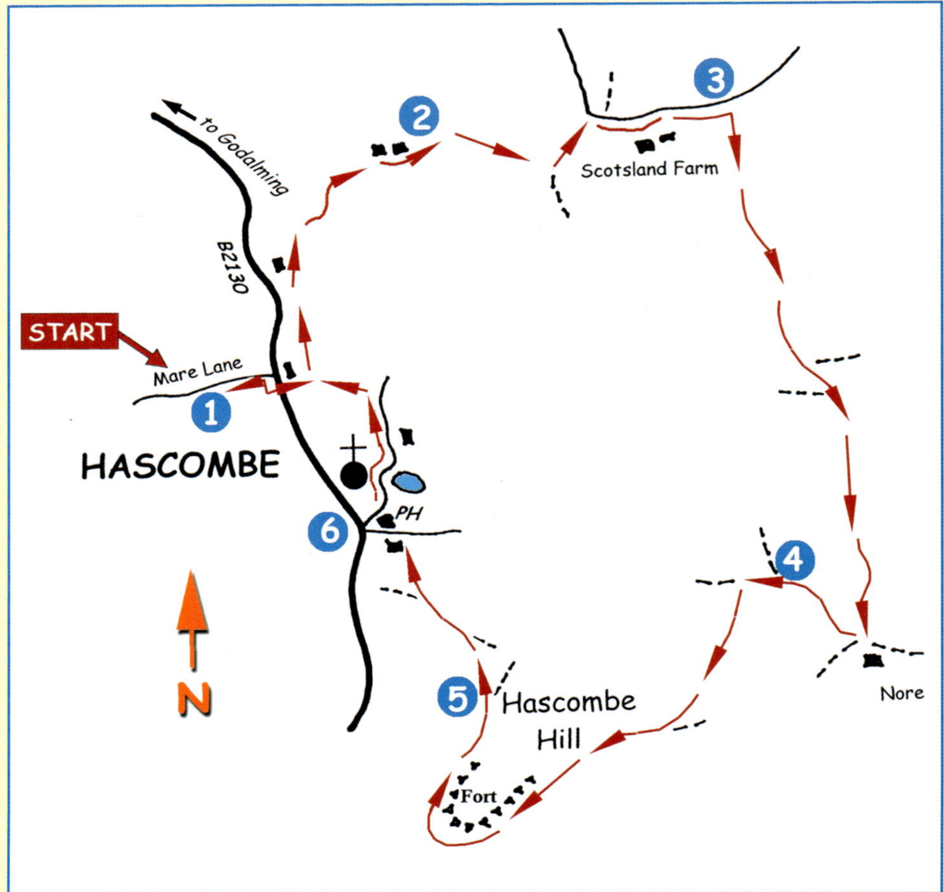

to have been erected by Bronze Age man although the great era for building hill forts came towards the end of the Iron Age period.

Iron Age man was very adept at recognising defensive positions that, with a little help from themselves, would offer protection from marauding tribes during times of trouble. The classic inland hill fort consisted of a promontory with three naturally steep sides where the addition of defensive earthworks would make attack difficult. The fourth side containing the entrance was protected by artificial ramparts made from stone and wood. Several hill forts of this type exist in Surrey: Holmbury above Ewhurst, Anstiebury near Holmwood, St Georges Hill at Weybridge, Dry Hill near Dormansland and this one at Hascombe.

As Iron Age civilisation developed, tensions between tribes sometimes arose and a group would withdraw into the enclosure for protection. These defensive positions had other uses during times of peace and could show the wealth of the tribe as well as acting as corrals for their cattle, administrative centres and even as places of worship. The largest might enclose a small village while the smallest would offer protection to just a single homestead or two.

Iron Age hill forts in Britain proved no match for the invading Roman armies although a few, it seems, remained in use as settlements for the new Romano-Britons. Others were turned into garrisons during the Roman occupation, but the majority were either destroyed or abandoned. After the Romans left Britain, some hill forts were restored and re-occupied as protection from Anglo-Saxon invaders, who in turn sought refuge in them from waves of invading Vikings. As peace eventually fell across Britain, the hill tops were abandoned and the people moved to the more hospitable valleys below, as here in Hascombe.

THE WALK

1 Walk back to the B2130 and turn right to meet the village spring in 30 yards.

Many of the villagers prefer drinking the water that issues from this spring than that piped to their homes.

Cross the road to a path beside Fountain Cottage and follow it to soon meet a T-junction with a bridleway. Go left here and soon ignore a bridleway to your left. Continue ahead, pass stabling and ignore another bridleway to the left. The bridleway narrows now and continues alongside rolling fields with majestic woodland on your left.

2 After passing a couple of isolated houses the way makes a short steady climb through woodland and meets with the Greensands Way long-distance path. Fork left here on the signed GW path that goes downhill and remain on it as it bends to the left and ends at a quiet lane. Turn right along the lane and pass by the beautiful buildings of Scotsland Farm.

Hascombe's scenic village pond

Recorded as Scottyslond in 1524 and Scotchland in 1684, the farm is named after the family of a John Scot who originally lived here.

❸ Continue on the lane until a signed bridleway is met on your right. Follow this lovely bridleway for 1 mile and ignore all side paths, as it leads you along the bottom of the hill with panoramic views. Finally, after passing through woodland the bridleway meets a junction of paths by a gate with a cottage beyond. Turn right here and when the path soon divides by a tennis court, go right on an uphill bridleway.

❹ At the crest of the hill keep ahead and continue downhill for 45 yards to meet a signed footpath on your left. Follow this path and when it divides either side of a beech tree with several trunks, keep left. The path leads you along the top of the ridge and you should ignore all side paths. Some 20 yards after passing a massive beech tree to your left that has large boughs reaching down the slope, keep left at a fork to reach the wooded ramparts of Hascombe hill fort. The path now circles the hill fort where you get some sdea of how easily this hilltop could be defended.

Hascombe Hill was devoid of trees until the 18th century and offered the builders of the fort far-reaching 360° views over the surrounding countryside. The broad path you are following below the rim of the hill was originally a man-made ditch. Finds in this ditch during archaeological excavations indicate that it was dug around 100 BC.

5 At a fork by a large beech tree and a directional post, take the left fork and continue downhill. At a second fork when the wide track sweeps left, keep ahead to meet a T-junction and a marker post in 60 yards. Turn right here and soon cross a stile and pass the side of a small wooden building to meet a lane. Turn left along the lane to rejoin the B2130 beside the White Horse pub.

6 Pass the front of the pub and continue along Church Road where you soon pass the village pond. Remain on Church Road until Lower House is met. Turn left here on a bridleway and soon ignore a stile on your right. On a right-hand bend in the bridleway look out on your left for the footpath you walked earlier. Follow the path to rejoin the village spring, from where it is just a few yards back to Mare Lane and the end of the walk.

> **REFRESHMENTS**
>
> Near the end of the walk the circuit passes the White Horse pub where the good food and sunny garden are favourites of walkers. Open 11 am to 3 pm and 5 pm to 11 pm each weekday and all day at weekends. Telephone: 01483 208258.

The beautiful buildings of Scotsland Farm

OCKLEY AND THE ROMAN ROAD BUILDERS

Length: 6 miles

The pump on Ockley village green

HOW TO GET THERE: Ockley is 6 miles south of Dorking on the A29.

PARKING: Park at the southern end of the village green by the cricket pavilion. There is alternative parking in the lay-by on the A29 opposite the Inn On The Green pub.

MAP: OS Landranger 187 (GR 147402).

INTRODUCTION

This fascinating walk over level ground begins beside Ockley's superb village green before soon immersing itself in this remote part of Surrey. Easily followed paths, tracks and green lanes lead through peaceful woodland and pass ancient Wealden farmhouses little changed since Tudor times. The halfway point comes when the route meets lovely Okewood church, said to be the remotest in the county. Traversing a pretty woodland dell cut through by brooks, the way makes its return along a wonderful green lane before crossing the scenic parkland of Jayes Park and passing its lake to rejoin Ockley. This route may not be suitable in winter or after prolonged rain because of the sticky Wealden clays.

HISTORICAL BACKGROUND

What the Romans called their road between London and Chichester has been lost in time, but since then it has gone under the name of Stone Street or Stane Street. Nowadays mapmakers tend to use the latter, Saxon, version, as *stane* was their word for stone.

Thought to be one of the last major roads the Romans built in England, it dates from the 3rd century AD and is believed to be purely military as it touched no important towns along its route. Much of the modern-day A24 follows its course from London as it goes through Clapham, Tooting, and Epsom before

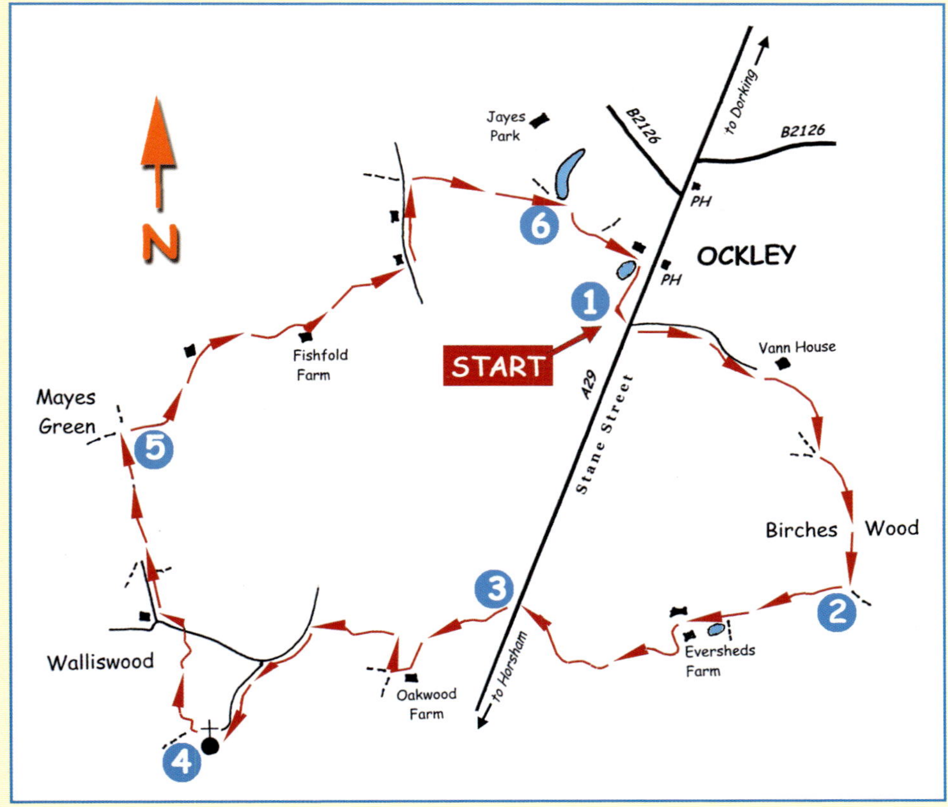

heading for Dorking where, through expediency, it bends and passes through the Dorking Gap.

The next and perhaps longest straight section comes as it leaves Dorking and passes through Ockley, Billingshurst and Pulborough – now the A29 main road – and continues on its way past Bignor, the site of an important Roman villa. From here it continued uncompromisingly straight over the top of the South Downs to Boxgrove Common on the seaward side where the modern A285 follows its course into *Noviomagus*, or Chichester as we know it today, and the nearby Roman port of Fishbourne.

To negotiate the treacherous Wealden clays at Ockley, the Romans raised their road on a causeway 1½ metres high; quite a feat when you take into account that it was also around 6 metres wide. A section of the road unearthed on the firmer greensand soils north of here in Redlands Wood, shows that when the natural surface was good, the road was raised by only a few centimetres with a wide ditch on either side, probably to mark its route. One mile north of Ockley, where the modern road bends sharply east at the entranceway to Buckinghill Farm, the old Roman causeway continues and can clearly be seen standing almost 1 metre above the fields on either side.

THE WALK

1 If you parked in the lay-by, then walk across the green to meet the cricket pavilion at its southern end.

Many believe that Ockley was the site of a great battle between the armies of King Ethelwulf of Wessex and the invading Danes in AD 851. After sailing up the Thames and making landfall in Kent, the invaders sacked Canterbury before continuing on to London where their next victory was against King Beorhtwulf of the Mercians. Enthused by these easy victories, they turned and marched southward as they headed towards their next objective, Winchester.

Whilst these skirmishes were taking place, news had reached Wessex where King Ethelwulf quickly raised a powerful army and began a march eastward with the intention of cutting the invaders off. After a few days, both armies finally clashed here at Ockley in what has been described as one of the first decisive battles in English history. Ethelwulf's superior forces annihilated the Danes and those that escaped death at Ockley were later hunted down and ruthlessly killed.

Tradition has it that the brook that feeds the pond beside the green at Ockley ran red with Danish blood and a report in the Saxon Chronicle 400 years later stated that they were 'so heavily defeated that by sunset there were none left to bury their dead'.

Walk back to the A29 and cross to Friday Street opposite. Follow this quiet lane and continue through a gateway by Vann Cottage to finally meet the ornate gates of Vann House. Here seek out a bridleway 8 yards to the right of the gates and

The house of Jayes Park seen from the path that crosses its parkland

follow it to meet a T-junction in woodland by a low directional post. Turn left here, cross a wooden bridge and 40 yards later keep right at a fork. Now press on along a bridleway through woodland, continuing ahead at a couple of crossing tracks.

2   When the track finally meets a T-junction by a directional post with a field seen through the trees beyond, go right and follow the bridleway out of the woodland. Ignore a bridleway on your left by a pond and continue ahead to farm buildings. Now follow a cart track between farm buildings and the large house of Eversheds Farm.

Thomas de Everesheved was recorded as living here in 1255 although this house is Tudor with a remodelled Georgian frontage.

Press on along the cart track and 140 yards after passing through a dip and crossing a stream, ignore a left fork and continue ahead. Pass a modern house and 40 yards later when opposite a large barn, go right through a gate and follow a track to meet the A29 main road.

3   Cross the road and continue along the drive of Middle Lodge. When this remote house is reached, continue on a bridleway to the left of the gate. Pass through a gate by the yard of Oakwood Farm and turn right. In 100 yards continue through a field gate and keep right at a fork to meet a stile ahead. Ignore the stile and pass through a gate to its right and follow a narrow bridleway along the edge of woodland. At a second gate maintain direction along a field edge and pass through a third gate on your right to continue on the bridleway to meet a lane. Go left along the lane and when it soon reaches a road junction, turn left on a lane signed to Okewood church. The road ends at the remote church, which is well worth a visit.

REFRESHMENTS

The Inn On The Green pub offers a good selection of cooked food (telephone: 01306 711032), while the Old Bakery and Post Office a few yards south of the pub provides fresh take-away sandwiches as well as hot and cold drinks – perfect for a picnic on the green.

The 13th-century church was originally a chapel of ease to Wotton. There is a story that during the 15th century, Sir Edward de la Hale and his son were hunting wild boar in the forest when his son was thrown from his horse in front of an injured boar. The boar charged the prone boy but before Sir Edward could react, an arrow from an unseen forester finished the boar off. In gratitude Sir Edward vowed to serve God by way of restoring and endowing this little forest chapel. Unfortunately it also attracted the Victorian 'restorers' who almost doubled its size, although it still retains its original red ochre wall paintings.

4   Pass through the gate to the churchyard and in 10 yards go right on a narrow path through woodland and soon cross a stream. In 80 yards when the path divides, turn right over a bridge and climb out of this small dell. Cross a stile and continue on the left side of a field, after which you follow the path beside a garden to reach a road opposite the gates to Gatton Manor. Turn left along the road and then right by Okewood Cottage and continue along Trap Lane. After passing a cluster of houses, ignore signed paths to left and right and press on ahead along a wonderful byway until it ends at a T-junction.

5   Now turn right along a second byway that finally meets the gateway of Holdenbrook Farm. Fork right here along a concrete drive through woodland and follow the lane until it finally ends at Mole Street. Turn left along Mole Street and 230 yards after passing Winks Cottage, turn right over a stile and follow a signed path along the edge of woodland. Cross a stile at its end and go left over a planked bridge and 20 yards later turn right and cross the centre of a large field. After passing to the right of a group of trees nearest you, a stile will be seen at the far side.

6   Cross the stile and go ahead over a stream and pass the end of a scenic lake, with the large house of Jayes Park beyond, to reach a field. Turn right along the field edge and at the apex of a bend, turn left by a directional post and cross the field, aiming to the right of a house to meet Ockley's lovely duck pond. Ahead and to the left are the lay-by and the Inn On The Green, while a short walk to the right alongside the pond brings you to the cricket pavilion and the end of this great walk.

Painting the Devil – the Normans at Chaldon

Length: 4½ miles

Chaldon's wonderful Norman church

HOW TO GET THERE: Coulsdon Common is on the B2030, 2 miles south-east of the A23 at Coulsdon.

PARKING: At the open common, turn west into Fox Lane by the Fox pub sign and continue to the end of the road and the free car park.

MAP: OS Landranger 187 (GR 317568).

INTRODUCTION

This interesting walk begins by crossing the beautiful rolling downland of Happy Valley, where wildflowers display themselves en masse during spring and summer. After passing through the valley you reach Chaldon's hidden treasure, the ancient church of St Peter and St Paul where a visit to view the remarkable Norman wall painting is a must. The route levels out now and continues through

Chaldon village on quiet lanes before meeting with an old drover's road that leads back to Coulsdon Common, where it passes the door of the Fox pub.

HISTORICAL BACKGROUND

During 1870, a surprising discovery was made at Chaldon for, in the early Norman church of St Peter and St Paul, under a thick layer of whitewash, a red ochre painting depicting the Ladder of Salvation was uncovered. This startling painting is believed to have been the work of a Norman monk in 1170 and is the oldest and most important English wall painting in existence.

Measuring over 5 metres in width and 3½ metres in depth, the painting is in wonderful condition and illustrates the dividing line between the deliverance of souls and the horrors of Hell. Christ is shown triumphantly standing on the Devil, who is lying on a bed of nails, while St Michael stands to his left holding a set of scales for the weighing of souls. In the centre of the painting rises the Ladder of Salvation where figures representing good souls climb to heaven while sinners fall and are consumed by the flames of Hell.

Huge devils support a bridge of nails over which cheating tradesmen, holding the tools of their trade, pick their way carefully. The man with a hammer is a

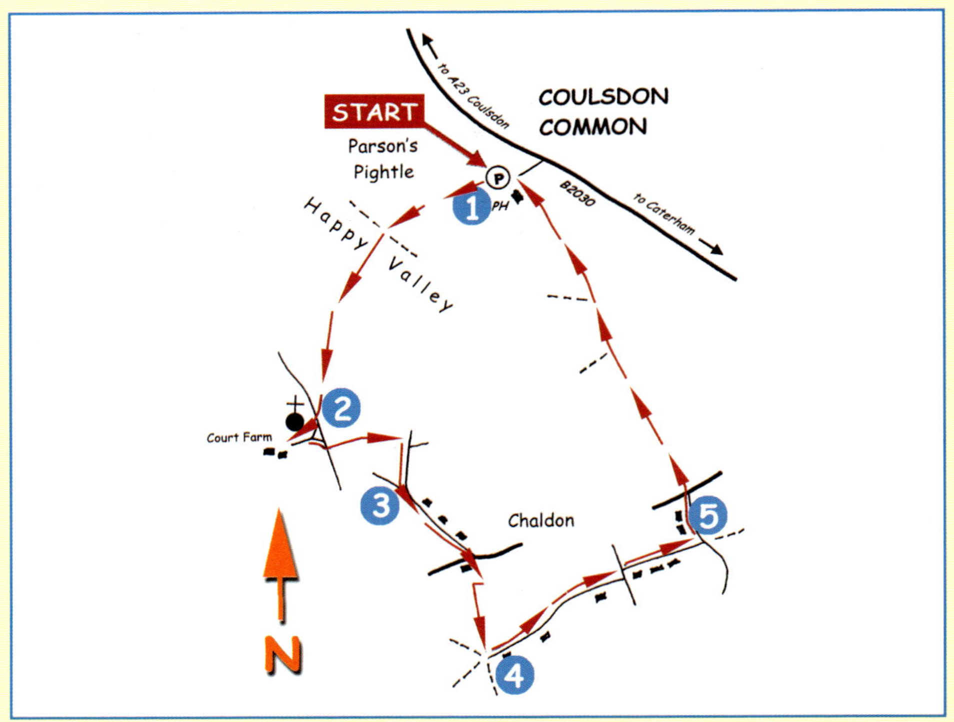

The massive Norman wall painting inside Chaldon's church

blacksmith while another with a bowl is a milkman, both terrified of the abyss below where a moneylender sits among the roaring flames, with a large purse hanging from his neck and bags of gold from his belt. He has no eyes and gold coins pour from his mouth while demons stab at his head with pitchforks.

Wherever the monk could find space, he has inserted the Seven Deadly Sins; *sloth* represented by three souls trying to stand on a beast, *gluttony* by a pilgrim grasping a bottle, *pride* by a woman raising her arm which is being bitten by a dog, *anger* by two fighting figures, *lust* by a couple embracing, *avarice* by the figure of the moneylender and *envy* by two figures, one with hair longer than the other.

The artist has very skilfully woven the legends and stories of his day into the painting to produce this dramatic scene. People at that time were profoundly religious and Hell was a real place to be feared – the message would certainly not have been lost on them.

THE WALK

① With your back to the road, walk away from the car park on a wide tarmac path and when it goes downhill and bends to the right, turn left on a steep downhill stepped path signed to Chaldon church. Cross a bridleway at the bottom and continue up the other side of the valley. Pass through a tree line and follow a well-trodden path over the field ahead. At a corner of woodland, go diagonally left over the next field to meet a quiet lane at the far side.

② Turn left along the lane to meet a road junction by a triangular island of trees in 70 yards. Go right here to the church of St Peter and St Paul.

When visiting the church, please leave muddy shoes and boots in the porch and, to ensure pigeons cannot enter the building, please remember to close both doors behind you as you enter and leave.

After a fascinating visit, pass by the right side of the island of trees to rejoin the lane and turn right for 30 yards before going left on a signed public footpath alongside a field. At the field end continue ahead alongside woodland to meet a T-junction with a track. Turn right here and when a tarmac residential road is reached, continue ahead to a T-junction with another road beside Corner Cottage.

3   Turn left along this quiet road and pass a few well spaced houses within their large gardens to reach another T-junction. Here go ahead and seek out a stile to the left of a driveway opposite. Now follow a well-trodden path ahead and then right as it skirts a paddock. Cross a stile on your left and continue through a ribbon of woodland and alongside a field.

4   At the field end, cross a stile to meet a junction of paths and a directional post inscribed 'Five Ways'. Here turn left and remain ahead on a signed footpath along a private drive that leads you past fields with views and occasional houses amidst fragrant gardens. At a road junction, turn left for 30 yards before going right on another signed footpath along a private drive named The Heath.

5   The Heath ends at a T-junction with Roffes Lane where you should ignore a footpath opposite. Turn left now along Roffes Lane and pass a couple of wonderful Arts and Crafts houses to your left before meeting another T-junction. The route now continues ahead on a broad bridleway opposite, where you should ignore the occasional path to left and right.

As this bridleway nears its end, you will see a housing development behind a tall wall which once formed the boundary of the Guards Depot of Caterham Barracks. The tall barrack buildings have been ingeniously included in the development as apartments while the bricks from those buildings that were demolished have been re-used in the low rise housing.

When the bridleway ends at a road, pass through a gate opposite and continue through woodland to the Fox public house, from where it is just a short distance leftwards to rejoin the car park where this enjoyable walk ends.

REFRESHMENTS

The Fox pub is just a few yards from the start point of the circuit and serves a good choice of cooked food throughout the day. Telephone: 01883 330401.

WALK 5
SURREY'S ROYAL CASTLE – GUILDFORD

Length: 4½ miles

Guildford's castle keep

HOW TO GET THERE: The walk starts from St Martha's Hill car park, easiest found from Chilworth, on the A248 between Albury and Shalford. From a few yards east of the level crossing, follow Blacksmith Lane which soon becomes Halfpenny Lane and in 1 mile look out for St Martha's Hill car park on your right.

PARKING: St Martha's Hill car park.

MAP: OS Landranger 186 (GR 021484).

INTRODUCTION

This wonderfully varied walk packs in peaceful woodland tracks, a picturesque riverside path, Guildford Castle and the panoramas from Pewley Hill. Beginning from below the wooded slopes of St Martha's Hill, the route takes an ancient track through woodland before reaching the river Wey and following its towpath into Guildford. After exploring the castle grounds, and perhaps Guildford's interesting High Street just yards away, the circuit begins its return. A steady climb to the top of Pewley Hill that should not trouble the average person is rewarded by the stunning views this vantage point offers and from here easily followed paths lead you back towards St Martha's Hill to complete this interesting walk.

HISTORICAL BACKGROUND

Approaching Guildford Castle from under Castle Arch in Quarry Street you immediately step into antiquity; the arch still retains the grooves in the stonework where the portcullis was raised and lowered, and built into the fabric is a fine old house that is now the home of the Surrey Archaeological Society. The castle itself was built by the Normans soon after the Battle of Hastings and consisted of a typical 'motte and bailey'. The large square keep was added later during the 12th century and is constructed of local Bargate stone, replacing an earlier chalk shell keep.

In 1154 the castle became the Royal residence for King Henry II, who is credited with establishing courts around the country where local magistrates were first granted the power to make legal decisions in the name of the Crown. Many years later a great-grandson of his, Edward I, came to stay in the residence. Edward was

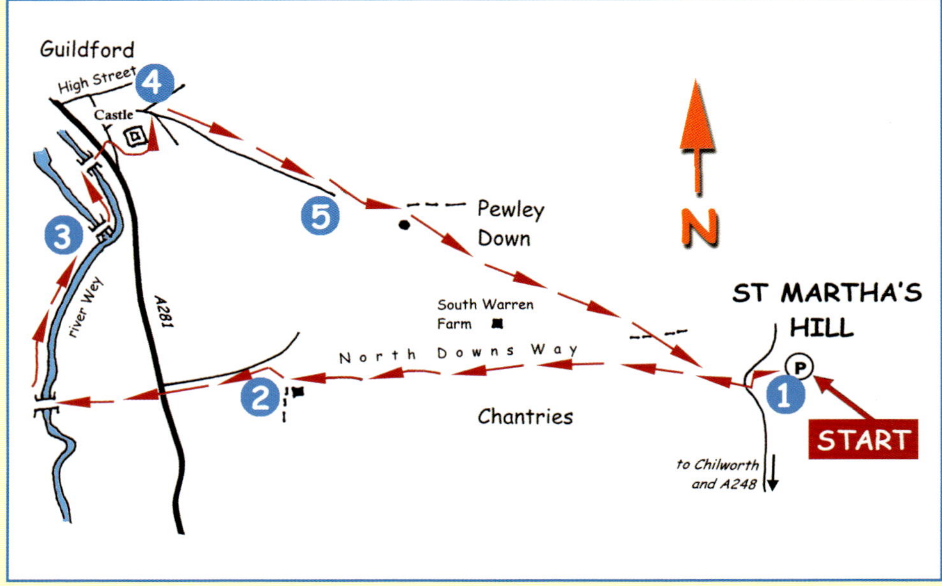

popularly known as 'Longshanks' due to his 6 ft 2 in frame which would have towered over the average Englishman of the time. His first marriage to Eleanor of Castile produced fifteen children and after her death he went on to marry Marguerite of France who, in turn, gave birth to a further three children making this, even in his day, a very large family.

Edward was a fierce man and showed his ruthlessness when defeating Simon de Montfort and his supporters at the Battle of Evesham in 1265. De Montfort died on the battlefield and although he was a cousin to the king, Edward showed no mercy to the surviving members of his family and hunted them down ferociously.

The castle never saw warfare and much of it had already fallen down by the 14th century, but the keep continued to play a role as a prison for both Surrey and Sussex until the jail moved to Southwark during the 16th century. In 1611 Francis Carter bought the castle remains and the extensive grounds which he let out for farming. He lived in the keep until it became uninhabitable during the 1630s when the roof collapsed and he erected the house that is now home to the Archaeological Society.

The keep was restored in 1885 and the grounds opened as a pleasure garden three years later. Conservation work was carried out on the tower in 2003 and part of it is now open to the public during the summer months. The rest of the castle has almost disappeared and only the indistinct remains of the private chambers of King Edward I remain, but these are now mainly covered by well-groomed flower borders, fine spreading trees and close-cropped bowling greens.

The keep is open April to September 10 am to 5 pm daily; March and October on Saturdays and Sundays only.

THE WALK

1 Seek out an information board at the edge of the car park and pass it to meet an open area with a sandy track beyond. Turn right along the sandy track and soon cross the drive of a house named Southernway. Press on along the signed North Downs Way long-distance path to meet with Halfpenny Lane. Turn left along the road for 40 yards before turning right along the North Downs Way. At a fork in 100 yards, keep left and continue on the long-distance path as it passes between fields and through woodland for 1 mile before reaching a junction of tracks beside Chantry Cottage.

2 Go ahead here along a tarmac drive signed as the North Downs Way to reach a residential road named Pilgrim's Way and bear left along it.

A couple of centuries ago a pesthouse (plague hospital) occupied a site beside what was then a rough track well outside the environs of Guildford. That rough track is now this

Part of the circuit follows the bank of the river Wey

smart suburban road and the hospital, now named Cyder House, makes a fine residence.

Follow the road to reach a T-junction with a main road (the A281). Here go ahead and cross a large meadow.

This meadow was the site of Shalford's medieval fair that attracted merchants from far and wide. John Bunyan, who lived in Shalford for a while, is believed to have drawn his inspiration from the fair to write the Pilgrim's Progress.

Press on through a tree line on a well worn path to meet the river Wey and cross a footbridge. Turn right along the river bank and follow it towards the houses of Guildford.

3 Turn left at Millmead Weir and pass Guildford Boathouse to reach Millmead Lock. Go right over a bridge by the lock to meet the main road, which you should cross via a pedestrian crossing 20 yards to your left. Go ahead up Rosemary Alley, where the old timber-framed houses lean towards each other. Turn right at the top of the alley to meet Castle Arch. Pass through the arch and fork left in 40 yards to enter the castle grounds. The route follows a path to the right of the keep to meet a gate opposite Tunsgate Square, a modern shopping centre, the other side of which is the town's interesting High Street.

After exploring the keep and castle grounds, or Guildford's historic High Street, return to this gate from where the walk continues.

4   When facing the entrance to Tunsgate Square, turn right along the road and at a road junction turn right into South Hill. After 50 yards fork left into Pewley Hill and follow it to its end. A glance over your shoulder gives you a great view of Guildford's cathedral.

The odd roofline of the large house at the junction with Semaphore Road is explained by its name: Semaphore House (see walk 14).
    Near the end of the road is Pewley Point, the site of a fort built to protect London but now mostly built upon and private (see walk 15).

5   At the road end, pass between posts to reach the superb vantage point of Pewley Down. Bear left along the top of the hill and make for a toposcope that points out distant features. In 140 yards after passing the toposcope, fork right on a chalky downhill path with a hedgerow to your left. Follow this path between fields to the foot of the hill and press on ahead at a junction of paths as it enters woodland. When the path meets with the North Downs Way, follow it leftwards and retrace your steps back to St Martha's Hill car park and the end of this great walk.

WALK 6

FARNHAM CASTLE – THE BISHOPS' RESIDENCE

Length: 4 miles

The keep at Farnham Castle

HOW TO GET THERE: Farnham is on the A31 and 10 miles west of Guildford. From the A31 Farnham by-pass, turn north at traffic lights into South Street, first left into Union Road then continue along Downing Street to its end. Go left into West Street and in 200 yards turn right into The Hart and at its end right again into Long Garden Way, where the car park is to be found.

PARKING: Upper Hart pay and display car park (Sundays free) in central Farnham.

MAP: OS Landranger 186 (GR 837470).

INTRODUCTION

This undulating walk is through some of the best parkland scenery to be found in Surrey. Beginning in Farnham town centre – itself an intriguing place to explore – the route follows quiet residential roads that bring you to rolling fields with magnificent views into Hampshire. As the way turns north it enters parkland where it follows quiet drives and wide tracks through great scenery. The parkland is idyllic and the route easy to follow and all too soon the tracks return you to Farnham by its old castle. After visiting the castle, it is only a short walk along Castle Street, one of the best Georgian streets in England, before you find yourself back at the car park and the end of this superb circuit.

HISTORICAL BACKGROUND

Henry of Blois, Bishop of Winchester and grandson of William the Conqueror, began building Farnham Castle in 1138, leading to occupancy by successive Bishops of Winchester until 1955, it being an ideal stopping place between Winchester and London.

 The first fortification was a typical Norman motte and bailey castle but lasted only 17 years before being razed to the ground by Henry II. It was rebuilt 50 years later, this time more substantially with a stone keep that encased the motte and was protected by an outer curtain wall. The next incursion came in 1216 when

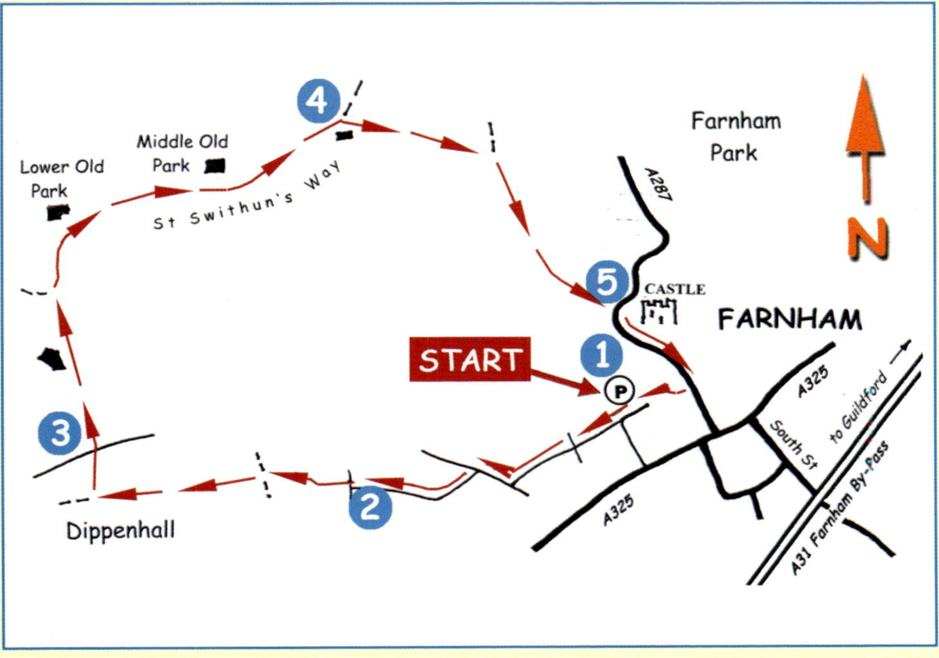

Louis, Dauphin of France, invaded and took Farnham, Guildford and Winchester with little opposition but his occupation was to last only ten months before he was thrown out and the Bishop reoccupied his castle.

During those early times a couple of man-made stretches of water were created to the south of Farnham at Frensham, which acted as fisheries to stock smaller pools nearer the castle for the Bishop's table. The diocese was second only in importance to that of York and kings and queens were entertained here; the most recent Queen Victoria.

Over the centuries various buildings and fortifications were added, including domestic buildings and a brick entrance tower during the 15th century, but that did not stop an incursion during the English Civil War in 1648 when the fortifications were breached and destroyed. Further buildings, mainly domestic, have been added since then, the best by Bishop Morley in the 17th century.

During the Second World War, the castle was home to the Camouflage Development and Training Centre, manned by a band of men with skills that ranged from architects, carpenters and accomplished surrealist artists such as Roland Penrose and Stanley William Hayter, to Jasper Maskelyne, a stage magician. The department, known as the Magic Gang, was charged with creating clever deceptions that included making jeeps look like tanks and tanks look like trucks in their thousands. Their biggest achievements came when, to protect Alexandria from German night bombers, they built a mock-up of the town's night lights three miles away in the Egyptian desert, and managed to hide the Suez Canal by the clever use of spinning mirrors.

The castle's domestic buildings have been occupied for the last 50 years by an International Training and Conference Centre and are not open to the public although the keep is, and may be visited between April and September. A charge applies.

THE WALK

1   When facing Waitrose supermarket from the car park, go right along Falkner Road and, at a crossroads, continue ahead along Beavers Road. At a T-junction, turn right for 150 yards before turning left into Waynflete Lane.

2   At the end of Waynflete Lane, cross a road and go ahead on a signed footpath and fork right on the waymarked path in 65 yards. The path leads you through a shallow valley and over a stream. Here continue through a small meadow and at the top of a rise, go over a farm track and cross a stile. Keep ahead along the left side of a field to meet and cross a stile at its end. Now maintain direction along the right-hand edge of the next field and at the crest of the hill and 120 yards before a clump of pines are met, turn right by a way marker and descend to a hitherto unseen road.

The Windsor almshouses in Castle Street

3   Cross the road and continue on a track to the right of the entrance to Burles Farm. About 6 yards before the ornate gateway to Burles House, follow a path rightwards that skirts the grounds before continuing between fields and ending at an estate drive. Turn right along the drive that forms a section of the St Swithun's Way long-distance path.

The St Swithun's Way long-distance path is 34 miles long and begins at Winchester Cathedral in the heart of the Saxon capital of England. Passing through the Itchen Valley, it makes its way through the towns of Alresford, Alton and Chawton before ending at Farnham, where the route continues to Canterbury via the North Downs Way long-distance path.

Remain on this wonderful drive as it passes Lower Old Park and then Middle Old Park, a very splendid mansion house where the drive ends. Here continue ahead on a wide track that finally ends at a junction of tracks beside a house.

4   Ignore a track to your left and press on ahead on a track that finally ends at a T-junction. Turn right here and remain on this track as it descends towards

Farnham and houses begin to appear. The track finally ends at a T-junction with the A287 and you should cross to steps opposite. Turn right along the pavement to soon reach the entrance to Farnham Castle.

5   After visiting the castle, return to the roadside pavement and continue leftwards to soon meet wonderful Castle Street. Press on along Castle Street and pass the Windsor almshouses on the left side of the street.

A plaque on the wall of the almshouses reads 'Erected by Andrew Windsor in 1619 for the relief of eight poor honest old impotent persons'. Castle Street was built this wide to host the markets that were held along its length over the centuries.

Some 90 yards later cross the road and continue along Long Acre Walk, signposted to Lion and Lamb Yard, Upper and Lower Hart car parks. Bear right at Waitrose to return to the car park.

A lovely track through Old Park

RUNNYMEDE – KING JOHN AND THE MAGNA CARTA

Length: 3½ miles

The Magna Carta memorial

HOW TO GET THERE:
Runnymede is 1 mile west of Egham and junction 13 of the M25.

PARKING: From the A30 Egham bypass roundabout, take the A308 in the direction of Windsor and 1 mile after passing the Runnymede Pleasure Grounds, park in the National Trust pay and display car park on the river bank.

MAP: OS Landranger 176 (GR 997731).

INTRODUCTION

This wonderful level walk is full of interest and combined with a picnic makes a splendid day out. Beginning on the bank of the river Thames, the route heads for the foot of Coopers Hill, where it passes the serene John F. Kennedy and Magna Carta memorials. The path takes you through the famous water meadows and meets with Langham Pond and Meadow, where you are guaranteed to spot wildlife. After leaving this tranquil place, the way continues over the water meadows to reach the banks of the river Thames and from here the route follows the water's edge through the Runnymede Pleasure Grounds and back to the National Trust car park. This walk may not be suitable after prolonged rain during winter.

HISTORICAL BACKGROUND

Runnymede's water meadows are famous as the site of a momentous meeting in 1215 when England's powerful barons forced King John to sign the Great Charter, or, as it has become more commonly known by its Latin name, Magna Carta. The medieval English throne had developed into the most powerful in Europe but after King John took power at the beginning of the 13th century all had changed. Earlier, his older brother Richard the Lionheart, had left him in charge of Ireland while away on the Third Crusade but John's inept leadership led to him being brought home prematurely.

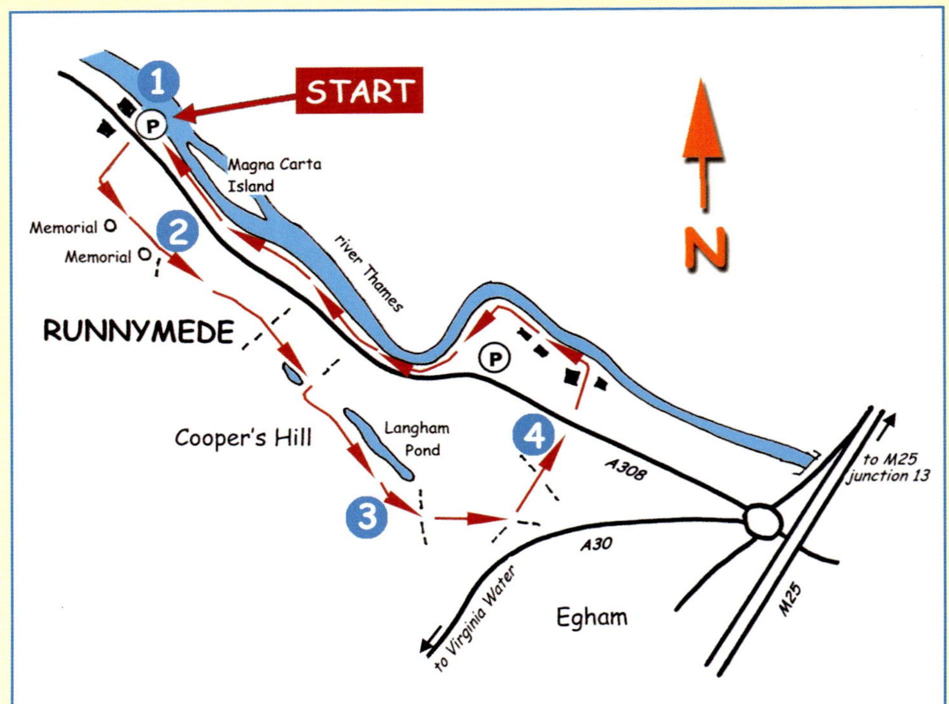

When Richard was captured in 1192 and imprisoned in Austria, John tried to seize the Crown but, without the backing of the powerful English barons, his attempt failed and it wasn't until Richard's death seven years later that he finally acceded to the throne. The growing dislike the barons had of him was compounded in 1207 when he fell out with the Pope over who should be Archbishop of Canterbury. John was excommunicated and England put under Church law, a situation that lasted until 1213 when he was forced to surrender to the Pope.

This catalogue of failure proved too much for the barons, who led a revolt against him and forced him to come to Runnymede on 15 June 1215 to sign the demands written in the celebrated document. The charter to which he affixed his great seal gave English people rights that they had never previously had but, in truth, it was intended to benefit the barons rather more than ordinary folk. Even so, it has filtered down through the ages and has been the foundation of English law which has been copied throughout the world.

The 61st clause was the longest and was known as the 'security clause' as it was based on the medieval practice of 'distraint', which gave 25 barons the right to meet and overrule the king's decisions. After the barons had left Runnymede, John claimed that he had only signed the document under duress and he went on to declare that he had no intention of abiding by it, a statement that immediately threw England into civil war.

This was another battle King John was going to lose as by now he had very few supporters and during the conflict that ensued, he made his escape across the Wash in Lincolnshire; his baggage party mistook the tides and was engulfed by the incoming water causing the loss of all his treasure. Now in flight, his valuables gone and with little support, he fell ill with dysentery and his last days were spent on the road where he expired on 18 October 1216.

THE WALK

The historic Runnymede meadows were given to the National Trust in 1929 by Lady Fairhaven in memory of her husband who died that same year. The Fairhaven Lodges either side of the road near the car park were designed by Edwin Lutyens.

The name Runnymede, or Runingmed as it is spelt in the Magna Carta, indicates that this area was already well known as a meeting place, as 'runinge' in Middle English means 'taking council' while 'mede' is another name for meadow. During Alfred the Great's time, the Witan Council, an early form of government, was held here.

1 From near the car park entrance, cross the road at 'Keep left' signs and continue ahead on a grassy path. Follow the path as it swings left below Coopers Hill to meet an information board in 200 yards at the edge of woodland. A short excursion here to the John F. Kennedy Memorial and a little piece of America is well worthwhile.

The dignified John F. Kennedy memorial

The winding path is constructed from 60,000 hand-cut granite setts and leads to the John F. Kennedy Memorial. The large dignified slab of Portland stone stands in an acre of ground given to America by the people of Britain and is inscribed with a part of the assassinated president's Inaugural Address.

As you return to the information board, note how the steps magically 'vanish'. The route continues along the foot of the hill where you will soon meet with the gate of the Magna Carta Memorial.

The Magna Carta Memorial is designed in the form of a classical temple and was given by the American Bar Association in 1957. Nearby are two oak trees planted in 1997, one by the Queen to mark National Tree Week and the other by John Marshall, Secretary to the Army of the United States of America. Hopefully the trees will live for many centuries.

2 From the memorial gate, maintain direction through a gate, ignoring another one on your right. Now press on ahead with a ditch and tree line on your right and when you reach a directional sign to the Air Forces Memorial, maintain direction ahead. As you pass a wetland pool, cross a stile on your right and continue on a planked walkway and cross a second stile. Now continue ahead alongside beautiful Langham Pond.

Langham Pond and Meadow is an important SSSI (Site of Special Scientific Interest) and a remnant of an old ox-bow lake formed when the Thames changed its course. It is a fine example of marsh and open water and is home to herons, kingfishers, 20 species of dragonfly and the greater water-parsnip; a rarity in Surrey.

Ignore a gate on your left and continue ahead to a kissing gate under an oak tree.

3 Pass through the kissing gate, cross a stream and go diagonally half right aiming for the houses of Egham in the distance. Keep ahead at a crossing path in 60 yards and when near a hedgerow on your left at another crossing path, go left and continue alongside the hedgerow. When the hedgerow bends leftwards, keep ahead on the path to meet a stile seen in the distance beside the A308 main road.

4 Cross the road and go ahead alongside an industrial building to meet the bank of the river Thames. Now turn left along the bank towards the Runnymede Pleasure Grounds. The café is near the entrance to your left. The route continues alongside the river bank until you finally meet with the National Trust car park and the end of this short, but splendid walk.

REFRESHMENTS

The route passes through the Runnymede Pleasure Grounds where a café serves a good selection of simple hot and cold snacks and drinks. The Pleasure Grounds are also an ideal picnic site, or for a remote picnic surrounded by nature try Langham Pond halfway round the circuit.

THE POWER OF WATER – HAXTED MILL

Length: 5½ miles

Haxted watermill museum

HOW TO GET THERE: The walk starts at Marsh Green, 3½ miles east of Lingfield on the B2028.

PARKING: Some 200 yards after passing the Wheatsheaf pub, bear left on a small road beside the village green and park near St John's United Reformed church.

MAP: OS Landranger 187 (GR 439443).

INTRODUCTION

Although beginning just over the border in Kent, the majority of this superb field path walk is in Surrey. After leaving the hamlet of Marsh Green, the route soon meets with the river Eden and follows its course to the outskirts of Edenbridge and the Kent Brook. The circuit follows the brook for a while before entering Surrey, where the panoramic views over the Eden Valley from the field paths are outstanding. The way continues through the hamlet of Haxted and visits the old watermill, from where the circuit begins its return over level fields to pass Starborough Castle where only the moat remains. With just a couple of field paths remaining, the route all too soon returns to Marsh Green.

HISTORICAL BACKGROUND

The Romans first introduced the watermill to Britain although it is believed that the ones they built had horizontal wheels, but by the time of the Norman invasion a thousand years later, the waterwheel had become vertical as we know it today. The Domesday Book records 114 watermills in Surrey, the greatest clusters being seven mills in Battersea followed by six in Farnham. These would all have been quite small and inefficient, probably with a single undershot paddle wheel driven directly by the force of a stream where often the flow dwindled to a trickle during dry summers, leaving the mill without power.

Watermills remained largely unchanged until the 14th century. Then, as Europe came out of the Middle Ages it suffered crisis after crisis; the Great Famine began its two-year ravage in 1315, the peasants were in revolt, and 30 years later the Black Death took its toll on the population. These calamities added to a general decline in farm labour as the population moved from the countryside to seek their fortune in the towns. To overcome some of these shortages in labour, landowners began to turn to technology for more productive methods of milling, and water, as yet untamed as a source of power, became a major part of their answer.

Dams were constructed across streams running through valleys, creating large bodies of water made manageable by the use of simple sluice gates. These gates controlled the flow of water to the paddle wheels via a man-made leat while a second leat was employed to bypass the mill when power was not required. Over time other types of waterwheel came into being – backshot and breastshot – but by the 18th century the most powerful of all, the overshot wheel was in use. This new waterwheel also employed the force of gravity and proved to be twice as powerful as those of the undershot type, when even a small source of water was able to drive three or four pairs of stones together.

Although the Domesday Book records a mill at Haxted, nothing from that time exists today and the present mill dates from 1580, making it one of the oldest in existence in Surrey. The overshot wheel here drove three pairs of stones that remained in use until the mill's closure in 1945.

After undergoing many years of restoration, the mill is now a museum and is open to the public from Easter to the end of September between 10 am and 3 pm (closed Mondays); October to Easter 10 am to 2 pm Sundays only.

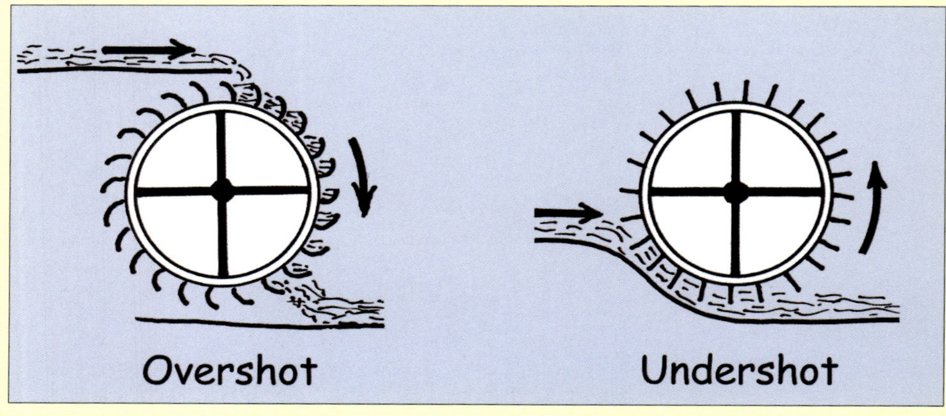

The field paths offer panoramic views

THE WALK

1   Seek out a public footpath to the left side of St John's church and soon enter a field. Continue along the left side and after passing through a kissing gate bear right between fields to meet with a cart track. Go ahead along the cart track until it finally ends in a field. Keep ahead along the right side of the field to soon cross a bridge over the river Eden on your right.

2   Immediately after crossing the river, turn right and follow a distinct grassy path along the river bank. Keep to the path when it heads away from the river by a Second World War pill box and remain on a well trodden path along the right-hand side of two fields. At the end of the second field, fork right to rejoin the river bank. At a plank bridge by a second wartime pill box, ignore the bridge, turn left and continue with a hedgerow and the tiny Kent Brook close to your right. At the end of this field resist the temptation of a path to your right and continue ahead alongside the next field. Maintain direction through a third field and at its end turn right to meet the bank of the Kent Brook.

3   Follow the bank of the brook leftwards and soon ignore a concrete farm bridge on your right. Keep ahead along the right-hand side of a field and cross a stile in the hedgerow ahead. Now go diagonally left for 35 yards before turning right on an indistinct grassy path on an upward slope. Pass through a tree line and continue ahead towards another tree line with barns beyond. When the trees are met, turn left alongside them and at their end, turn right over a brook. Press on ahead along a field edge and at its far corner, turn right on a wide path. Continue ahead here over two stiles to meet with a road.

4 Turn left alongside the road to reach Haxted watermill and the fine Riverside Brasserie. To continue the walk, 25 yards beyond the watermill, turn left over a stile and go ahead along the left side of a field. At the field end cross a small bridge and continue to a stile in the hedgerow opposite. Now turn left along a road and soon ignore a right fork. Keep to the road until it bends sharply right.

5 Go left over a stile signed as the Vanguard Way and turn left for 25 yards before turning right along the right-hand side of a field. Cross a stile at its end and keep to the right-hand side of the next field before crossing a stile to a cart track. Turn right along the track to meet a tarmac drive by the Coach House. Continue along the drive for 30 yards before turning left over a stile. Go ahead along a field edge before turning left over a stile to the drive of Starborough Castle.

Starborough was spelt 'Sterburgh' in 1369 and the castle probably takes its name from Richard Sterr who is recorded as living here in 1312. During the Civil War, Parliamentary troops were garrisoned at the castle and they later demolished it to stop it falling into Royalists hands. Only parts of the moat are visible from the route.

6 Cross the drive and a stile before continuing along a boundary fence to reach and cross a stile in the field corner. Turn right for 15 yards before going left and continuing over the crest of a low hill to meet and cross a stile. Turn right here before turning left over another in 25 yards and cross a plank bridge. Now follow a fenced path that skirts a field and ends at a driveway to a house. Turn right along the drive for 40 yards before turning left on a signed footpath that continues through woodland and finally ends at the B2028. Turn left along the road to return to Marsh Green and the end of this walk.

THE MILLERS OF OUTWOOD

Length: 5 ¼ miles

Outwood Mill was built in 1665

HOW TO GET THERE:
Outwood is 3 miles south of Bletchingley and the A25. Follow Outwood Lane south from the centre of Bletchingley.

PARKING: At Outwood Common turn right on a track opposite the mill to reach the National Trust car park.

MAP: OS Landranger 187 (GR 326456).

INTRODUCTION

This great field walk is along level paths and cart tracks through pastoral scenery that is quite stunning in early summer when the meadows are carpeted with wildflowers and the hedgerows garlanded by wild roses. After leaving Outwood

Common and its old windmill, the way heads across fields with panoramic views as far as the North Downs, where it meets with a cart track that traces the edge of fields before joining a peaceful drive by Lodge Farm. The circuit now follows the drive that serves but a handful of houses and along the way passes the magnificent 17th-century Lower South Park Farm. Continuing along scenic tracks and through woodland, the way finally crosses a couple of fields to return to Outwood Common.

HISTORICAL BACKGROUND

The origin of the windmill in Britain is shrouded in mystery, although one theory is that the early Crusaders saw them being used by the Saracens and brought the idea back with them. What is certain, though, is that the majority of the 5,000 mills recorded in the Domesday survey in 1086 were driven by water with the remainder having their stones turned by oxen. The first references to wind-powered mills date from the late 12th century and these would have probably been rather crude fixed structures built to face the prevailing breeze.

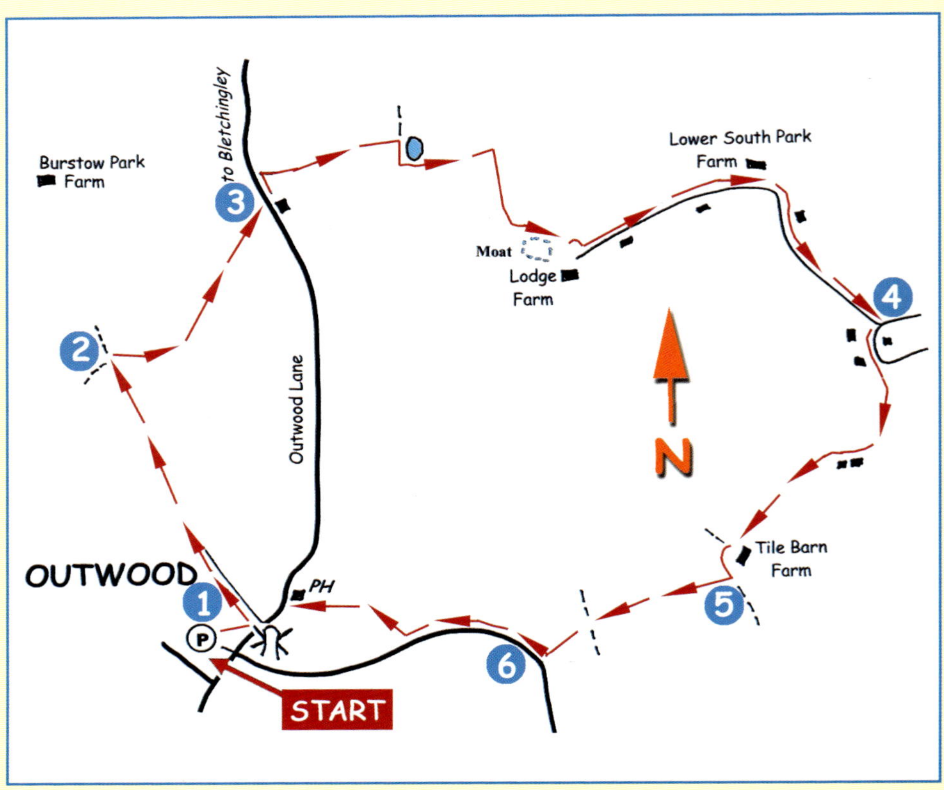

The three basic types of windmill. All were turned to face the wind automatically by a fantail with gearing although early post mills required manual turning.

Over the centuries, several types of mill came into being: the first was the post mill, as at Outwood. This type is limited by size as it swivels the whole body of the mill, weighing in at around 25 tons, on a single post to face the wind, but by the 17th century much larger smock and tower mills had evolved. The smock mill, so named as it resembled the smock worn by farmers of the day, was constructed of wood and usually octagonal in shape, while tower mills were of brick and normally round. In both types only the cap, or cupola, that carry the sails and wind shaft revolve to face the wind. Millers were generally thought of as rogues because they obtained their payment by taking a proportion of the grain measured in a 'toll-dish'. It was a system open to abuse and many succumbed to temptation, a fact mentioned in the verse:

> Miller, miller, dusty poll,
> How many gristings have you stole?
> One of wheat and two of rye,
> Hang the miller six feet high.

Outwood mill is the oldest working post mill in the country, although the word 'working' needs to be qualified as it now only grinds flour on selected weekends as a demonstration for the tourists who visit here. Built in 1665, it is rumoured that locals climbed to the roof a year later to watch the Great Fire of London raging 22 miles away to the north.

The delightful track at Outwood

By 1790 two brothers owned the post mill, but after a quarrel one of them constructed a rival within the grounds in competition. The new mill was a much larger smock mill and, being a more modern and efficient design, should have put the older post mill out of business quite easily, but it totally failed in its challenge. Maybe the brother misjudged the character of the farmers who remained loyal to the old mill; another possible misjudgement could have been in thinking that he would attract business from further afield. This plan would surely have been foiled by the thick clay of the Wealden tracks that prevented heavily laden wagons reaching such a remote spot.

The smock mill ceased working in 1914 and as time passed it become more and more dilapidated until finally, during a storm in 1962, it collapsed. Apart from some old photographs that show its dominating size, no proof of its existence can be seen today.

The post mill is open every Sunday from Easter Sunday to the end of October, from 2 pm until 6 pm.

THE WALK

1 From the car park, face the mill and go diagonally left across the common, passing the gate of Chapter House to soon reach a lane. Turn left along the lane, pass Windmill Garage and later ignore a right fork. When the lane ends beside a couple of cottages, go ahead, cross a stile and continue ahead through a meadow. Press on along the right-hand edge of the next field and at its end, cross a stile.

2 Turn right here and continue along the right-hand side of this, and a second field. Pass through a line of trees and go diagonally left across the centre of a field to meet and cross a stile in a hedgerow. Continue over the next field aiming for a stile 60 yards left of power cables. Press on across another field and cross a stile to the left of a house seen through trees to meet a road.

3 Cross the road and continue leftwards along it and when it soon bends right, turn right on a signed bridleway along a cart track. Follow the cart track along the side of woodland and when it ends at a T-junction, turn right along another track. Pass a pond on your left and follow the track left through a tree line. Now remain on the track as it follows the edge of a couple of fields before continuing between fences and reaching a concrete drive by the gates of Lodge Farm.

The indistinct remains of a moat are in the right-hand field a few yards before the drive to Lodge Farm is met.

Turn left along the drive and remain on it until it finally ends at a T-junction in woodland.

4 Turn right at this T-junction and when the drive soon bends left beside the gateway of Brooklands, go ahead on a cart track and continue through woodland. After passing a couple of isolated cottages, the entrance gate of Tile Barn Farm is met. Continue ahead through the gate and when approaching the large re-modelled barn, follow the bridleway rightwards around the garden and ignore a stile on your right.

5 In 120 yards at a gate and junction of bridleways, turn right and continue through woodland. After prolonged rain in winter this bridleway can become very muddy but there is a relief footpath to its left. Follow the bridleway until it finally ends at a road beside Hornecourt Cottage.

6 Turn right along the road and look out for a stile on your right before a left bend. Cross the stile and go diagonally left across the corner of a field to meet a stile in a blackthorn thicket. Cross the stile and continue along a field edge with the sails of Outwood mill ahead of you. Go over a stile on your right to quite handily meet the Bell Inn, with the road beyond. Outwood Common, the National Trust car park and the end of this lovely walk are a few yards away to your left.

BRITAIN'S EARLIEST CANAL – THE WEY NAVIGATION

Length: 4 miles

A narrowboat approaching Newark Lock

HOW TO GET THERE: Ripley is 1 mile west of the A3 and 2 miles south of junction 10 of the M25. When entering the village from the A3, turn right onto a track 100 yards west of the Half Moon pub.

PARKING: Continue along this track for 150 yards to a parking area near the cricket green.

MAPS: OS Landranger 187 and 186 (GR 053571).

INTRODUCTION

This superb level walk begins on the village green at Ripley before following a path that brings you to the Wey Navigation, where colourful narrowboats cruise the waters and negotiate the locks. After following the towpath and passing the stark ruins of Newark Priory, the way heads for Pyrford and its glorious Norman church, always worth an investigation. From here the circuit begins its return by following a quiet lane and cart track before rejoining the wonderful towpath and its resplendent wildlife. After passing the ancient grounds of Pyrford Place, the way turns towards Ripley and passes Ockham mill before continuing through peaceful woodland and bringing you back to the huge village green at Ripley.

HISTORICAL BACKGROUND

Sir Richard Weston of Sutton Place, near Guildford, did much to improve early agriculture and in 1618 was the man who introduced clover and turnips to Britain. He also decided to improve his estate by designing a canal as a means of irrigating the meadows. At that time many large estates had ornamental 'canals' designed into their formal gardens but, at 3 miles long, Sir Richard's was much more extensive. To control the water level he constructed a pound lock that still exists today at Stoke, near Guildford.

Sir Richard's peaceful existence was ended in 1642 by the Civil War when, being a Royalist Catholic, he was forced to flee to Holland and forfeit his estate. During his time in exile surrounded by waterways he turned his thoughts back to Sutton Place and the 3-mile long canal he had created. At the end of the war,

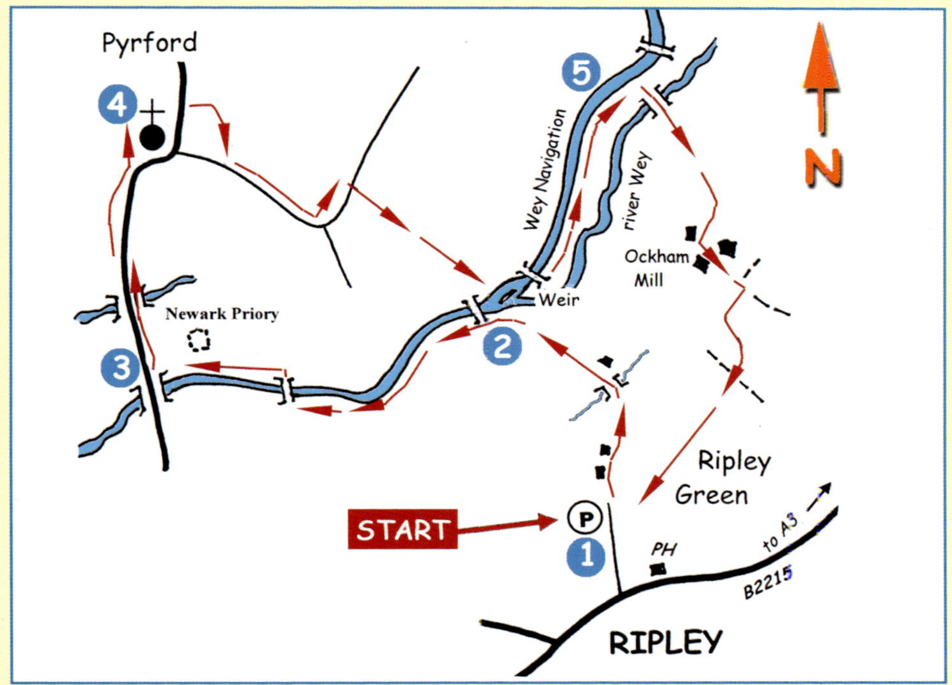

he petitioned the government for the return of his estate and after it was granted, he, together with others, by an Act of Parliament in 1651 began an enterprise to make the river Wey navigable between Guildford and the Thames.

With the use of locks, they bypassed the wildly meandering parts of the river by digging new channels while straighter sections had their banks raised and reinforced with thousands of wooden hurdles. The River Wey Navigation finally opened to traffic in 1653, the first of its kind in Britain, and remains almost exactly as Sir Richard would remember it.

The Navigation brought wealth to its owners and Guildford prospered; corn, cloth, paper, wool and gunpowder from local industries now had direct access to London, while coal and building materials made the return journey. The annual return from tolls began to flood in: £5,860 by 1800 representing 57,500 tons of cargo, while at its peak in 1838 they had reached £7,763 for the 86,000 tons carried. Unfortunately, improved road transport and the coming of the railway to Guildford in 1845 saw tolls begin to decrease until by 1948 only £1,398 was raised.

Wey Navigation barges were built at Guildford and were unique to the canal being 70 ft long by 14 ft wide, a measurement dictated by the size of the locks. Some were assisted by a single distinctive red sail which enabled them to continue along the Thames unaided and, fully laden, they could weigh as much as 90 tons. Surprisingly, more often than not they were towed by a small team of men called bow-haulers.

A uniquely British invention came to the Wey Navigation during the early 19th century in the shape of the narrow boat, still seen today crewed by pleasure seekers. Although they remained 70 ft long, their beam was only 7 ft and these new craft offered more flexibility of haulage, while the owners developed a previously unseen art form in boat decoration.

The Navigation continued to lose trade to the roads and railways and its last owner, William Stevens & Sons, the predominant carrier, finally entrusted the Wey Navigation to the National Trust in 1964 before ceasing trade in 1969.

THE WALK

1 From the parking area, continue along the track and remain on it on when it bends left by a field gate. After crossing a stream the track ends by a couple of houses and you should continue ahead on a signed path between fields to reach the bank of the Wey Navigation by Walsham Weir.

2 Turn left along the towpath and after passing through a meadow, Newark Priory comes into view in the water meadows to your right.

Newark Priory was founded in the late 12th century by Rual de Calva and his wife Beatrix de Sandes during the reign of Richard the Lionheart. During the 13th century John Peckham, the Archbishop of Canterbury stayed here several times but three centuries later, Henry VIII dissolved the monastery and sent all its church plate to London.

At Newark Lock, cross a bridge and continue along the right-hand bank to reach a road.

To the left here are the footings of Newark Mill that ceased working in 1942 and burned to the ground in 1966. It was Surrey's largest watermill.

A 17th-century summerhouse in the grounds of Pyrford Place

3   Go rightwards along the road on the pavement and when this ends, cross to the pavement on the left-hand side. At a right bend, continue ahead uphill on a signed path to Pyrford's wonderful Norman church and memorial cross.

The church has a Tudor porch and a Norman door surround with zig zag carving, while the interior has remnants of Norman red ochre painting decorating the walls. (See walk 4 for the most complete Norman church painting in Britain.)

The Saxons called the settlement Pyrianforda but by 1086 it appeared as Peliforde in the Domesday Book. The meaning is 'ford by a pear tree'.

4   From the memorial cross, go down to the road which you cross and continue on a path in the graveyard. Ignore a stile ahead of you and turn right along the top edge of the graveyard to a small parking area. Continue through this to join a lane at its entrance and turn left, soon passing Wheelers Farm. In 200 yards after passing the entrance to Warren Farm Home Park, turn right on a track signed as a footpath. The track brings you to Walsham Lock where you should cross a bridge and go left on the towpath. Here, you will notice quite graphically the difference between the canal and the river Wey below on your right. Press on along the towpath and pass an interesting summerhouse on the far bank.

The blue plaque on the summerhouse wall states that John Donne (1563-1631) lived here for four years. He didn't, he actually stayed at Pyrford Place, a moated manor house in the grounds of which the 17th-century summerhouse sits. A large 20th-century building containing apartments now occupies the site.

Donne, secretary to Sir Thomas Egerton, Lord Keeper of the Seal, fell in love with Ann More, an heiress of the Loseley estate near Guildford and believing that she would be barred from marrying a person of his status, they eloped. After being tracked down by her powerful relatives, Donne lost his job and was thrown into jail for a short period but after his release they married and stayed with her sister and husband, Sir Francis Wolley, for four years at Pyrford Place.

Donne eventually found a role for himself in the Church and after climbing back up the social ladder became Dean of St Paul's Cathedral in 1621. His sermons were eloquent and some lines are still quoted today: 'No man is an island', for instance, and 'Never send to know for whom the bell tolls', a line that Hemingway borrowed for his novel on the Spanish Civil War.

5 Continue along the towpath until a low marker post is met on your left with a bridge just coming into view ahead of you. Turn right here and head away from the canal.

The bridge is called Pigeon House Bridge after a large dovecot that once stood nearby in the grounds of Pyrford Place. In the 16th century pigeons and doves graced the menus of many large houses, while their droppings were a valuable commodity in the gunpowder industry (see walk 11).

Soon cross the river Wey and press on along the path to finally meet a cluster of fine houses by Ockham mill.

This trackway, known as Wharf Lane, led from Ockham mill to Pyrford Wharf, sited by the short marker post.

Turn left by the mill, pass through double gates to join a lane, and in 100 yards turn right on a signed bridleway through woodland and cross a small bridge. At a second bridge by a junction of paths, continue ahead to rejoin Ripley's village green, where the path continues ahead to meet the parking area where this superb walk ends.

REFRESHMENTS

A good selection of lunchtime and evening home-cooked meals are offered by the Half Moon pub in Ripley High Street. Telephone: 01483 224380.

FIRE AND BRIMSTONE – THE GUNPOWDER MILLS OF CHILWORTH

Length: 4 miles

The ruins of the incorporating mills seen on the walk

HOW TO GET THERE: The walk begins at Chinthurst Hill, 4 miles south of Guildford off the B2128, midway between Shalford and Wonersh.

PARKING: Chinthurst Hill car park, 200 yards south of the A248 and B2128 junction.

MAP: OS Landranger 186 (GR 014463).

INTRODUCTION

This lovely walk begins by crossing Wonersh Common before climbing easily through magnificent native woodland to reach the hamlet of Blackheath. With the only uphill section of the circuit behind you, the way begins to descend into the Tilling Bourne valley, where the views are stunning. The return begins by following a path through woodland and beside leats that once supplied power to the Chilworth gunpowder works. Birdsong rings out from every tree, and although the woodland is littered with the remains of this once important industry, nature has the upper hand – caution should be taken if exploring the ruins. As the way leaves the site it passes through Chilworth and joins a bridleway that brings you back to Wonersh Common from where it is just a short walk to the car park to end this interesting circuit.

HISTORICAL BACKGROUND

Black powder is thought to have been invented by the Chinese around 1000 BC, but its only use was for fireworks and rockets. It took many centuries for the invention to come out of China and it wasn't until the 10th century that Arab warlords acquired the secret formula and began using its explosive power to great effect against the Crusaders, although it was more frightening than destructive. History records that the Chinese also invented what could be referred to as the first cannon, as during the wars against the invading Mongols they used copper tubes loaded with black powder to propel projectiles at the invaders.

   The first recorded mention of black powder in Britain is in the writings of Roger Bacon, a Franciscan friar and philosopher who in 1248 wrote, 'We can, with saltpetre and other substances, compose artificially a fire that can be launched

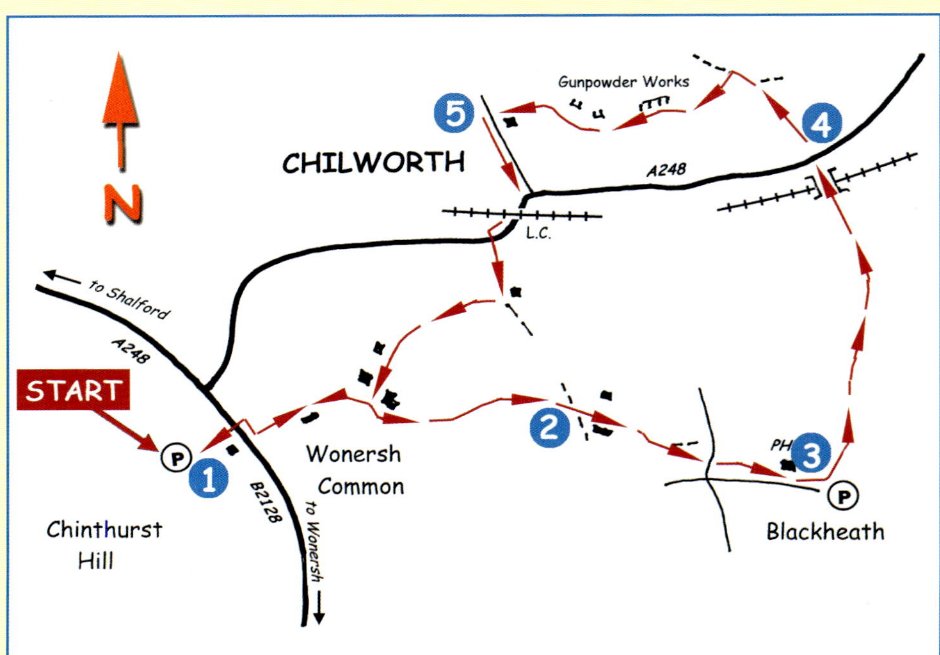

Millstones lay abandoned in the woodland

over long distances…'. Who invented the first true cannon as we know it today is not recorded but by 1326 the Republic of Venice had placed an order for several for the defence of its castles and from that moment on, the invention spread rapidly throughout Europe.

In 1626 the East India Company built gunpowder mills on the Tillingbourne at Chilworth, adding to the already well established paper and corn mills. Three simple ingredients – charcoal, saltpetre and sulphur, or brimstone as it was once called – mixed in the right quantities were all that was needed to produce gunpowder. The Tillingbourne provided a good supply of water to power the machinery and alder from the local woodland provided the finest charcoal. Naturally occurring saltpetre was initially imported from India and Africa but the discovery that it could be manufactured from earth gathered from dovecots to which dung, urine and lime were added, meant that it could be collected locally.

The Chilworth Gunpowder Mills became among the most important and largest in Britain but production was not without incident and numerous explosions occurred over the years. The corning house proved a hazardous place to work as this was where the gunpowder was granulated by forcing it through sieves, a process that in 1760 killed two workers and injured many others. At their height, the works employed 400 people but danger was a grim reality and one of the largest explosions happened in 1864 when 1½ tonnes of gunpowder exploded with further loss of life. Transportation proved no less safe as two bargemen that year were also killed by an explosion as they transported their load along the Godalming Canal.

Gunpowder's major drawback was that when fired, it produced large clouds of smoke, a problem highlighted by several generals who expressed their concerns about giving orders on a battlefield hidden by smoke. Although a Frenchman developed a smokeless explosive in 1880, it was Alfred Nobel seven years later who invented cordite, a smokeless powder that was more powerful and able to propel a bullet as far as 1,000 yards with great accuracy.

Chilworth Gunpowder Mills, by now owned by Nobel Industries, a subsidiary of a German company with German managers and foremen, kept abreast of these developments and the first cordite mill in Britain was opened here in 1892 with production also concentrating on making a safer version of nitro-glycerine – dynamite. These new developments did not bring greater safety for the workers though, as the last and biggest explosion happened in 1901 when a spark from a worker's hobnail boot ignited the powder he was loading onto a wooden tram and caused a secondary explosion in the corning house with the loss of six lives and many injured. The works finally ceased production in 1920 and the 27-acre site is now a Scheduled Ancient Monument.

THE WALK

1   Walk back to the car park entrance and cross the B2128 to the pavement opposite. Turn right alongside the road and soon turn left along the drive to Great Tangley where the circuit joins with the Downs Link long-distance path. Some 80 yards after passing the entrance to Great Tangley Manor, fork right and ignore a footpath on your right.

Hidden behind the hedgerow here is Great Tangley Manor House built in 1584 and one of Surrey's most impressive half-timbered houses.

Now continue on a bridleway that soon begins a steady climb through beautiful native woodland.

2   When a crossing bridleway is reached beside the rear of a couple of extensive gardens, press on ahead to a drive. In 80 yards after passing an entranceway to a large house, fork right on a narrow bridleway and keep ahead at a crossing path to meet with a quiet lane. Cross the lane and press on ahead along the signed bridleway that handily ends at the Villagers pub, the only watering hole on the route.

3 Go right to meet a road and continue leftwards along it and soon turn left along a private road just before reaching Blackheath Common car park.

In 80 yards after rounding a left bend, fork left on a path between posts beside a vehicle barrier. Go ahead over a crossing path in 40 yards and continue through woodland. When by the gate of Lingwood House, continue on a signed path to its right. Keep left when the path divides and when it ends at a railway bridge, press on ahead to meet the A248.

4 Cross the A248 and continue ahead on a farm track signed to Longfrey Farm. In 30 yards after entering woodland, cross a stream and turn immediately left on a well-trodden path by an information board that gives details of the various ruins.

You have now entered the site of the Chilworth Gunpowder Works and the leat here once provided the power for the mills. To your right are the ruins of the charcoal mill and mixing house while a little further along the path are the substantial ruins of the incorporating mills. Old granite millstones litter the area and several millraces tumble through the woodland.

Continue along this path as it passes through the woodland and at a small clearing ignore a left fork. The path ends at an iron gate beside West Lodge – the original works entrance.

Although not on the route, just 40 yards along the left fork are the remains of a swing bridge over the Tilling Bourne where horse-drawn wagons once pulled their loads to Chilworth station.

5 Turn left here along Blacksmith Lane and when it meets the A248, go right and cross a level crossing. In 90 yards turn left on a track alongside the entrance to a house named Tangley Mere. Pass a football pitch and children's playground to reach a fork in the bridleway beside a house. Go right here and follow the path back to Great Tangley Manor House, where you should turn right and retrace your steps back to the car park to complete this lovely circuit.

MOOR PARK – HOME TO JONATHAN SWIFT

Length: 7 ¼ miles

Moor Park House

HOW TO GET THERE: The walk begins at Tilford village. From the A3 south of Guildford, go west at Milford Junction on the B3001. After going through Elstead and passing the Donkey pub, turn left on a road signed to Tilford and follow the signs to the village.

PARKING: By Tilford village green. Cross the bridge, turn left and park in the parking area fronting the river.

MAP: OS Landranger 186 (GR 873433).

INTRODUCTION

This easy to follow walk begins in the pretty hamlet of Tilford that sits at the junction of the river Wey's North and South branches. For most of the way the route is along old byways and cart tracks that pass through majestic peaceful woodland. After an easy climb over Crooksbury Common and passing the Soldiers Ring, an ancient earthwork, the way heads for Moor Park where it discovers Mother Ludlam's cave. From here a short and worthwhile excursion (an addition of ½ mile to the circuit) may be made to the tranquil ruins of Waverley Abbey, from which Sir Walter Scott drew inspiration for his famous novel *Waverley*. As the route continues, it follows a byway through lovely woodland before rejoining Tilford's appealing village green.

HISTORICAL BACKGROUND

Jonathan Swift was born in Ireland in 1667 and received his education at Trinity College, Dublin, but because of his indiscipline he only achieved a degree *speciale gratia*. An uncle had paid for his education although Swift later ungratefully wrote that he was 'given the education of a dog'. He left Ireland and settled in England where he gained employment as secretary to Sir William Temple at Moor Park.

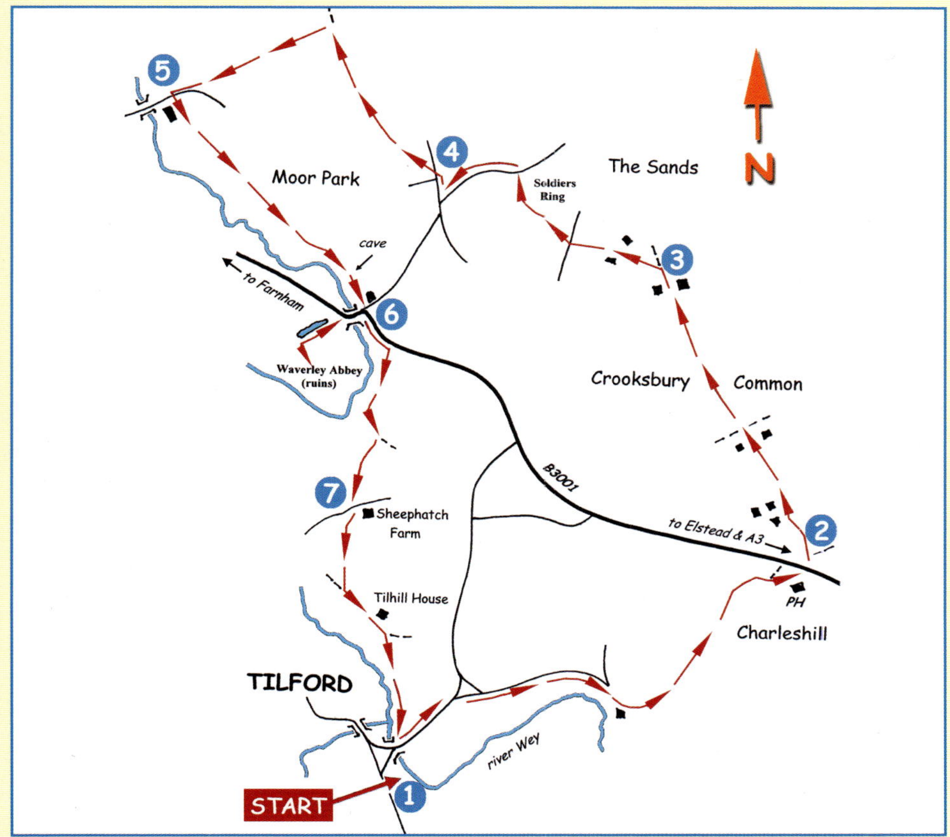

Sir William, a prominent Whig statesman, had already written his *Essay on the Gardens of Epicures*, an important work of its day based on experiments that he had carried out in the large formal gardens at Moor Park that included an ornamental canal. Some parts of Sir William's formal garden remain and were extended in the early 18th century and although Moor Park House is now a school, at its core is his 17th-century house.

While at Moor Park, Swift fell in love with Esther Johnson, a young girl on the estate whom he called 'Stella' in his early poetry. Swift went on to become a prolific and brilliant satirist and political pamphleteer, but the works that made him famous in his time were two of his books: *Tale of a Tub*, his first major work and possibly his best, and *Battle of the Books*, a brilliantly written satire where an epic battle is fought in a library with books coming alive in an attempt to settle the arguments between classical and modern authors.

Undoubtedly though, his most enduring book, penned after he left the service of Sir William, is *Gulliver's Travels*, a savage satire written in 1726 concerning the corrupt English establishment of his day. So condemning was it of the powers-that-be that he did not dare put his name to it at first for fear of being locked up.

After Sir William's death, Swift and Stella moved to Ireland where their love affair continued, but not without scandal as by then Swift had become Dean of St Patrick's Cathedral in Dublin. Their open secret finally ended in 1728 on her death at the age of 47, while he survived her for a further 17 years, most of which were spent with increasing mental health problems. They lie buried together in Dublin's cathedral, the city of his birth.

THE WALK

1   From the parking area, walk back over the bridge and continue along the village street. In 100 yards after passing Upper Street Farm turn right into Whitmead Lane and continue along it until you reach the gatehouse of Whitmead. Here continue ahead on a byway through woodland and, at a fork, go right to pass the Donkey pub and reach a road.

The pub is named after the donkeys that were once stabled here to assist heavily laden carts up the steep hill.

2   Cross the road and continue on a bridleway along a wide track. Remain on this lovely track as it passes a cluster of houses built in local ironstone and with extravagantly carved bargeboards. At a vehicle barrier continue ahead over Crooksbury Common, where the heather is a blaze of colour in late summer, and ignore any side paths.

3   The path finally meets with a tarmac drive by a couple of isolated houses. Continue ahead for 100 yards before turning left on a bridleway along a dirt track

The forlorn ruin of the lay brothers' refectory at Waverley Abbey

beside the gateway to Longlands. When the track ends at a road, go ahead through woodland on a bridleway marked by blue painted posts. After circling the indistinct remains on an ancient earthwork known as the Soldiers Ring, a road is met. Turn left along the road to meet a T-junction.

④ Turn right along Crooksbury Road and soon fork left on a bridleway beside Compton Way. Pass the rear of gardens and continue through woodland to meet the North Downs Way path at a marker post and steps. Turn left on the long-distance path and when it leaves the woodland, continue ahead alongside a field to reach a road. Now go downhill to the gateway to Moor Park House

⑤ Turn left through the gates, pass the house and remain ahead on a track where, near its end, it passes a cave before continuing close to a house to reach a road. Turn right here to join a road junction in 20 yards.

One infamous owner of Moor Park decided in 1879 to bar locals from using this path and chained the entrance gates. After being confronted by several hundred angry men and women wielding sticks and sledgehammers, the chain was broken and the path re-opened, as it quite fortunately has remained so to this day.

The cave, known as Mother Ludlam's Hole, was reputedly occupied by a benevolent witch of that name and many legends have grown up about her and a large cauldron that now resides in Frensham church. The most likely explanation of the cauldron was

made in Salmon's History of Surrey published in 1736, where he wrote that it was 'filled with ale and used for the entertainment of the village at the wedding of poor maids'. Many churches in the Middle Ages owned such a cauldron for use in village celebrations.

REFRESHMENTS

Facing Tilford village green is the popular Barley Mow pub where good food and beers can be enjoyed in a sunny riverside garden. Telephone: 01252 792205.

During the 18th century the cave became a much visited grotto feature with seating for visitors placed along either side. Iron cups were suspended on chains for those who chose to drink the cool water from the small spring that issues from within the darkness. A century later William Cobbett wrote: 'Alas, it is no longer the enchanting place that I knew…' and he went on '… the ground opposite, which was a grove chiefly of laurels, intersected by closely mown grass walks, has now become a poor ragged-looking alder coppice'.

The alder coppice is now an SSSI (Site of Special Scientific Interest) and a nationally rare habitat, while the cave entrance has been sealed for over a century for safety reasons; the only visitors now are the three species of bat that make it their home.

6   The way continues left along the road signed to Godalming, Milford and Elstead.

For the excursion, go ahead at this junction, cross a mill race and then turn left into a parking area. Press on alongside a stew pond believed to have been dug by the monks of the abbey to hold fish for their table, to reach the peaceful abbey ruins.

Founded in 1128, Waverley Abbey was the first monastery to be built in Britain by the Cistercian order; Fountains, Rievaulx and Tintern abbeys followed 25 years later. After the dissolution of the monasteries, much of the facing stone was transported to Loseley and incorporated into the new manor house.

Return to the road junction and turn right to continue the route. After 300 yards, turn right on a signed byway through woodland. At a junction with a footpath, turn right on the signed byway and continue through woodland until it ends at a road by the 17th-century barn of Sheephatch Farm.

7   Cross the road and go rightwards along a track. In 35 yards fork left, pass by a house with a unique dry stone wall and continue through woodland. When the track is joined by another from the right, bear left to soon pass Tilhill House. At the end of its grounds fork right on a downhill bridleway to rejoin the bridge at Tilford, where to the right is the village green and the end of this superb walk.

THE FOUNDING OF TWO GREAT HORSE RACES – THE DERBY AND THE OAKS

Length: 5¼ miles

Looking back along the finishing straight at Epsom racecourse

HOW TO GET THERE: The walk begins at Walton on the Hill which is on the B2220 signed from the A217 Tadworth roundabout.

PARKING: Turn left opposite Mere Pond as you enter Walton on the Hill and park along Deans Lane.

MAP: OS Landranger 187 (GR 227553).

INTRODUCTION

This great walk is virtually road-free and makes a good family outing where children can explore the route ahead to their heart's content. Beginning alongside Mere Pond in Walton on the Hill, the way follows a track across the common and passes a few isolated cottages before joining a bridleway that leads all the way to Walton and Epsom Downs. The circuit climbs the breezy downs and crosses the hallowed turf of the racecourse to meet the halfway point at the grandstand. As the way begins its return, it crosses The Hill, a popular spot for racegoers who flock here for the funfair and bookmakers' stalls on race days. After re-crossing the downs, a bridleway is joined beside Nohome Farm which returns you to Walton on the Hill to complete this enjoyable circuit. For obvious reasons, this walk is not suitable during race days.

HISTORICAL BACKGROUND

Epsom, already a well known spa town, saw the first recorded horse race on Epsom Downs in 1661 but racing didn't start in earnest until 1730 and it was almost a century later that the first grandstand was built.

Not far from Epsom Downs, to the south of Carshalton, stood a mansion called the Oaks, previously known as Lambert's Oaks after a family that had lived there

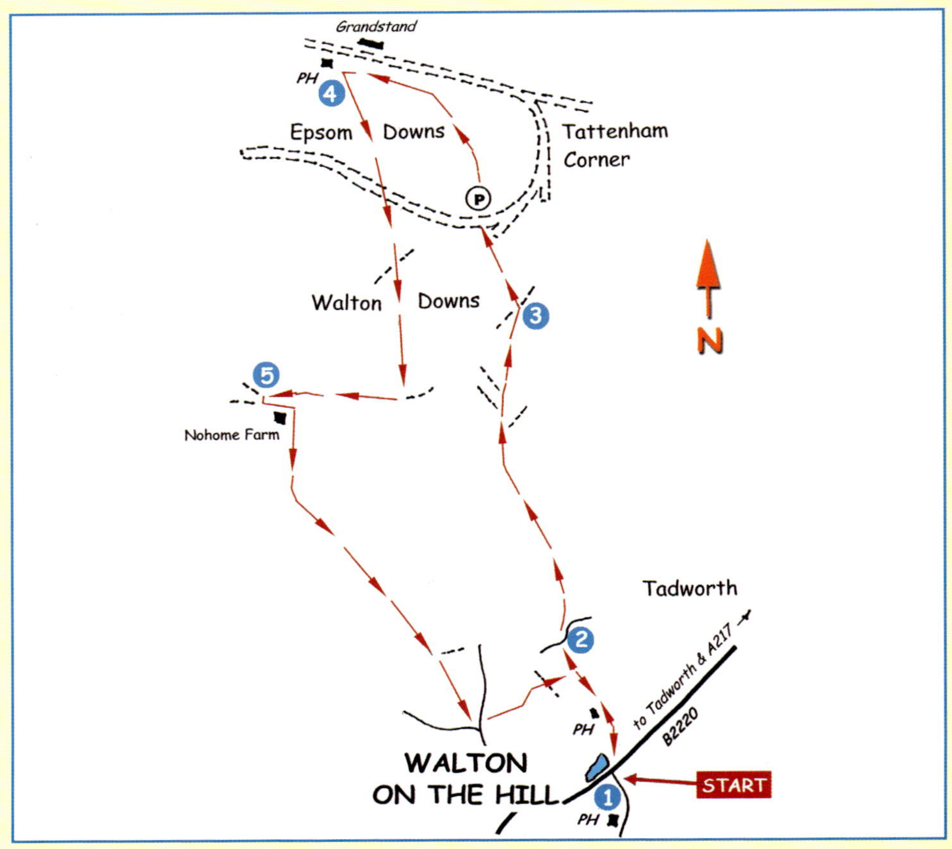

since the 14th century. Set within parkland reminiscent of a 'Capability Brown landscape, it had been rebuilt during the 1770s in the Italianate style and was owned by Edward Smith Stanley, the 12th Earl of Derby. In 1779, during one of the Earl's house parties, he organised a horse race for three-year-old fillies to be run at Epsom for the entertainment of his house guests and in honour of the event, they in turn named the race after his house, and so the Oaks was born.

The next year and another house party at the Oaks saw the inauguration of a second horse race, but this time the guests were undecided what to call it. The two contenders were Sir Charles Bunbury, a leading racing figure of the day and the Earl of Derby. A coin was tossed and had it dropped the other way we would all be watching the Bunbury each year rather than the Derby, although Sir Charles had the consolation of owning *Diomed*, the winner for that year.

In the beginning the course covered only one mile but was soon extended to its present-day one mile four furlongs; the races are both the same distance. Since those early days, the Epsom Derby and the Oaks have become classics in the horse-racing calendar and the left-handed course that follows the contours of the rolling downs is described as 'testing'. From the start line the runners begin a long uphill climb before sweeping downhill on a left-hand curve that gets tighter and tighter until they finally round Tattenham Corner at full speed, an impressive sight if you are standing by the rails here. It was at Tattenham Corner in 1913 that the suffragette Emily Davis fatally threw herself under King George V's horse, *Anmer*.

The straight is long and continues slightly downhill with an awkward camber of over 2 yards from right to left that can often affect challenging horses, and as the runners approach the stands they negotiate a short uphill section to reach the winning post, making the course a true test for the finest of thoroughbreds.

Many notable Derby records have been created here, among them the smallest field to take part at only four horses in 1794 and the largest ever at 34 runners in 1862; Lester Piggott becoming the youngest winning jockey at 18 in 1954; and *Shergar* winning by the widest margin ever recorded for the race, an incredible 10 lengths, in 1981. Sadly, two years later he was kidnapped by masked gunmen, generally believed to be an IRA unit and held to ransom for two million pounds. Negotiations failed and the greatest horse to grace Epsom was never seen again.

Although the original stand no longer exists, quite surprisingly the charmingly proportioned Prince's Stand of 1879 still graces the course albeit somewhat dwarfed by the large modern counterparts that have been built alongside it. As for the Earl of Derby's Carshalton house, that was pulled down in the late 1950s and Oaks Park is now a public amenity.

THE WALK

① From Deans Lane, cross the B2220 to meet a track to the right of Mere Pond and in 35 yards follow the right fork, ignoring a bridleway to your right. Continue

The route begins alongside Mere Pond

along this track as it passes a few isolated cottages and the Bell pub.

This little country pub is still known locally as 'The Rat', a name it had when just a beer house prior to it becoming a fully licensed pub in 1950.

Press on ahead along a dirt track and when it ends by the gates of a cottage and a coal duty post, continue ahead to soon meet a quiet drive. Turn right here and soon left on a bridleway by the gate of Bridle Cottage.

Coal duty posts once marked the boundary around London where tax became due on coal entering the capital. Originally introduced to help rebuild London after the Great Fire of 1666, the tax remained in force until 1889. The inscription '24 & 25 VICT CAP 42' refers to chapter 42 of the statue book during the 24th and 25th years of Queen Victoria's reign. Some duty posts were cast with an incorrect inscription and to facilitate a correction plate, several letters were ground off.

2 Now follow the bridleway as it continues behind large gardens. At the end of housing, at a fork in the bridleway, keep left and at a second fork in 50 yards, keep right. At a third fork in a further 45 yards, keep right again and follow the bridleway until it ends at a racehorse training track with open downs ahead of you.

3 Cross the training track and continue ahead on an indistinct path aiming for a radio beacon on top of the hill.

Quite surprisingly the downs are privately owned and it wasn't until an Act of Parliament in 1936 that the public were given the right of access for 'air and exercise' on foot although all racehorse training activities still take priority over other users before midday.

At the top of the rise go ahead on a sandy track to meet and cross the racecourse. Pass through a car park where ahead and right is Tattenham Corner while ahead and left is the grandstand, the halfway point of the circuit and you should make your way over the open downs to reach it.

4 The route continues left at the grandstand where you meet a junction of drives by the Rubbing House pub.

A horse trough here inscribed CICERO was donated by Lord Rosebery, one-time Prime Minister, and commemorates his Derby winner of 1906.

The Rubbing House is named after the paddock, Rubbing House Field, where horses were taken after each race. By 1801 a pub called the Rubbing House had been built on the site but it was consumed by fire in 1857 and was rebuilt as the Downs Hotel where guests could watch the racing from a long balcony. In 1968 the building was refurbished and the name returned to the Rubbing House.

Turn sharp left here on a tarmac drive that goes down a dip and climbs The Hill to rejoin the racecourse near the 9-furlong marker post. A glance to your right here will give you an idea of just how tough the course is; the Derby start is a further 3 furlongs down the slope. Cross the course and go ahead on a track through woodland to meet a T-junction. Remain ahead here on a grassy path, continue through a gap in the trees ahead and press on down a slope to meet a training track where you should turn right at the far side on a bridleway.

5 At a junction of tracks, turn left and in 20 yards turn left again to meet Nohome Farm. Here go right on a bridleway signed to Walton on the Hill. At its end in 1 mile when it meets Hurst Road, turn sharp left by a triangle of grass and in 12 yards turn right on a path beside the gateway of a house called Pilgrims. Follow this path until it ends by the coal duty post met earlier. Turn right now and retrace your steps back to Mere Pond to complete this fascinating walk.

CHATLEY HEATH – A MESSAGE FROM THE ADMIRALTY

Length: 7 miles

The well preserved semaphore tower

HOW TO GET THERE: The walk begins at Downside, 1½ miles south of Cobham. From Between Streets in Cobham, go south along Downside Bridge Road and in 1½ miles turn left at a crossroads.

PARKING: Park alongside the village green at Downside, opposite the Cricketers pub.

MAP: OS Landranger 187 (GR 108580).

INTRODUCTION

This lovely walk is level, varied and interesting. After leaving the pretty village green at Downside the route soon crosses the M25 motorway and continues through scenic fields to reach the tiny hamlet of May's Green. From here a lovely path through native woodland and over fields brings you to the outskirts of Ockham, where a bridleway is joined that leads you across the disused runway of Wisley airfield. Soon Ockham Common is met and waymarked paths lead you through beautiful scenery to the semaphore tower, where picnic tables are set out in a clearing of the woodland. A quiet track and hedgerow-lined drive bring you to Martyr's Green from where it is just a short walk back to Downside village.

HISTORICAL BACKGROUND

It was in 1684 that Robert Hooke first outlined his design for a visual telegraphy system to the Royal Society in London but his concept was never taken up and it lay dormant for almost a century. The next time the idea for a long-distance communication system surfaced, it was proposed by a French engineer named Claude Chappe who found his government more enthusiastic. After two years of experimentation on what he called the *télégraphe*, meaning 'far-writer', he was appointed by the French government to improve communications throughout France, firstly by building a line of 15 semaphore telegraph stations between Paris and Lille, a distance of around 140 miles.

His system employed the use of two black moveable wooden arms; one at each end of a T-shaped mast. Each arm was capable of seven positions, giving a total of 196 symbols; a typical message could travel the entire distance in 30 minutes, a huge improvement from when despatch riders where employed. To enable messages to be sent quicker and to be more secure, Claude also developed a code book for his semaphore operators. By using this book the operator could convert the basic arm movements into over 8,400 words and phrases. Eventually the French government commissioned over 550 semaphore stations throughout France, and Napoleon, never one to miss an advantage, even had his own portable version.

Seeing the success of the French semaphore, Britain began experimenting with their own system using opening and closing shutters which gave 63 combinations but proved less visible at distance. Later a design by Captain Popham incorporating a single mast and two moveable arms achieving 48 combinations was developed but this was soon superseded by an improved version by Colonel Charles Pasley. Similar to Popham's single mast, his design allowed each arm to be set in eight positions, giving 64 code combinations. The stations were positioned on high ground at intervals of between five and ten miles apart and were manned by a staff of two – one using a telescope trained on the up station while passing on the message to the second, who operated the

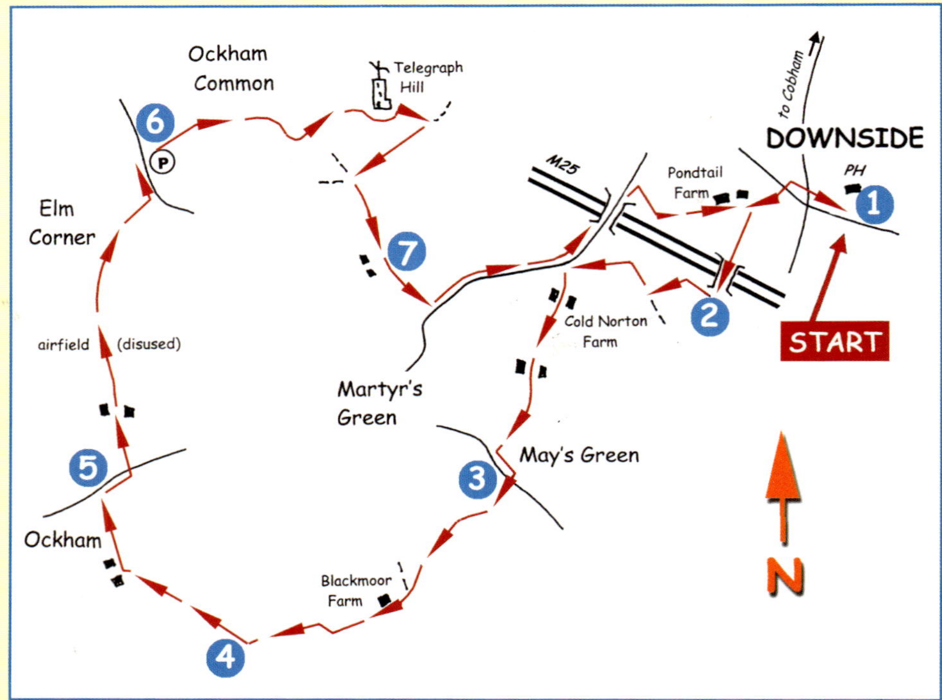

arms. Although the semaphore was a vast improvement, some despatch riders were still employed between the Admiralty offices and outlying stations because of poor visibility caused by the London smog, but the biggest drawback for all semaphores was that they were unable to operate at night.

Chatley Heath semaphore station was built in 1822. It was one of a line of 15 between the Admiralty in London and Portsmouth Harbour and is the only survivor. The next station north was at Esher while the nearest south was at Pewley Hill on the outskirts of Guildford. The optical telegraph system finally ceased in 1847 and was superseded by the newly invented electric telegraph.

The station is open from 12 noon until 5 pm on Saturdays, Sundays and bank holidays between April and October and on the first Sunday of each month between November and March.

THE WALK

1   Walk back to the crossroads, go ahead along Chilbrook Road and at the main gate of Pondtail Farm go left through a pedestrian gate. Follow the drive, where the landowner has thoughtfully planted a new hedgerow containing a good mix of indigenous shrubs. At the farmyard, go left over a stile and continue alongside a hedgerow. At the end of the hedgerow, cross a stile to your left, go over a farm track and stile opposite. Now turn right for 10 yards, go over a stile and continue on a bridge over the M25.

At 118 miles long, the M25 is the biggest ring road in the world, and at a cost of £909 million, the most expensive in Britain. This section between junction 8 at Reigate and junction 10 at Wisley was one of the last sections to be completed and was opened in 1985.

2   At the far side of the bridge pass through a field gate and turn right. When beside radio masts bear left and at a T-junction, turn right. After 200 yards turn left over a stile and continue on a path through a ribbon of trees. When the path ends at a road, turn left for 20 yards before turning left again along the driveway to Cold Norton Farm. Pass through the farm gate, go ahead between buildings and continue on a well signed path that leads you through small paddocks to reach a farmyard. Here, go ahead between two buildings and press on across a field to reach a farm track. Bear left along the track to meet a lane which soon ends at a T-junction.

3   Go left along the road and in 280 yards seek out a bridleway on your right. Now follow this through woodland as it traces an ancient bank and ditch.

Many of these banks and ditches date back to the Iron Age and once marked the border of a local chieftain's territory. Later many parish boundaries were marked in the same way.

At the end of woodland, continue ahead along a cart track to meet a farm drive. Go ahead and pass by Blackmoor Farm, ignore the drive when it bends left and keep ahead on a signed bridleway. After 90 yards, by a marker post, turn right on a footpath. At a vehicle barrier, turn right and in 30 yards when beside the gate of Stumps Grove Farm, turn left on a woodland path.

4   At the edge of woodland, cross a stile and go diagonally rightwards over a field. At the far side pass through a ribbon of woodland before maintaining your original direction over the next field to a stile in its corner. Now go ahead for 30 yards to meet a waymarked path. Turn left here, then right beside a barn in 40 yards. Keep ahead now alongside a field and through woodland to reach a road.

5   Turn right alongside the road before soon turning left along the drive to Bridge End Farm. At the farm, go ahead between buildings and soon between Armco barriers and cross the disused runway of Wisley airfield.

Pointing the way to the tower

Wisley airfield first became operational in 1944, when the aircraft manufacturer Vickers test flew its heavy bombers from here. Later, owned by the British Aircraft Corporation, test flights continued during 1948 on a prototype Vickers Viking, the first post-war British airliner to enter service. By 1952 a concrete runway 6,700 ft long had been constructed and a few years later saw test flights of the VC10 and BAC 111 airliners. The airfield closed in 1972 and the buildings were demolished in 1979.

At the far side of the runway follow a path through gates to soon join a byway, where you go ahead to meet a road in 60 yards. Turn left along the road to meet Ockham Common Pond car park on your right.

6   Turn right through the car park and pass by a vehicle barrier. Keep ahead on a wide path through woodland and follow red waymarked signs to reach Chatley Heath Semaphore Tower and welcome picnic seats. The route continues close to the right side of the tower along a tarmac drive. After 80 yards turn right on a downhill bridleway with an ancient bank and ditch on your left. At the foot of the slope by a junction of tracks, turn left on a bridleway signed to Ockham Lane.

REFRESHMENTS

The Cricketers on Downside village green offers a good selection of lunchtime and evening food. Telephone: 01932 862105.

7 At the end of this lovely track, go ahead along a tarmac drive to its end at a T-junction. Turn left here along the road and remain on it until it crosses the M25 motorway. In 100 yards after the bridge, turn sharp right on a signed bridleway and when it soon turns away from the motorway pass through a gate signed Pondtail Farm. Now follow the right side of a field to reach the farm buildings. Go ahead through the main gate and pass an ornamental pond, where you should continue along the drive and retrace your steps back to Downside village green.

The village green at Downside and the Cricketers pub

WALK 15

WAR FEVER AND THE FORT ON BOX HILL

Length: 5¾ miles

A section of the old fort

HOW TO GET THERE: The walk starts at Brockham, 1½ miles east of Dorking off the A25.

PARKING: Follow the signs to Brockham, cross the river Mole and park in Wheelers Lane beside Christ Church at the southern end of the village green.

MAP: OS Landranger 187 (GR 197494).

INTRODUCTION

This fairly energetic walk begins beside the picturesque village green at Brockham before crossing the river Mole and climbing 425 ft to the top of the North Downs.

The climb which, taken slowly, is not beyond the average family, is only a small section of this scenic route and once on top of the ridge, a level walk brings you to the well-known and popular vantage point of Box Hill where an information centre and café mark the halfway point of the circuit. After circling the old fort, the way descends the open hillside where breathtaking panoramic views across Surrey and Sussex are on offer. At the foot of the grassy slopes, the route re-crosses the river Mole before joining a lovely track that brings you back to Brockham.

HISTORICAL BACKGROUND

Box Hill certainly makes its presence known to those who pass through the only break in the line of the North Downs at Dorking. Facing the Dorking bypass is a 400 ft high chalk cliff known as 'The Whites', created by the river Mole that cuts along its base.

The cliff provides a sanctuary for the ancient box woodland from which the hill is named. Box (*Buxus sempervirens*) is an evergreen shrub or small tree that once grew in abundance on the hill and became a valuable commodity; an account in

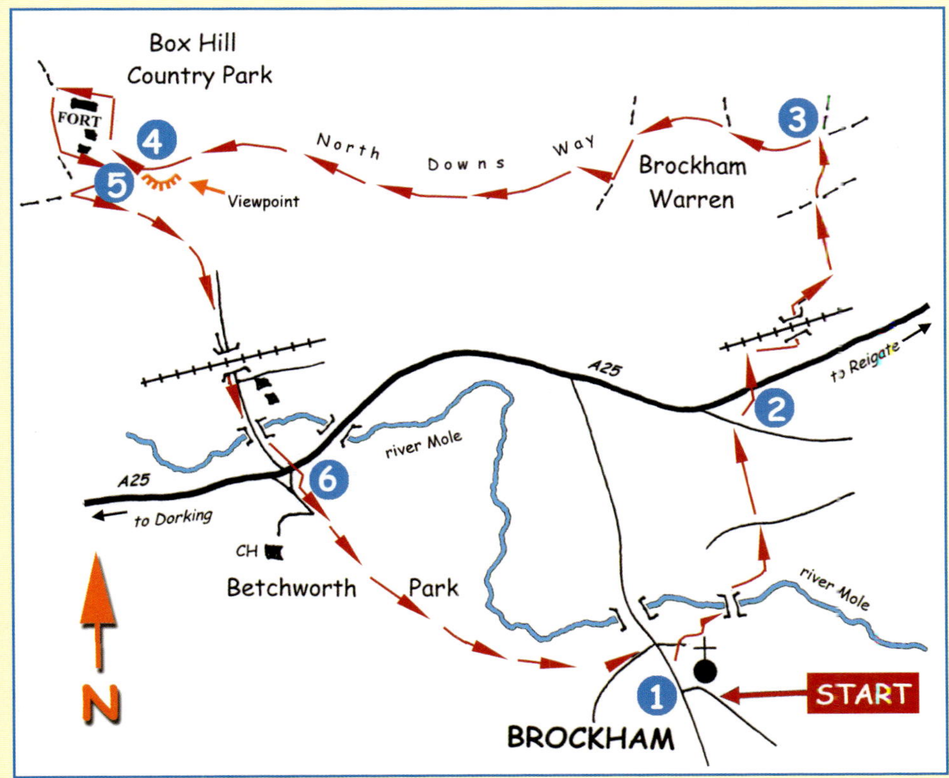

1797 states that Sir Henry Mildmay sold the rights for cutting trees over 20 years old at Box Hill for the then enormous sum of £20,000. Because of its dense, fine grain the wood was highly prized by wood block engravers as it enabled them to carve their illustrations with precision. More latterly its commercial use has been restricted to the young evergreen shoots used in florists' wreaths.

Many people have written about the beauty of the area, perhaps the first being Celia Fiennes who, towards the end of 17th century wrote: '…it's a great height and shows you a vast precipice on the farther side and such a vast vale full of woods, enclosures and little towns; there is a very good river that runs by a little town called Darken …'.

On the crest of Box Hill is a fort that was one of 13 built to protect London from invasion. They were erected in the last years of the 19th century by a Government that had not lost its fear of France, even though 80 years had lapsed since Napoleon Bonaparte had run rampant throughout Europe. Still gripped by the fear of invasion from across the English Channel, they planned a strategic defence line of forts to the south of London along the escarpment of the North Downs and the Hog's Back near Guildford.

The forts are somewhat misnamed as they were never equipped or fortified to the same extent as the earlier Napoleonic coastal defences. The next fort to the east was at Brockham Hills while the nearest westward was at Denbies above Dorking, both now demolished. They were designed by General Hamley, a military strategist who firmly believed that volunteer forces could play an important part in the defence of the capital. His forts contained limited artillery and were really not much more than fortified assembly and supply depots designed to protect nearby trenches and to supply provisions for the troops lining the hill tops. In 1906 the government finally regained its composure when the Royal Navy launched HMS *Dreadnought*, a revolutionary type of warship, and the forts were soon abandoned.

THE WALK

1   From Wheelers Lane walk back to the village green and follow a tarmac path along its right-hand side. Turn right on a lane by the Duke's Head pub and in 50 yards, when beside the village pound, go left through a pedestrian gate and continue on a tarmac path. After crossing the river Mole, bear right on a rising track and keep ahead to meet a T-junction with a road. Continue on a gravel drive opposite and keep ahead when it is met by another from the right. Cross a road and press on ahead on a signed footpath that soon ends at the busy A25.

2   Go ahead over the A25 with caution and cross a stile to enter a field. Follow a line of power cables to the far side where you should cross a stile and turn right along the field edge with a railway line to your left. At the field end turn left under a railway bridge and in 12 yards turn right over a stile. Now go diagonally

The panoramic view from the Salomon memorial and toposcope

right on an indistinct path aiming for a marker post 30 yards to the left of a pylon. From this post turn half left and continue to the tree line at the top end of the field. Cross a stile to meet a T-junction in 10 yards. Turn right now and in 10 yards fork left on an uphill path through woodland.

3   When a well-used crossing path signed as the North Downs Way is met, turn left along it. For the next 1¾ miles follow the clearly-marked North Downs Way and acorn signs. At one point the path begins to descend the hillside and here make sure you don't miss a right turn up steps after 320 yards on your right. Continue along the North Downs Way until you come to the popular open hillside by the Salomon memorial.

The viewpoint and toposcope memorial is in memory of Leopold Salomon, who gave Box Hill to the National Trust in 1923.

4   Follow a tarmac path to the right of the memorial to reach a National Trust shop and the Fort Café, where tables are set out on the lawn. The way continues leftwards on a bridleway 35 yards after the garden where the fort is soon reached. Pass close to the side of the fort on a narrow path and continue through a strip of woodland to meet a wide stony track. Turn left here to soon pass an unusual gravestone.

This stone marks the grave of Major Peter Labelliere, an eccentric resident of Dorking who, on his death in 1800, left two specific wishes; the first that his landlady's two youngest children dance on his coffin to show that there should be rejoicing rather than sadness at death and secondly, that he be buried upside down, reasoning that in this topsy turvy world he would meet his maker the right way up. For years afterwards locals celebrated his death by picnicking and dancing on the site.

After passing the gravestone, keep left at a fork in the track and pass the entranceway to an unseen house in the woodland to rejoin the garden of the Fort Café, where you should retrace your steps to the Salomon memorial.

The flint house among the trees at the end of the drive is called Swiss Cottage and is where John Logie Baird carried out some of his first experiments with television in 1930.

5   When facing the memorial and the panoramic view, go right on a wide path across the open hilltop that soon enters woodland. After 90 yards, and just before a clearing is met, turn sharp left on an easily missed path that now descends diagonally across the face of the hillside. Maintain direction at the foot of the hill and continue along a tarmac lane. At a road junction keep right and at the end of the road, cross a footbridge over the river Mole to meet the A25.

6   Although the way continues ahead along the drive to Betchworth Park Golf Club opposite, it is safer to turn left alongside the A25 for 50 yards and cross the road via a pedestrian refuge. Go along the golf club drive and in 70 yards continue along it leftwards. When the drive turns right towards the clubhouse, continue ahead on a signed bridleway along an old coach road that initially passes between fairways and later farmland to finally end at a lane. Go left here along the lane and cross Tanner's Brook to rejoin Brockham village green where Christ Church, Wheeler's Lane and the end of this great walk are to be found to the right.

ENGLAND'S MICHELANGELO – G.F. WATTS OF COMPTON

Length: 4½ miles

The Watts Gallery in its country setting

HOW TO GET THERE: Compton is on the B3000 ½ mile east of the A3 just south of Guildford.

PARKING: In the lay-by outside the village hall, The Street, Compton. When travelling from the A3, the lay-by is on the right in the centre of the village. The convention on parking is either nose or tail to the kerb. If the lay-by is full, there is additional roadside parking in Spiceall, a further 150 yards west.

MAP: OS Landranger 186 (GR 956468).

INTRODUCTION

This lovely walk passes through delightful countryside as well as being packed full of interesting history. The route begins by heading east and soon passes 16th-century Loseley House, for centuries the home of the More family. A lakeside in the grounds is set out with tables and makes a good picnic spot. The walk then turns north and joins with the scenic North Downs Way long-distance path, which it follows below the Hog's Back until the Watts Gallery is met. Entry to the unique one-man art gallery is free and refreshing nourishment can be had at the adjoining tea rooms. Continuing on, you come to the Watts Memorial Chapel, a creation by the great man's wife. As the route returns along the village street it passes many old cottages and Compton's famous 12th-century St Nicholas' church. Allow plenty of time to enjoy this fascinating walk.

HISTORICAL BACKGROUND

George Frederick Watts was born in 1817 and became one of the most important artists of his time. For most of his life he lived and worked in London, but spent some time in Italy after which he returned for a short stay with Henry Prinsep and his wife at Little Holland House in Kensington, a Bohemian centre for artists and writers. His 'short stay' lasted for 24 years and over that time he became good friends with many of the Pre-Raphaelites, and even influenced some of the younger ones, although he himself ploughed his own furrow and his style throughout remained largely Classicist.

His first noted work came in 1842 and was entitled *Caratacus Led in Triumph through the Streets of Rome*, for which he won a prize. By 1865 Watts had found a patron in Charles Richards, a Manchester man who began buying his work. This

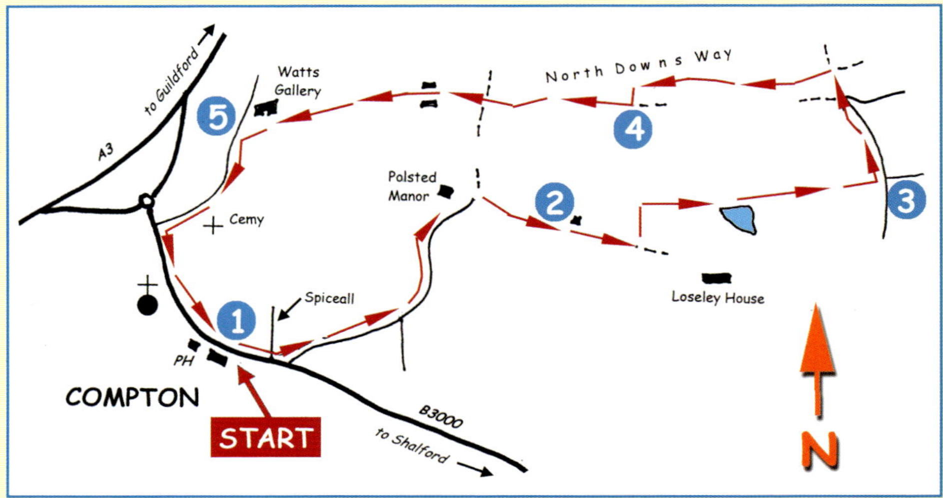

provided him with a decent income and in 1877 he exhibited for the first time at the Grosvenor Gallery. Now firmly established and living in Melbury Road, London, he converted his studio into a gallery during 1881 and over the next few years twice stubbornly refused a Baronetcy although he did later accept the Order of Merit.

In 1891, and not in the best of health, he and his wife Mary, a skilled craftswoman herself, left London and its smog behind to move to the country near their friends at Compton and so, at the age of 74 he had a substantial house designed and built in Down Lane and named it Limnerlease. To display his work, they had the Watts Gallery built across the road from the house in 1903. The architect was Christopher Turnor who pursued the Arts and Crafts style for the building, which was intended not only to house the artist's work, but also to act as accommodation for the apprentices of his wife's successful pottery.

Watts died in 1904, the year the gallery opened and true to his socialist principles it has remained free of entry ever since. Sadly, much of his most important work resides in galleries around the world, but there is enough here to immerse yourself in. The gallery is Grade II listed and remains one of the few single-artist galleries in Britain today. The building, which requires constant remedial maintenance work, was featured in the BBC television series *Restoration Village* in 2006 and came second in the national final.

The gallery is open on Monday, Tuesday, Friday and Sunday from 2 pm until 6 pm (4 pm in winter) and Wednesday and Saturday 11 am to 1 pm and 2 pm to 6 pm (4 pm in winter). Closed on Thursday.

THE WALK

1   From the lay-by, cross the road and turn right along the pavement and soon cross the end of Spiceall. Maintain direction over a large grassy area to meet a quiet lane which you now follow leftwards. Remain on this lane and ignore side turns. When it finally ends 60 yards after passing the entrance gate to Polsted Manor, turn right along a cart track.

2   Along the way pass by Polsted Lodge gate house and press on along an avenue of horse chestnut trees to a second gate beside a Loseley sign. Turn left here and follow a narrow path that skirts the grounds of Loseley House. Cross two stiles in quick succession and continue ahead alongside a field edge.

Across the parkland is Loseley House, a beautiful Elizabethan mansion built in 1562 by Sir William More using many of the facing stones from Waverley Abbey near Farnham, while the interior has wood panelling from Henry VIII's Nonsuch Palace.

Soon cross a stile on your right to meet the bank of a scenic lake, a good picnic spot. Continue along the bank and cross a second stile before pressing on ahead

St Nicholas church, with its wonderful Norman arches and rare two-storey sanctuary

on a well trodden path through two fields. After passing between a couple of cottages, meet with a road.

3 Turn left here on the rising lane and at a hairpin bend with Sandy Lane, keep ahead. Ignore a bridleway on your left in 20 yards, but 35 yards later turn left over a stile and continue on the signed North Downs Way long-distance path.

4 At the foot of a dip when the track turns sharply rightwards, go left for 15 yards before turning right on the North Downs Way path through woodland. When a junction of tracks is met in a dip, press on ahead and remain on this wonderful path until it meets a lane beside the Watts Gallery and Tea Rooms.

5 After visiting the gallery, turn left along the narrow lane. *It is safer to remain on the left side of the lane as it offers slightly more room for pedestrians.* The route soon passes the not to be missed Watts Memorial Chapel, a true masterpiece of imagination that mixes Italian Romanesque, Art Nouveau and Celtic art.

Mary Watts and her craftsmen built this memorial chapel in honour of her husband. The chapel is open to the public and displays her wonderful terracotta ornamentation.

Continue along the lane until it ends at a T-junction and then turn left alongside The Street where many old cottages will be passed. Look out for St Nicholas' church on the right.

Parts of St Nicholas' date from the 11th century but it is best known for its very rare 12th-century, two-storey sanctuary, with a guard rail that is one of the earliest pieces of Norman woodwork in the country, while below is a finely executed vaulted lower chamber. The church boasts two arches with deeply carved decoration that display the exquisite workmanship of the Norman stonemason, while under the protection of a couple of Perspex sheets is an earlier Saxon window with a horn frame and medieval graffiti carved into the internal stonework.

Press on alongside The Street to soon return to the village hall lay-by, or Spiceall if you parked there, to complete this interesting walk.

REFRESHMENTS

The Watts Gallery Tea Shop on the route offers teas, coffee, home-made cakes and light lunches. Next to the village hall is the Harrow Inn, long known for its good food. Telephone: 01483 810379.

A ONE-WAY TICKET TO BROOKWOOD – THE LONDON NECROPOLIS

Length: 3 ¼ miles

A section of the military cemetery, with the Brookwood Memorial beyond

HOW TO GET THERE: The walk starts at Pirbright, which is on the A324, 4 miles north of Guildford.

PARKING: When travelling from the Guildford direction, turn right in Pirbright beside the White Hart and park in a lay-by beside the village pond. Additional parking can be found around the village green.

MAP: OS Landranger 186 (GR 947559).

INTRODUCTION

This unique and quite fascinating walk begins in the centre of Pirbright village and soon passes the grave of the great newspaperman and explorer, Sir Henry Morton Stanley who discovered Dr Livingstone in the African jungle. After passing through quiet woodland, the route continues in Brookwood's pristine military cemetery, the last resting place for so many brave men and women from around the world. As the way begins to make its return to Pirbright it passes through the civil cemetery where the vast expanses of grassland, heathland and woodland habitats are so important to wildlife and have quite rightly been included on the National Register of Parks and Gardens of Historic Interest, as well as a Site of Nature Conservation Importance. Dogs are not permitted in either cemetery.

> *The owners of the cemetery have kindly given permission for this route through their property to be published but have requested that any group visits, both large and small, seek written permission in advance.*
>
> **For further information: www.brookwoodcemetery.com**

HISTORICAL BACKGROUND

By the mid 19th century London had run out of room to bury its dead and so in an effort to solve the problem, an enterprising group of businessmen got together

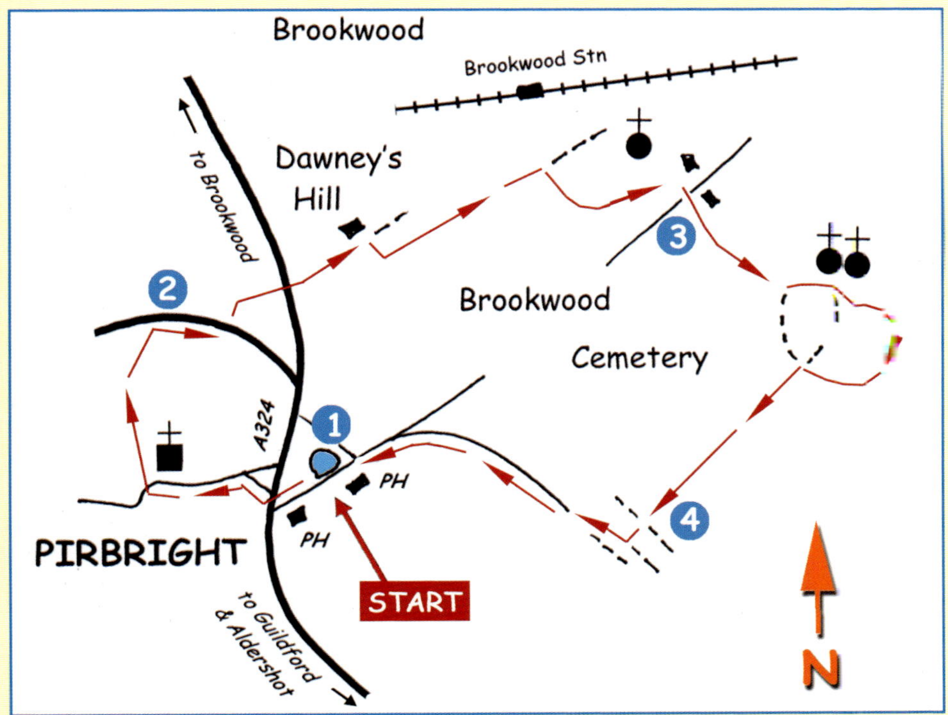

and formed the London Necropolis & National Mausoleum Company, which was established by Act of Parliament two years later. After purchasing 2,000 acres of land at Brookwood from Lord Onslow they began to plant redwood trees and, rather unusually, to construct two purpose-built railway stations, one for Anglicans and the other for Nonconformists.

The cemetery, then the largest in the world, opened in November 1854 and specially converted London & South Western Railway trains began their daily service from a private terminus beside Waterloo Station in London, which issued special one-way tickets for the coffins. Utilising the company's main line to Brookwood, the trains then transferred to a branch line that ran through the cemetery, stopping first at North station for the Nonconformists before continuing on to the Anglican South station. The terminus at Waterloo continued to send London's dead to Brookwood until it was destroyed by bombing during the Second World War. It was never rebuilt and the service ceased. The tracks through the cemetery were ripped up soon after the war and both stations became derelict and by the mid 1970s were demolished.

Although no longer the largest cemetery in the world, Brookwood remains the largest in England and is the last resting place for over 235,000 people. It is quite unique in its rural vastness and it far surpasses the London cemeteries it came to replace. Although the original company relinquished its interest in 1970, the cemetery is still in private hands and remains open for burials. The owners have kindly given permission for walkers following this route to use the paths through the cemetery, but please see the boxed information above regarding any organised groups visiting.

THE WALK

❶   From the village pond, walk back to the White Hart, cross the A324 road and bear off rightwards along a residential road to soon meet Church Lane. Turn left along the lane and as you round a right-hand bend, pass by the graveyard of St Michael and All Saints' church.

In the graveyard is a large granite monolith marking the grave of Sir Henry Morton Stanley; the same Stanley who uttered those immortal words 'Dr Livingstone, I presume' after an epic journey through dense African jungle in search of the missionary during 1871. The two then explored what is present-day Tanzania and established that Lake Tanganyika was not the source of the Nile. During a later expedition, Stanley solved the last great African mystery by tracing the course of the river Congo to the sea. The inscription 'Bula Matari' is the name given him by his African porters and means 'rock breaker'.

In 45 yards after passing the church lych gate, turn right over a stream and continue on a narrow path along a ribbon of woodland until a road is met.

The former Anglican chapel now houses the St Edward Brotherhood

2   Turn right alongside the road and when the entrance gate of Pirbright village primary school is reached, go left through a small parking area. Then 30 yards after passing the gate of Surrey Wildlife Trust's headquarters, turn right on a path and continue through a small cluster of houses to rejoin the A324. Cross the road and continue along a magnificent avenue of pines to reach the gate of Brookwood Military Cemetery. Go through a pedestrian gate and after 40 yards turn right on a tarmac drive, passing by the Brookwood Memorial that honours those with no known grave. Keep to this drive as it soon bends left and continues through these magnificent grounds.

The military cemetery is administered by the Commonwealth War Graves Commission. Among the graves are twelve holders of the Victoria Cross ranging in rank from private to brigadier general, although great courage holds no rank.

When the closely cropped grass, regimented memorials and pristine tarmac come to an end, continue ahead through a pedestrian gate beside a vehicle gate and enter the civil cemetery where, in contrast, you will find a riot of nature. Soon turn right along Western Avenue and as it nears its end look out for a striking new black headstone on your left.

The newly-erected headstone was placed here in April 2007 by the Scots Guards

Association to honour one of their forgotten war heroes who had lain here for 138 years in an unmarked '2nd class grave'. Private William Reynolds earned a Victoria Cross during the battle of the river Alma, the first major battle of the Crimean War of 1854-1856. After surviving the battles of Alma, Balaclava, Inkermann and Sebastopol, he was invested with his medal by Queen Victoria in June 1857. Sadly, just twelve years later he succumbed to illness and died at the Strand Union Workhouse in London, aged 42.

REFRESHMENTS

The Cricketer's (telephone: 01483 473198) and White Hart (telephone: 01483 799715) pubs are near the starting point and both serve a good selection of food.

At the end of Western Avenue turn right to meet with a road.

3   Cross the road and continue ahead along St Cyprians Avenue. Remain on the curving drive to reach the buildings of St Edward Orthodox Church and Brotherhood.

The former Anglican chapel is now home to the St Edward Brotherhood, named after an early king of England who was murdered in AD 979 at the tender age of 17 on the command of Queen Elfrida, his jealous stepmother, in order that her own son, Ethelred the Unready could become king. Many subsequent miracles surrounding King Edward's remains elevated him to the title of 'Martyr' and his relics were enshrined in 1001; seven years later he became a saint.

In 1931 a casket believed to contain his bones was discovered and the owner of the land began long discussions with the major churches to find a suitable resting place. After many years it was only the Russian Orthodox Church in Exile that met his criteria and so in September 1984 a ceremony of enshrinement took place in the brotherhood's then newly-acquired church within the London Necropolis.

Turn right opposite the church. Ignore St David's Avenue on your immediate right and take St Chad's Avenue to the left of it. The drive first curves left before curving rightwards after it passes a double gate. At a wide crossing path, turn left along St Mark's Avenue and remain on this until it ends at the edge of woodland.

4   As you enter woodland, a junction of paths is met. Ignore those to left and right and press on ahead to soon meet a T-junction. Turn right here and in 8 yards go left to meet with a byway. Now turn right to join Chapel Lane in 30 yards. Go rightwards along the lane and at its end turn left alongside the road to pass the Cricketer's pub and return to the village pond and the end of this fascinating circuit.

LAVISH EDWARDIAN SPLENDOUR – POLESDEN LACEY

Length: 5¾ miles

Polesden Lacey, now owned by the National Trust

HOW TO GET THERE: The walk begins at Ranmore Common, which can be reached via the A24 at Dorking. From opposite Dorking Station go west along Ashcombe Road and at its end turn right into Ranmore Road. In 1¼ miles pass by a car park on your left and continue for 1 further mile.

PARKING: Ranmore Common National Trust car park.

MAP: OS Landranger 187 (GR 126501).

INTRODUCTION

This very easy to follow undulating route begins on a wide track in native woodland and crosses a shallow valley to the parkland of Polesden Lacey. The circuit passes the entrance to the grounds and a visit to the house will add a further two-thirds of a mile to the length of the walk. The way skirts the extensive parkland as it turns and begins to head back, passing the remote Tanners Hatch Youth Hostel along the way. Continuing on a broad cart track through majestic woodland, the circuit heads for Ranmore where it joins with a section of the

North Downs Way long-distance path. After following the escarpment for a while, a short bridleway all too soon brings you back to the car park to end this great walk.

HISTORICAL BACKGROUND

Polesden Lacey is one of Surrey's premier grand houses and is set within beautiful grounds on top of the North Downs. During its lifetime it has undergone many alterations and rebuilds since it was first recorded in 1336. Its most famous owner was Sheridan, the great poet and playwright, who bought the house in 1804 and absorbed himself totally in playing the country squire and creating hugely lavish parties for his friends.

This tradition of opulence was carried on a century later by the Grevilles when they purchased the house in 1906 and had it remodelled to suit their lavish entertainment needs. It has been written that society hostess Mrs Greville came

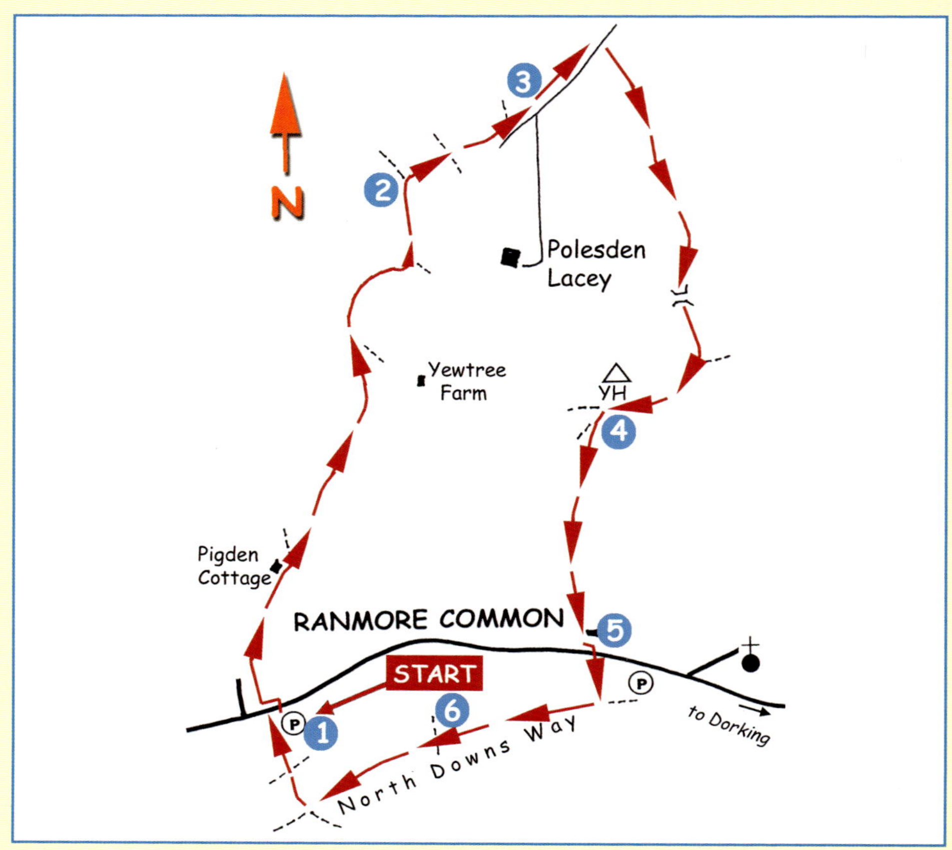

from a rather dubious background and that she was actually the illegitimate daughter of William McEwan, the founder of the brewery business that still carries his name. Whether or not she was his daughter and for whatever reason, she was supported by his great wealth and she, on coming of age, joined London high society where she first met Ronald, her future husband, and his great friend Edward VII.

The Grevilles already owned a large fashionable home in London but her fiercely competitive nature fed the need to outshine other society hostesses of the day and so Polesden Lacey was purchased. These were times of plenty for the rich and her lavish parties became legendary, with glittering guest lists that included many Royals; in 1923 the house hosted King George VI and Queen Elizabeth the Queen Mother who spent their honeymoon here.

Mrs Greville's collection of fine paintings, furniture, porcelain and silver is displayed in the reception rooms and galleries, just as it was at the time of her celebrated house parties. The final gesture of her immense generosity came on her death when she bequeathed the house and its contents to the National Trust, in whose hands it safely remains.

Polesden Lacey house is open mid-March to the end of October between 11 am and 5 pm from Wednesday to Sunday. The gardens are open each day throughout the year. Admission fees apply to both.

THE WALK

❶ From the most westerly car park entrance, cross the road and go ahead to meet a wide grassy track in 20 yards. Turn left here to soon meet a stony byway in a dip where you should now turn right. Remain on this old byway and ignore a left fork 100 yards after passing lonely Pigden Cottage. Ignore any side paths as the byway leads you through a shallow valley.

❷ After 1½ miles, a distinct fork in the byway is met and here you should take the right fork and pass along the left-hand side of two fields to meet a cart track. Maintain direction ahead here to the tarmac drive of Polesden Lacey. *(If you intend to visit the house, turn right here and pass the gatehouse.)*

❸ The route continues ahead along a fine avenue of young beech trees. At the top of a rise at the end of the parkland, seek out a signed bridleway on your right. Now remain on this superb track as it leads you back through the valley and brings you to the door of Tanners Hatch Youth Hostel after 1¼ miles.

❹ In 35 yards after passing the hostel, ignore a footpath ahead and bear left on a cart track and 30 yards later keep left at a fork. Remain on this track as it leads you through magnificent indigenous woodland before ending at the road on Ranmore Common.

The fine view over Dorking from the route

⑤   Turn left alongside the road for 40 yards before turning right on a signed footpath through woodland until it ends at a T-junction with the North Downs Way long-distance path. Turn right here and in 20 yards fork right along the long-distance path.

This track has been adopted as part of the 153 miles of the North Downs Way long-distance path that begins in Farnham and ends at Dover via Canterbury. It was first called the Pilgrims Way by Victorian mapmakers, although being a Neolithic trackway it pre-dates pilgrimage to the tomb of Thomas Becket, Archbishop of Canterbury by some 8,000 years.

⑥   When a byway crosses the North Downs Way path, keep ahead on the long-distance path but ½ mile later at a crossing bridleway, turn right up a short hill. Now keep ahead on the bridleway to soon meet with the car park and the end of this great walk.

REFRESHMENTS

There is a good tea room within the grounds of Polesden Lacey though it can only be accessed by paying an admittance charge to this National Trust property. Otherwise there is plenty of choice in nearby Dorking.

MOSQUITO
Squadrons of the
ROYAL AIR FORCE

MOSQUITO
Squadrons of the
ROYAL AIR FORCE

Chaz Bowyer

LONDON
IAN ALLAN LTD

First published 1984

ISBN 0 7110 1425 6

Published by Ian Allan Ltd, Shepperton, Surrey;
and printed by Ian Allan Printing Ltd at their works
at Coombelands in Runnymede, England.

Contents

Acknowledgments

In compiling this tribute to the Mosquito I have yet again been most fortunate in my friends and acquaintances, whose selfless generosity supplied no small number of the illustrations herein. Each is owed a sincere debt of gratitude. They are (in alphabetical order); Sqn Ldr R. C. B. — 'Chris' — Ashworth, RAF Retd; Sqn Ldr A. F. — 'Tony' — Carlisle, DFC, RAF Retd; Jerzy Cynk; Gp Capt J. R. — 'Benny' — Goodman, DFC, AFC, RAF Retd; Peter H. T. Green; E. — 'Ted' — Hine of the Imperial War Museum Photo Library; Stuart Howe; R. — 'Reg' — Mack of the RAF Museum, Hendon; K. — 'Ken' — Munson; Rev John D. R. Rawlings; Bruce Robertson; Ray C. Sturtivant; Flt Lt A. — 'Andy' — Thomas RAF; Dave Vincent in Australia; Elayne Ware of *Flight International* Photo Library; and never least, Dave Gray of Walkers Studios, Scarborough. And for splendid help and numerous photographs when I visited the former de Havilland 'Archives' at Hatfield some 12 years ago, Philip Birtles and 'Ted' Hunt, whose dedication to preserving the history of de Havilland aircraft and history is rarely matched.

Introduction

The de Havilland 98 Mosquito was one of very few aircraft designs in Royal Air Force annals to have been an immediate success on its introduction to firstline operational use — in simpler words, a 'winner' from the outset. It also proved to be one of the most adaptable aircraft ever to wear RAF livery, shouldering with aplomb a truly astonishing range of roles with equal accomplishment and, indeed, often outshining other aircraft types designed specifically for each of those roles. Day and nightfighter, fighter-bomber, pure bomber, intruder, pathfinder, anti-shipping hunter, photo-reconnaissance 'eye', minelayer, meteorological 'sniffer', high speed courier — all were grist to the 'Mozzie's' mill. In all nearly 8,000 Mosquitos were actually built, in some 50 distinct variants or versions, until production ceased in November 1950. These, among other allocations, fully or partly equipped more than 100 RAF-controlled squadrons between 1941 and 1955. The first Mosquito war sortie, a photo-recce of the Brest area, was flown on 17 September 1941, while the ultimate Mosquito operational sortie in RAF firstline service was flown from Seletar, Singapore, on 15 December 1955. Thus, the RAF owes a huge debt to the Mosquito, and particularly to the men and women whose foresight, faith, skills and courage created, produced, and flew the design to its deserved permanent niche in RAF history.

This book, therefore, is primarily a record and reminder of the Mosquito's enormous contribution to the RAF's constant endeavours to preserve freedom during the fateful years of World War 2 and the post-bellum decade. Its contents are deliberately restricted to those squadrons and other units which operated Mosquitos in RAF service, under direct RAF control only; the design's doughty service with other air forces may be traced readily in many of the published sources quoted in the bibliography, as can greater detail of particular Mosquito units, personnel, operations, etc. Hence, the squadron 'histories' herein are patently much condensed, and confined in the main to those periods, bases, etc concerned with the operation of Mosquitos. My original aim to provide at least one representative photograph of each squadron's Mosquitos has proved (apparently) impossible to achieve, due in part no doubt to the contemporary officialdom's hysterical obsession with so-termed 'security', which regarded even possession of a camera as virtual treason. Again, a few photographs used here are frankly of poor reproductive quality, but are deliberately included for their historical value.

Chaz Bowyer
Norwich

Squadrons Nos 1-110

No 4 Squadron

Formed originally at Farnborough in September 1912 from a nucleus supplied by No 2 Squadron, No 4 Squadron flew general army co-operation and reconnaissance roles from then until 1944, apart from a brief disbandment period from September 1919 to April 1920. From 1939 the Squadron was equipped successively with Lysanders, Tomahawks and Mustangs until August 1943, in which month the unit was reorganised for photo-reconnaissance duties only. For this role 'A' Flight received Spitfire XIs and XIIIs for high-level work, while 'B' Flight flew Mosquito XVIs. By March 1944 'B' Flight comprised six Mosquitos but two months later these were phased out and No 4 Squadron became an all-Spitfire unit for high-level PR duties only. Disbanded at Celle, Germany, on 31 August 1945, its remaining personnel and aircraft were absorbed by No 2

Mosquito VIs of No 4 Squadron, 1949 at Celle. In the centre (white overall) is Sqn Ldr C. P. N. Newman, DFC (OC Squadron).

Squadron — in effect, a return to No 4 Squadron's origins — but on the same date a new No 4 Squadron was 'born' at Volkel by the simple process of renumbering the resident No 605 Squadron AAF there. The 'new' No 4 Squadron flew Mosquito FBVIs in a pure bomber role until July 1950, and was then tasked with low-level fighter attack and consequently exchanged its aircraft for Vampire FB5 jets.

Main bases

Odiham	August 1943
Sawbridgeworth	November 1943
Aston Down	January 1944
Sawbridgeworth	March 1944
Gatwick	April 1944
Volkel	August 1945
Gilze-Rijen	September 1945
Gutersloh	November 1945
Wahn	November 1947
Celle	September 1949
Wunstorf	July 1950

Aircraft examples flown
HJ756; MM273, 'P'; MM299, 'Q'; MM309, 'U'; MM315, 'T'; MM361, 'W'; NT181, 'H'; PZ165, 'E'; RS625; RS678, 'T'; RS679; SZ967; TA539, 'D'; TA122; VL728, 'F'.

Commanding Officers

Sqn Ldr R. H. D. Rigall	March 1943
Flt Lt A. S. Baker	December 1943
Sqn Ldr R. J. Hardiman DFC	December 1943
Sqn Ldr W. Shepherd	May 1944
Sqn Ldr C. D. Harris St John DFC	May 1945
Wg Cdr M. P. C. Corkery	September 1945
Wg Cdr R. L. Jones	May 1946
Sqn Ldr B. Everton-Jones	November 1947
Sqn Ldr C. P. N. Newman DFC	September 1949

No 8 Squadron

After disbandment as a Liberator 'Special Duties' unit at Minneriyah on 15 November 1945, No 8 Squadron was reformed at Khormaksar, Aden, on 1 September 1946 with the renumbering of No 114 Squadron. With a bomber role initially the Squadron flew Mosquito FBVIs (eg TE702) but in March 1947 the unit began receiving Tempest fighters, and by May 1947 had relinquished its Mosquito aircraft.

Commanding Officers

Wg Cdr P. E. St E. O'Brien DFC	September 1946
Sqn Ldr F. W. M. Jensen DFC, AFC	February 1947

No 11 Squadron

A Spitfire unit of the Allied occupation forces in Japan from May 1946, No 11 Squadron was disbanded there on 23 February 1948, but on 4 October 1948 the Squadron was re-formed at Wahn, Germany, where No 107 Squadron was retitled. At first No 11 Squadron's Mosquitos FBVIs retained No 107 Squadron's 'OM' codings on some aircraft. In August 1950 its Mosquitos began being replaced by Vampire FB5 jet fighters, and from 11 August the Squadron's prime role was officially changed to ground attack.

Main bases

Wahn	October 1948
Celle	September 1949
Wunstorf	August 1950

Aircraft examples flown
NS898; SZ984 (EX-C); TA489 (OM-D); TA581.

Commanding Officers

Flt Lt J. Welsh	June 1948
Sqn Ldr I. W. Hutchison	October 1948
Sqn Ldr J. M. Rumsey	March 1949
Sqn Ldr D. H. Seaton	August 1950

No 13 Squadron

Though disbanded as a Boston bomber unit at Hassani, Greece, on 19 April 1946, No 13 Squadron was re-formed at Ein Shemer, Palestine, on 1 September that same year when

Above:
PR34, RG268, 'F' of No 13 Squadron.
via R. C. B. Ashworth

Below:
PR34, VL618 of 13 Squadron.
Hawker Siddeley Aviation

No 680 Squadron, a unit which had flown Mosquito IXs and XVIs for the previous two years, was renumbered. The unit role now became photo-reconnaissance and (principally) aerial photo-survey of most Mediterranean and adjacent territories, occasionally extending its coverage as far south as Rhodesia. By the close of 1951 the Squadron had begun receiving replacement aircraft, Meteor PR10s, and by February 1952 had ceased Mosquito operations.

Main bases

Ein Shemer	September 1946
Kabrit, Egypt	December 1946
Fayid, Egypt	February 1947

Aircraft examples flown

PF633, 'D'; PF678, 'H'; RG242, 'A'; VL617, 'N'; VL618; VL619; VL620.

Commanding Officers

Wg Cdr A. H. W. Ball DSO, DFC	September 1946
Wg Cdr A. M. Brown DFC	November 1946
Sqn Ldr R. N. Hampson	March 1947
Sqn Ldr J. C. T. Hewell DSO, DFC	December 1948
Sqn Ldr L. V. Bachellier AFC	December 1949

No 14 Squadron

As a Coastal Command Wellington XIV unit, No 14 Squadron was disbanded at its Chivenor base on 1 June 1945, but on the same day the unit was 're-formed' at Banff by the retitling of No 143 Squadron. Its 'new' equipment was Mosquito FBVIs and it continued 143's anti-shipping strike role until 31 March 1946, on which date it was again disbanded. The next day, however, saw No 14 Squadron take over the Mosquito XVIs and, later B35s formerly belonging to No 128 Squadron at Wahn when the latter unit was renumbered; the Mosquito B35s beginning to arrive in December 1947. Further re-equipment and a change of role came in February 1951 when No 14 Squadron became a fighter unit flying Vampire FB5s.

Main bases

Banff	June 1945
Wahn	April 1946

Wg Cdr R. W. Cox, DSO, DFC, AFC, and Sqn Ldr Allinson with Mosquito B35, VP178 of 14 Squadron at Celle, c1950. *via RAF Museum*

Celle   September 1949
Fassberg   November 1950

Aircraft examples flown
HR373; HR436, 'J'; PF544, 'F', PF612, 'G';
PF618; PZ415; PZ466; RF646; RS501; RS625;
MM192; RS704, 'B'; TA694, 'S'; TA707;
TH999, 'A'; TJ141; TK602; VP202; VR799.

No 16 Squadron

The inclusion of No 16 Squadron here as a Mosquito unit, though justifiable in the context of official documentation, is at least questionable. Having served in various roles throughout World War 2, by September 1945 the unit was flying Spitfires. On 17 September the Squadron was split into three Flights each of six aircraft, these being destined to join Nos 2, 26 and 268 Squadrons respectively, the remaining personnel returning from the Continent to Dunsfold, England a few days later, and the Squadron being officially disbanded on 20 October 1945. Due to an administrative foul-up, however, and before the 'original' Squadron's legal disbandment, two other squadrons were renumbered as No 16 Squadron simultaneously with effect from 19 September 1945, these being No 268 (Spitfires) at Celle, and No 487 Squadron RNZAF (Mosquito FBVIs) at Epinoy. In the event No 268 Squadron was disbanded in October 1945, but No 487 Squadron continued under its new number for some weeks before red-faced officialdom retitled the unit as No 268 Squadron retrospectively from 19 September 1945 (still ignoring the official paper existence of No 16 Squadron at that date).

No 18 Squadron

Another unit with only a brief Mosquito association, No 18 Squadron was a Lancaster GR3 unit based at Ein Shemer, Palestine when it was disbanded on 15 September 1946. It next reformed at Kabrit in the Suez Canal Zone on 15 March 1947 as a light bomber unit flying Mosquito FBVIs. Only weeks later the Squadron moved to the Far East where it remained until being renumbered as No 1300 (Meteorological) Flight at Changi, Singapore from 15 November 1947.

Main bases
Kabrit, Egypt   March 1947
Mingaladon   March 1947
Changi   September 1947

Commanding Officer
Sqn Ldr D. R. Lumley-George   March 1947

No 21 Squadron

Formed at Netheravon on 23 July 1915 originally, No 21 Squadron earned a high reputation for its dogged and courageous army co-operation work throughout 1915-18, and was eventually disbanded at Fowlmere on 1 October 1919. Its rebirth came on 3 December 1935 at Bircham Newton as part of the RAF's hasty expansion of the late 1930s, equipped initially with Hawker Hinds, then in August 1938 with Bristol Blenheim bombers. On 15 June 1939 the Squadron was honoured by being ceremoniously affiliated with the City of Norwich, being based at nearby Watton at the time. From the outbreak of war in 1939, as part of No 2 Group in Bomber Command, the Squadron saw virtually continuous operations in its Blenheims and, from November 1942, Lockheed Venturas. In July 1943 the Squadron began gradual re-equipment with Mosquito FBVIs, its first operations with the type being flown on 10 November 1943 by six Mosquitos, only to abort the sortie due to bad weather. On 25 November the Squadron commenced 'Day Ranger' sorties — in effect, pairs of aircraft raiding specified targets — attacking communication centres, oil depots, trains, rail yards, etc, in high-speed, low-level onslaughts, and in December commenced pinpoint bombing of the recently identified V1 'buzz-bomb' launching sites. At this period the Squadron was part of the Sculthorpe Wing, teaming up with Nos 464 and 487 Squadrons for joint operations on many occasions, and from 31 December being joined by No 613 Squadron. This interlinked operational effort was particularly emphasised on 18 February 1944 when

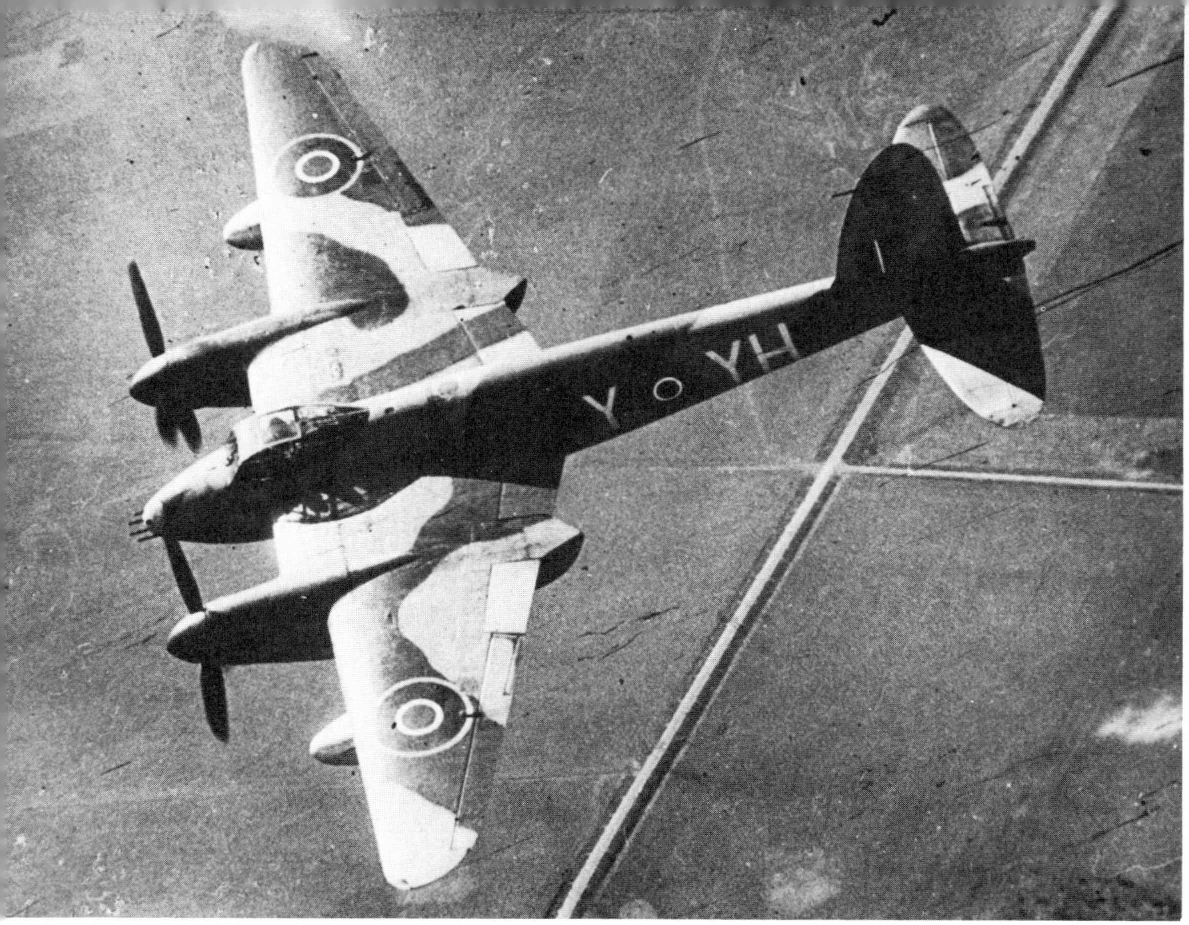

Above:
FBVI, PZ306, 'YH-Y' of 21 Squadron over France on 18 March 1945, crewed by Sqn Ldr A. F. Carlisle, DFC and Flt Lt N. J. Ingrams. *Sqn Ldr A. F. Carlisle, DFC*

Below:
FBVI of 21 Squadron (serial unknown) tucking in close, 1945. *via D. Vincent*

Right:
FBVI, LR356, 'YH-Y' of 21 Squadron on a 'Noball' operation in 1944. *Sqn Ldr H. Lees*

No 21 Squadron supplied six of the 19 Mosquitos, led by Gp Capt Percy Pickard, DSO, DFC, which blasted the German gaol at Amiens — an epic of precision bombing. By the spring of 1944 No 21 Squadron was undertaking a number of night intruder sorties over Europe, having started this form of offensive on 2/3 March when two crews attacked Montdidier airfield. On 26 March the Squadron added 'Flower' operations to its repertoire, while in late April the unit commenced experimental high-level night raids, led by *Oboe*-equipped Mosquito marker aircraft of No 109 Squadron. All these were preliminary raids to the imminent D-Day invasion of Normandy by Allied forces, and on the eve of that invasion, 5/6 June, No 21 Squadron put up 18 aircraft during 25 sorties, attacking enemy communications in the Caen area. For the following weeks this intense operational effort was maintained, mostly against any German movement or communications directly affecting the Allied invasion area. The unit next contributed to the preliminary air assault to the Allied airborne invasion of Arnhem, despatching 17 crews in the morning of 17 September 1944 to bomb Nijmegen. By then No 2 Group's Mosquito units had proved themselves especially proficient in attacking pinpoint objectives with deadly accuracy, exemplified on 31 October 1944 when Nos 21, 464 and 487 Squadrons sent 24 Mosquitos, led by Gp Capt Peter Wykeham-Barnes, DSO, DFC to bomb the Gestapo HQ at Aarhus University, Jutland, No 21 Squadron supplying eight of the aircraft. For the following three months atrocious weather severely restricted the Squadron's bombing, though on nights when this was possible every available aircraft was employed. On 21 March 1945 yet another Mosquito precision attack was mounted, this time against the Gestapo HQ housed in the Shellhaus building in Copenhagen. The 18-Mosquito formation (four from No 21 Squadron) was led by Gp Capt R. Bateson DSO, DFC and devastated its objective, though Mosquito 'T' (SZ977) of No 21 Squadron failed to return The unit's final operations of the war were flown on the night of 25/26 April, when 12 of the Squadron's Mosquitos intruded against rail and road transport at Wittenburg and Bad Oldsloe respectively. One of the Squadron's veteran aircraft had been LR385, 'D', which flew a total of 104 operational sorties between February and November 1944. After the cessation of hostilities No 21 Squadron remained based in Europe, at Gutersloh, operating an aerial courier service to Blackbushe from Furth during the Nuremberg Trials of war criminals. On 7 November 1947 the Squadron was disbanded.

Main bases

Sculthorpe, Norfolk	September 1943
Hunsdon, Herts	December 1943
Gravesend, Kent	April 1944
Thorney Island, Hants	June 1944
Rosieres-en-Santerre, France	February 1945
Melsbroek, Belgium	April 1945
Gutersloh, Germany	November 1945

Aircraft examples flown

DZ414; HP848, 'U'; HR162; 'HR345, 'N'; HR359, 'N'; HX957; HX958; HX959; HX969; HX976, 'F'; HX981; HX984; LR292; LR294, 'R'; LR301; LR353; LR373, 'A'; LR385, 'D'; LR402; LR403, 'U'; LR388, 'F'; MM398, 'J'; MM406, 'J'; NS834; NS843; NS889, 'E'; NS903; NS911; NS990, 'E'; NT124; NT170, 'N'; NT174; NT197; NT200; PZ297, 'A'; PZ305, 'D'; PZ306; PZ307; PZ314; PZ316; PZ382; PZ471; RS532, 'E'; RS551; RS573; RS599; SZ977, 'T'; SZ981; SZ995; SZ996.

Commanding Officers

Wg Cdr R. M. North DFC, AFC	June 1943
Wg Cdr I. G. Dale DFC	May 1944
Wg Cdr D. F. Dennis DSO, DFC, DFM	July 1944
Wg Cdr I. G. Dale DFC	October 1944
Wg Cdr V. R. Oates	February 1945
Wg Cdr P. A. Kleboe DSO, DFC, AFC	March 1945
Wg Cdr A. G. Wilson DFC	April 1945
Wg Cdr L. J. Joel DFC	May 1946

No 22 Squadron

Disbanded at Gannavarum as a Beaufighter unit on 30 September 1945, No 22 Squadron was re-formed at Seletar, Singapore on 1 May 1946 by renumbering No 89 Squadron, and flew Mosquito FBVIs briefly until again being disbanded on 15 August 1946.

Commanding Officer
Wg Cdr A. Pleasance CBE, DFC   May 1946

No 23 Squadron

From its original formation at Gosport on 1 September 1915, No 23 Squadron was always primarily a fighter squadron, adopting that role throughout 1915-18 until its disbandment on 31 December 1919, and resuming its traditional task when reformed at Henlow on 1 July 1925. From then until the outbreak of World War 2 No 23 Squadron was equipped successively with Sopwith Snipes, Gloster Gamecocks, Bristol Bulldogs, Hawker Demons and Bristol Blenheim IF fighters, and from 1940 specialised in the nightfighter role. In March 1941 the unit began replacing its outmoded Blenheim IFs with Douglas Havocs, but by 7 June 1942 the Squadron had received a single Mosquito TIII 'trainer' at its Ford base, and on 2 July the unit's first operational example of a Mosquito II (DD670) had arrived; this aircraft was flown on 6 July by Sqn Ldr B. R. O'B — 'Sammy' — Hoare, DFC (later Wg Cdr DSO, DFC) for the Squadron's first Mosquito intruder sortie. The next night saw Hoare destroy a Dornier Do17 over Montdidier in DD670, 'S', the first of four victims to fall to 'Sugar's' guns that month. For the next five months No 23 Squadron continued its Mosquito intruder role, then on 6 December was temporarily stood down from operations while re-equipping with 18 new Mosquito IIs specially fitted with long-range fuel tanks for an imminent detachment to Malta. This move began on 21 December when Wg Cdr Peter Wykeham-Barnes DSO, DFC led the Squadron off from Portreath in Mosquito DZ230, 'A-Apple' to fly to Gibraltar, and eventually arrived at Luqa, Malta on 27 December — the first Mosquito fighters to reach the island. Within 24 hours the Squadron commenced intruder operations against enemy targets in Sicily, and strafing raids along the North African coast, mixed with attacks on trains in southern Italy, followed soon after. By May 1943 the Squadron had accounted for 30 enemy aircraft destroyed or damaged, some 200 trains, and numerous other forms of vehicle, but not without losses. During May alone the Squadron mounted 233 sorties, claiming six enemy aircraft and 65 trains destroyed, but lost seven Mosquitos and their crews. On 1 July the unit received its first Mk VI Mosquito, and the first sortie on the new variant was flown in HJ716 on 17 July, a strafe of airfields near Rome. By 30 August the Squadron had flown its 1,000th sortie when

HJ675, 'YP-V' of 23 Squadron. *via RAF Museum*

YP•S
RL206

37230

Above left:
NF36, RL206, 'YP-S' of 23 Squadron.
via B. Robertson

Above:
PZ288 ('W') and 'V' of 23 Squadron en route to France.

Left:
Mk II DZ230, 'YP-A' of 23 Squadron, piloted by Wg Cdr P. G. Wykeham-Barnes DSO, DFC (OC Squadron) off Malta, January 1943. This was the first Mosquito to arrive on Malta (on 27 December 1942). *via RAF Museum*

Right:
Armourers loading the four 20mm Hispano cannons of a Mosquito FBVI. *Topix Agency*

HJ737, attacked targets at Taranto. Operations continued apace until Italy's surrender in early September, still based at Luqa, but thereafter the Squadron began operating from 'forward airfields' in Italy, though retaining its HQ base on Malta. Night intruder sorties were now the prime form of operations flown, mainly against the retreating German armies' communications and transportation systems, and by February 1944 the Squadron had raised its 'tally' to 33 aircraft destroyed in the air, 39 more on the ground, 331 trains and hundreds of other vehicles (including light shipping). From 9 April the Squadron commenced 'Day Ranger' sorties, roaming far and wide seeking suitable objectives, but flew its final sorties in the Mediterranean theatre on 2 May before returning to England to take up residence at Little Snoring airfield near Norwich. From here it began bomber support operations from early July as a unit of No 100 Group alongside No 515 Squadron (also at Little Snoring), these two units being the Group's main night intruders at that period. For this role No 23 Squadron's aircraft were modified to carry the American AI Mk XV (3cm) radar — known as *Ash* — in their nose sections, and later the AI Mk XV set. It meant several months of of trials and experimental work, but on the night of 31 December/1 January, Mosquito VI RS507 of No 23 Squadron made 100 Group's first claim, a Ju88, using the AI Mk XV radar. Continuing its main role of support for Bomber Command's main streams the Squadron began flying pure incendiary raids against German airfields in April 1945, usually carrying up to 80 of the standard RAF 4lb hexagonal incendiary bombs. The Squadron's ultimate operation took place on 2/3 May when, with Nos 141 and 515 Squadrons, it attacked Hohn and Flensburg; the 141 element incidentally carrying loads of napalm gel 'bombs'. No 23 Squadron remained based at Little Snoring until its disbandment on 25 September 1945. Re-formed at Wittering on 11 September 1946, the Squadron was equipped with Mosquito NFXXX and NF36 aircraft as part of the RAF's night interception arm, and retained its Mosquitos until May 1952, though replacements with Vampire NF10 aircraft commenced from October 1951.

Main bases

Ford	October 1940
Manston	August 1942
Bradwell Bay	September 1942
Luqa, Malta	December 1942
Sigonella, Italy	September 1943
Alghero	December 1943
Little Snoring	June 1944
Wittering	September 1946
Coltishall	February 1947
Church Fenton	November 1949
Coltishall	September 1950

Aircraft examples flown
DD670, 'S'; DD673, 'E'; DD687, 'E'; DD712, 'P'; DD795, 'J'; DD798, 'S'; DD800, 'V'; DZ229, 'C'; DZ230, 'A'; DZ235, 'W'; DZ238, 'H' and 'Z'; HJ674, 'B'; HJ716; HJ737, 'R'; HJ832, 'T'; HR201, 'K'; HR216, 'T'; HX804, 'P'; HX814, 'E'; HX896, 'D'; HX900, 'G'; HX944, 'Z'; LR254, 'X'; LR305, 'Y'; PZ172, 'C'; PZ176, 'B'; PZ187; PZ315, 'Y'; PZ437, 'O'; RS507, 'C'; RS548, 'V'; RK977, 'G'; RK998, 'A' and 'P'; RL141, 'B'; RL193, 'B'; RL243, 'E'; RL249, 'E'; RL257, 'B'; RL261, 'A'.

Commanding Officers

Wg Cdr B. R. O'B. Hoare DSO, DFC	March 1942
Wg Cdr P. G. Wykeham-Barnes DSO, DFC	September 1942
Wg Cdr J. B. Selby DSO, DFC	April 1943
Wg Cdr P. R Burton-Gyles DSO, DFC	September 1943
Wg Cdr A. M. Murphy DSO, DFC	December 1943
Wg Cdr S. P. Russell DFC	December 1944
Sqn Ldr P. G. K. Williamson DFC	September 1946
Sqn Ldr D. L. Norris-Smith	July 1947
Sqn Ldr V. S. H. Duclos DFC	October 1949
Sqn Ldr A. J. Jacomb-Hood DFC	December 1951

No 25 Squadron

Formed at Montrose on 25 September 1915 originally, No 25 Squadron was another unit which commenced life as a fighter squadron and, apart from a brief spell on day bombing duties in 1917-20, remained primarily a fighter unit throughout its long history. Disbanded initially

on 20 January 1920, it was soon re-formed three months later on 20 April at Hawkinge, equipped with Sopwith Snipes, and in the following two decades re-equipped successively with Gloster Grebes, Armstrong Whitworth Siskin IIIas, Hawker Fury Is and IIs, Demons, Gloster Gladiators, and, in December 1938, Blenheim IF fighters, the latter becoming its war equipment from 1939. As the first RAF squadron to receive Blenheim IFs, No 25 was also the first unit in firstline service in *any* air force to operate radar-equipped, operational nightfighters, its first AI-equipped Blenheim IFs being delivered on 31 July 1939, and having 15 AI Mk IFs and IVFs on charge on 3 September 1939, with a further six examples brought on strength by the end of that month. Thus No 25 Squadron became a pioneering protagonist of radar-guided night interception; a role in which it was to specialise for the rest of its existence. The Squadron's Blenheims were later replaced by Beaufighters, then Havocs (these for only a brief period), but on 21 October 1942 the first Mosquito Mk II arrived on the Squadron as the beginning of fresh equipment, and the Beaufighters were phased out by February 1943. By June 1943 the Squadron strength stood at 26 Mk IIs, though two months later 'C' Flight re-e-quipped with FBVIs for extended sorties across

NF36, RL123, 'G' of 25 Squadron at West Malling, 1950. *G. A. Heather*

Europe. In December 1943 the unit began receiving NFXVIIs, and therefore phased out its remaining Mk IIs, the latter type making its last sorties on the night of 21/22 January 1944. In the main the Squadron flew a mixture of 'Ranger', intruder, and night interception sorties during 1943-44, though in the early months of 1944 it achieved several night victories against raiding Luftwaffe bombers; an example being on the night of 19 March when the Squadron claimed five victims, three of these falling to Mosquito HK255 (Flt Lt Singleton), and two to HK278. During the following two nights No 25 Squadron added three more confirmed victories to its tally. From June 1944 the Squadron was one of many units engaged in intercepting V1 robot flying bombs being launched against England, and by October, when it moved base from Coltishall to Castle Camps, its crews had claimed 22 'buzz bombs' and at least three Heinkel He111 'carrier' aircraft destroyed. In October too the Squadron flew its first sorties with Mosquito XXX variants, on the 4th. For the final months of the war No 25 Squadron reverted to intruder patrols over Europe, inter-spersed with a few bomber-support operations

— the latter necessitating taking on charge again a number of FBVIs — up until the ultimate night of the hostilities. Unlike most wartime units, No 25 Squadron remained a firstline night interception fighter unit in the peacetime RAF, albeit at a quarter of its wartime strength for the first year. Then, in September 1946, it re-equipped with Mosquito NF36s, retaining this ultimate Mosquito NF Mark until July 1951 when its Mosquitos were finally exchanged for Vampire NF10s — thus becoming one of the first squadrons to operate jet nightfighters in the RAF.

Main bases

Church Fenton	October 1942
Acklington	December 1943
Coltishall	February 1944
Castle Camps	October 1944
Bradwell Bay	July 1945
Castle Camps	August 1945
Boxted	June 1946
West Malling	September 1946

Aircraft examples flown

DD733; DD746; DD748; DD752; DD755; DD756; DD759; DD782; DZ238; DZ258; DZ655; DZ685; DZ759; HJ645; HJ649; HJ653; HJ654; HJ713; HJ743; HJ757; HJ914; HK237; HK243; HK255; HK257; HK258; HK278; HK283; HK285; HK298; HK304; HK357; HK362; HP853; HX827; HK866; KA280, 'Z'; MM810, 'Y'; MT471, 'C'; MT483, 'S'; MT487, 'L'; MV524, 'T'; MV528, 'F'; NT245, 'D'; NT378, 'G'; NT425, 'H'; NT508, 'L'; NT541, 'P'; PZ200, 'A'; RK959, 'X'; RK960, 'B'; RK980, 'F'; RL120, 'A'; RL123, 'F'; RL124, 'G'; RL176, 'D'; RL181, 'C'; RL204, 'Y'; RL212, 'H'; RL243, 'G'.

Commanding Officers

Sqn Ldr E. G. Watkins AFC	September 1942
Sqn Ldr J. L. Shaw	March 1943
Wg Cdr S. N. L. Maude DFC	April 1943
Wg Cdr C. M. Wight-Boycott DSO	October 1943
Wg Cdr L. J. C. Mitchell	September 1944
Wg Cdr W. Hoy DFC	April 1945
Sqn Ldr R. Goucher DFC	December 1945

No 27 Squadron

Known from its inception on 5 November 1915 as 'The Flying Elephants' — a reference to its original equipment with Martinsyde G100 'Elephant' aircraft, permanently perpetuated in the elephant motif of its official badge — No 27 Squadron spent its first 30 years on a virtually continuous operational basis, fighting throughout 1915-18 in France, then flying 'war' sorties with few lapses over the North-West Frontier Province of India (now Pakistan) during the inter-war years, and remaining in India and Burma during 1939-45. It began its operational life in World War 2 as a Blenheim IF unit in Singapore in February 1941, the sole nightfighter squadron in the Far East then. Decimated in the subsequent Japanese invasion of Malaya, Java and Sumatra, No 27 Squadron reformed at Armada Road on 19 September 1942, and became the first unit to equip with Bristol Beaufighters in the Far East RAF, receiving its first example on 22 October 1942 and flying the first Beaufighter sorties on 24 December. Almost a year later, on 4 December 1943, the unit's 'A' Flight began *officially* converting from Beaufighters to Mosquitos, though in fact the Squadron had been operating a few Mosquitos since the first example, DZ695, arrived via Egypt on 11 April 1943 — the first Mosquito to be delivered to a Far East squadron. The intention was merely to equip one flight of the Squadron. The first premeditated Mosquito operational sorties by No 27 Squadron were flown by two aircraft on Christmas Day, 1943 when the Squadron Commander, Wg Cdr E. J. B. Nicolson VC in HX822 and Flg Off Thompson in HS811 made a strafe of Japanese railway traffic. The Squadron continued to fly mixed Beaufighter/Mosquito sorties in 1944, but on 9 March Wg Cdr Nicolson flew the unit's ultimate Mosquito operation — a general recce of Japanese airfields — and the unit's aircraft were exchanged for Beaufighters, several of the Mosquitos being sent to No 680 Squadron. Early teething troubles with the Mosquito in the humidity of jungle temperatures — mainly glue-rot in airframe jointing, but also fractious engines — had forced the change; air crews then engaged on tree-top level strafing and reconnaissance had

Mk II, DZ696 of 27 Squadron, 1943. Arriving on the Squadron on 2 May 1943, it crashed on 5 June, but was repaired and reallocated to No 681 (PR) Squadron on 13 June 1943.
via RAF Museum

little faith in the design, and preferred the doughty Beaufighter.

Main bases

Agartala	February 1943
Parasharam	February 1944

Aircraft examples flown

DZ695; DZ696; DZ697; HJ759; HJ760; HJ770; JH811; HJ813; HX821; HX822; HX945; HK946; LR310.

Commanding Officers

Wg Cdr H. C. Daish	December 1942
Wg Cdr E. J. B. Nicolson VC	August 1943

No 29 Squadron

A fighter unit throughout its history, No 29 Squadron was 'born' via fighter 'parents', when a nucleus from No 23 Squadron provided the unit's original personnel from 7 November 1915 at Gosport. Joining the war in France from 25 March 1916, by the Armistice on 11 November 1918, No 29 Squadron's pilots had claimed a total of 313 'victories' officially credited, apart from nearly another 70 in other categories. Reduced to cadre on 11 August 1919, the Squadron was then disbanded at Spittlegate (now Spitalgate), Grantham, on the last day of that year. Reformed at Duxford on 1 April 1923 with Sopwith Snipes, the Squadron later flew Grebes, Siskins, Bulldogs and Demons, and by the outbreak of World War 2 was equipped with Blenheim IF 'fighters'. Specialising in night interception, No 29 Squadron was a pioneer of nightfighter radar sorties, continuing this role when the unit re-equipped with Beaufighters

HK382
RU·T

NFXIII, HK428, 'K' of 29 Sqn with AI
Mk VIII in a 'thimble' nose radome. This
aircraft joined 29 Squadron on 28 January 1944,
destroyed a Ju88 on 17 June 1944, and later
served with the Central Gunnery School.
Hawker Siddeley Aviation

Left:
NFXIII, HK382, 'RO-T' of 29 Squadron at
Hunsdon. *Imperial War Museum*

Top:
Mosquito Bite. A No 29 Squadron Mosquito
demonstrates its fire-power on Hunsdon stop
butts by night.

Above:
No 29 Squadron Mosquito's return to Hunsdon,
1944. The crew escaped without serious
injuries.

from 2 September 1940 with the arrival of its first example, R2072. For the following two and a half years the Squadron steadily increased its success rate against German raiders, and included in its crews such outstanding pilots as John Braham, Guy Gibson (later VC), Wight-Boycott and Widdows; from early 1943 the Squadron began offensive 'Night Ranger' sorties over enemy-occupied Europe. In June 1943 the Beaufighters were finally replaced by Mosquito XIIs and the first all-Mosquito sorties were flown on the night of 15 June. The first Mosquito victories came on 23/24 August when aircraft HK164, HK175 and HK197 each claimed a German aircraft destroyed. In November the Squadron recorded its 60th aerial victory to date, while on the night of 24/25 February 1944 Squadron crews claimed five victims. By the close of 1943 the Squadron had received a number of Mosquito XIIIs and flew a mixture of these and Mk XIIs for nearly a year. In early 1945 it began receiving Mosquito NF30s, and flew its first sorties on this version on 14 April. Ten days later came the Squadron's last engagement in combat with the Luftwaffe, when WO Dallinson tackled two Messerschmitt Me262a jet fighters, destroying one and at least damaging the other. Remaining a unit of the peacetime RAF's night defences, No 29 Squadron added a number of Mk NF36 Mosquitos to its strength from 1946, but in 1951 all Mosquitos were exchanged for Meteor NF11s, the first example, WD585, arriving in January 1951, thus making No 29 Squadron the RAF's first jet nightfighter squadron.

Main bases

Bradwell Bay	May 1943
Ford	September 1943
Drem	March 1944
West Malling	May 1944
Hunsdon	June 1944
Colerne	February 1945
Manston	April 1945
West Malling	October 1945
Tangmere	October 1950

Aircraft examples flown
HK177; HK126; HK129, 'G'; HK140; HK143; HK164; HK167; HK169; HK174; HK175; HK189; HK197; HK382, 'I'; HK403; HK413, 'D'; HK418, 'P'; HK422, 'Z'; HK513; HK514; HK515; HK522, 'L'; KA119, 'Z'; MM446, 'Q'; MM463, 'J'; MM516; MM524; MM548, 'B'; MM568; NT386, 'B'; NT417, 'E'; NT429; NT431, 'J'; NT438, 'M'; NT490, 'O'; NT508, 'D'; PZ196; RK955; RK959, 'X'; RL116; RL122; RL124, 'D'; RL126, 'J'; RL127; RL130, 'W'; RL175, 'P'; RL192; RL210, 'Y'; RL231, 'C'.

Commanding Officers

Wg Cdr R. E. X. Mack DFC	June 1943
Wg Cdr P. W. Arbon DFC	February 1944
Wg Cdr G. F. Powell-Sheddon DFC	April 1944
Wg Cdr J. W. Allan DSO, DFC	December 1944
Sqn Ldr T. C. Wood DFC	December 1945
Sqn Ldr D. Hawkins DFC	February 1947
Sqn Ldr M. J. B. Young DFC	March 1949
Sqn Ldr M. Shaw DSO	July 1949

No 36 Squadron

Re-formed at Thorney Island on 1 October 1946 by renumbering No 248 Squadron, No 36 Squadron flew Mosquito FBVIs in a coastal strike role but was disbanded again on 14 October 1947.

Aircraft examples flown
RS610 (coded DM-Y); VP343 (T3).

Commanding Officers

Wg Cdr J. V. Hoggarth	October 1946
Sqn Ldr F. H. Stubbs	April 1947
Wg Cdr G. E. Horne	August 1947

No 39 Squadron

Reformed on 1 March 1949 as a fighter-bomber unit at Khartoum, flying Hawker Tempest F6s, No 39 Squadron moved to Egypt that year and re-equipped with Mosquito NF36s to become the sole nightfighter unit in the Middle East zone, until it was joined in this role by No 219 Squadron in March 1951. In November 1952 the Mosquitos were replaced by Meteor NF13s.

Main bases

Fayid, Egypt	September 1949

NF36, RL229, 'F' of 39 Squadron.
via R. C. B. Ashworth

Kabrit, Egypt   February 1951

Aircraft examples flown
RK973, 'E'; RK976, 'F'; RL113, 'C'; RL233,
'G'; RL241, 'B'.

No 45 Squadron

Equipped with Vultee Vengeance dive-bombers
at Kumbhirgram, India in January 1944, No 45
Squadron was withdrawn from operations that
month to convert to Mosquito FBVIs, the first
of these (LR250) arriving at Yelahanka on
29 February. After several moves of base, the
Squadron recommenced operations from
Kumbhirgram on 1 October, flying by night and
by day, attacking Japanese airfields and communications. From 1 May 1945 the Squadron,
along with Nos 47 and 84, flew 'Cab Rank'
sorties for the army, despatching the unit's final
war sorties on 12 May, by which date its crews
had dropped a total of 3,234 bombs on Japanese
targets. Postwar the Squadron maintained an
anti-shipping role, but in November 1945 began
re-equipment with Beaufighter Xs the last Mosquito leaving the unit on 12 December, though a
few Mosquitos were again used, albeit briefly, in
1948.

Main bases
Yelahanka, India   February 1944

**FBVI, RF957, 'OB-B', of 45 Squadron at Santa
Cruz, 1946.** *via RAF Museum*

Dalbhumgarth	May 1944
Ranchi	August 1944
Kumbhirgram	September 1944
Joari	April 1945
Cholavaram	June 1945
St Thomas Mount	October 1945
Negombo, Ceylon	May 1946

Aircraft examples flown

HP867; HP881; HP921; HP941; HR291;
HR368; HR371; HR404; HR514; LR250;
LR306; RF598; RF668, 'J'; RF778, 'T'; RF785,
'V'; RF792, 'X'; RF964, 'Z'; TE640, 'F'.

Commanding Officers

Wg Cdr H. C. Stumm DFC	January 1944
Wg Cdr R. J. Walker	May 1944
Sqn Ldr V. S. H. Duclos DFC	March 1945
Wg Cdr Etherton DFC	July 1945
Sqn Ldr G. O. L. Dyke	March 1946
Wg Cdr F. W. Snell DFC	April 1946
Sqn Ldr D. P. Marvin DFC	June 1946
Wg Cdr G. C. O. Key	November 1946

No 46 Squadron

No 46 Squadron first became operational with Beaufighters in May 1942, and was tasked with the nightfighter defence of the Suez Canal area, but by 1943 was mainly engaged in offensive day sorties over Sicily mixed with night intruder operations. It continued flying variegated offensive roles in the eastern Mediterranean zones until August 1944, in which month it received Mosquito XIIs and continued its night intruder role. However, by November 1944 the Squadron had virtually ceased operations, due mainly to insufficient appropriate objectives, and in December 1944 returned to England, where it re-equipped with Short Stirling C5s and became a long-range transport unit.

Commanding Officer

| Sqn Ldr C. E. Robertson | August 1944 |

No 47 Squadron

A Beaufighter X unit, based at Yelahanka, India in October 1944, No 47 Squadron received some Mosquito FBVIs in that month and flew both aircraft types operationally for few weeks before the Mosquitos were grounded in December. In February 1945 Mosquito sorties recommenced, flying both day and night sorties 'round the clock' during the final Allied advances in Burma, the ultimate war sorties by the unit's Mosquitos being flown on 12 August 1945. After the Japanese surrender the Squadron's Mosquitos were fitted for rocket projectile (RP) armament, and in November 1945 became involved in the Indonesian insurrection in the Netherlands East Indies, flying warlike sorties against rebel targets. The Squadron then disbanded at Butterworth, Malaya on 21 January 1946.

Main bases

Yelahanka	October 1944
Ranchi	November 1944
Kumbhirgam	January 1945
Kinmagon	April 1945
Hmawbi	August 1945
Kemajoran	November 1945
Butterworth	January 1946

Aircraft examples flown

HR301, 'O'; HR334, 'Z'; HR468, 'G'; HR486, 'G'; HR500, 'Q'; HR523, 'Z'; HR631, 'M';

Left:
Piratical emblem on one of 47 Squadron's Mosquitos on the Arakan front, Burma. *IWM*

Below:
Mosquito TIII, VT589, 'OT-Z' of 58 Squadron. *via RAF Museum*

HX943; RF649, 'J'; RF695, 'Y'; RF713, 'L'; RF763, 'B'; RF780, 'P'; RF818, 'K'; RF891, 'W'; RF942, 'H'; TE650, 'Y'.

Commanding Officers

Wg Cdr W. D. L. Filson-Young DFC	November 1943
Flt Lt J. H. Etherington, DFC	May 1945
Wg Cdr V. S. H. Bucles	June 1945
Wg Cdr G. H. Melville-Jackson, DFC	October 1945

No 55 Squadron

After a distinguished career throughout 1939-45, No 55 Squadron was equipped with Boston bombers in July 1946 when it exchanged these for Mosquito XXVIs. Before becoming fully operational with the latter, however, the Squadron was disbanded at Hassani, Greece on 1 November 1946.

No 58 Squadron

Re-formed at Benson on 1 October 1946, No 58 Squadron was equipped with Mosquito PR34s and a few Anson C19s, with a prime role of photo-survey of Great Britain in order to update ordnance maps, etc. It retained this role until mid-1953 when Canberra PR3 jets began replacing the Squadron's existing aircraft.

Main bases

Benson	October 1946
Wyton	January 1953

Aircraft examples flown
PF652, 'S'; PF671; PF668, 'Y'; RG178, 'R';
RG183, 'U'; RG193, 'D'; RG199; RG200, 'N';
RG212; RG300, 'A'; RG700; TJ124; TK656;
TW117; VA927; VR803; VT589, 'Z'; VT624,
'G'; VT625.

Commanding Officers

Wg Cdr A. D. Panton	October 1946
Wg Cdr A. Gadd DFC	September 1947
Sqn Ldr J. M. Rumsey	November 1947
Sqn Ldr M. M. Mair	February 1949
Sqn Ldr A. D. Maclaren DFC	May 1951
Sqn Ldr J. G. Bishop DFC	June 1951
Sqn Ldr R. A. Hoskin DFC, AFC	April 1952

No 60 Squadron SAAF

At the beginning of 1943 No 60 Squadron SAAF
was based at Castel Benito (now Castel Idris),
Tripoli, flying Baltimores (mainly) on PR sorties
over the North African battle zones in support
of the British 8th Army. At the end of January
two Mosquito IIs were allocated to the
Squadron, and the first Mosquito PR sortie was
flown, in DD744, on 15 February. Further Mosquito deliveries were slow, with two Mk VIs
and a Mk IV arriving in June, and the
Squadron's first Mk IX arriving on 29 July. At
the end of September 1943 the unit had just
seven Mosquitos, but by November it had a
total of 10 Mk IXs and one Mk VI on strength.
On 1 February 1944 the Squadron received its
first Mk XVI (MM287). The Squadron used its
Mosquitos for long-range PR sorties, penetrat-
ing deep into enemy territory photographing
objectives as far afield as Austria and southern
Germany, and relying on the Mosquito's speed
to avoid combat interception by enemy fighters,
but in March 1944 the Squadron had its first
'combats' (the Mosquitos were unarmed) with
Me262 jet fighters, opposition which the crews
were to continue to meet throughout the rest of
the war. Undeterred, No 60's crews flew a unit
record of 98 sorties in April 1944, despite the
fact that no more than seven aircraft were
usually serviceable at any given time. By 1945
the Squadron had suffered several losses to
Me262 fighters but continued to be the prime
long-range photo-recce unit with the Allied

armies in Italy, by which time its Mosquitos
were reaching deep into Germany. No 60
Squadron's final sorties comprised mapping
survey work over Austria, the Italian Alps and
the Italo-French border, followed postwar by
further photo-coverage of Greece and southern
Italy. On 15 July 1945 the Squadron was
officially 'stood down', and in August its crews
flew 10 Mosquitos back from Italy to Zwarkop
in South Africa for 'storage'.

Main bases

Castel Benito	January 1943
Senen	March 1943
Sorman	May 1943
San Severo	December 1943

Aircraft examples flown
DD743; DD744; DZ553; LR411; LR437;
MM287; MM366; NS520; NS644, 'G'.

Commanding Officers

Maj O. G. Davies DFC	February 1943
Maj E. U. Brierley	June 1943
Lt-Col O. G. Davies DFC	April 1944
Maj D. W. Allam	April 1944
Maj P. P. Daphne DFC	January 1945

No 68 Squadron

Re-formed at Catterick on 7 January 1941 as a
nightfighter squadron, No 68 flew Blenheim IFs
initially, but from May 1941 became a
Beaufighter unit, claiming its first night victim
on 17 June 1941. The Squadron continued to
operate Beaufighters for the next three years
until mid-1944 when Mosquito XVIIs began
replacement, the first operational sorties with
the new aircraft being flown on 9 July 1944. In
the same month a number of Mk XIXs arrived
— first flown on operations on 26 July — and at
the start of the new year both Marks began
being replaced by NF30s; this version was
operationally 'baptised' by No 68 Squadron on
21 February 1945. For much of its Mosquito-
equipped period No 68 Squadron was employed
combating German V1 flying bombs and their
Heinkel He111 'transporters', but as this threat
diminished and operational opportunities grew
less the UK-based RAF nightfighter force was

Above:
PRXVI MM366 of 60 Squadron, SAAF.
Lt-Col O. G. Davies DFC

Below:
Mosquito XIX, 'WM-Z' of 68 Squadron with its Czech crew, late 1944.

steadily reduced, resulting in No 68 Squadron being disbanded at Church Fenton on 20 April 1945.

Main bases

Castle Camps	June 1944
Coltishall	October 1944
Wittering	February 1945
Coltishall	February 1945
Church Fenton	March 1945

Aircraft examples flown

HK239; HK250, 'Z'; HK289, 'K'; HK296; HK307; HK348; MM680; NT273; NT317, 'J'; NT321, 'O'; NT368, 'L'; NT381; NT419; NT531; TA389.

Commanding Officers

Wg Cdr D. Hayley-Bell DFC	October 1943
Wg Cdr G. Howden DFC	August 1944
Wg Cdr L. W. Gill	February 1945

No 69 Squadron

Disbanded as a Wellington XIII unit at Eindhoven on 7 August 1945, No 69 Squadron was 're-formed' next day at Cambrai/Epinoy by the renumbering of No 613 Squadron, equipped with Mosquito FBVIs. The unit was again disbanded on 28 March 1946, only to reform four days later at Wahn, where No 180 Squadron was duly renumbered; this time to fly Mosquito BXVI. During the following 18 months the unit's aircraft acted mainly as communication couriers, particularly for the Nuremberg War Trials, but on 6 November 1947 it was disbanded.

Main bases

Cambrai/Epinoy	August 1945
Wahn	April 1946

Aircraft examples flown

LR348; PF455; PF515; PF612; PZ229; RS611, 'R'.

No 81 Squadron

A former fighter squadron from 1941 to 1946, No 81 Squadron was re-formed at Seletar, Singapore on 1 September 1946 by the contemporary practice of renumbering an existing unit, in this case No 684 Squadron. Initial Squadron equipment comprised nine Mosquito PR34s, though in August 1947 the Squadron also acquired seven Spitfire PR19s when No 34 Squadron disbanded. The prime role for No 81 Squadron was aerial survey of Malaya, West Thailand, Java and adjacent areas, a task later widely extended to include Hong Kong, Burma,

Above:
**PR34a of 81 Squadron, piloted by
Flt Sgt Anderson, 'beats up' its base, Seletar,
Singapore in May 1953 at deck height.**
Flight International

Below:
**Mosquito PR34a RG314 of 81 Squadron and its
crew after flying the ultimate Mosquito sortie in
RAF firstline use, at Seletar, Singapore, on
15 December 1955.** *via RAF Museum*

Borneo, et al. In June 1948, however, Operation 'Firedog' — the eventual 12-year campaign against Chinese Communist terrorists attempting to overthrow constitutional control of Malaya — officially commenced, and No 81 Squadron became the foremost photo-reconnaissance squadron in the Far East Air Force. Having flown the ultimate RAF Spitfire operational sortie on 1 April 1954, it fell to 81 Squadron also to fly the final Mosquito sortie in RAF firstline service when RG314 made a brief local flight on 15 December 1955. By that date No 81 Squadron had completed 6,619 sorties during the 'Firedog' operations. In the same month re-equipment with Meteor PR10s was completed.

Main bases

Seletar	September 1946
Changi	October 1947
Tengah	February 1948
Seletar	March 1950

Aircraft examples flown
PF620; PF622; PF652; PF668; PF677; RG177; RG189; RG205; RG211; RG235; RG239, 'M'; RG254; RG255, 'P'; RG262; RG308; RG314; VL614; VL622.

No 82 Squadron

As the first RAF squadron to receive and operate the Vultee Vengeance dive-bomber — from November 1942 — No 82 Squadron built up a reputation as one of the most efficient and accurate bomber units operating over Burma in 1943-44. On 4 July 1944 it began converting from Vengeances to Mosquito FBVIs, and recommenced operations by October. A structural failure in one of No 82 Squadron's Mosquitos that month led to all aircraft of the type being grounded throughout the Far East — the result of high temperatures and humidity literally rotting glued jointings in Mosquito airframes — but within a month operations had been resumed. From 19 December the Squadron commenced intruder sorties with its full strength of 10 aircraft, attacking all forms of Japanese road, rail and river communications both by day and by night. By February 1945 it had 12 aircraft on strength and was engaged mainly on daylight operations, bringing it into occasional air combat with enemy fighters. In March 1945 No 82 Squadron flew a total of 269 individual sorties — its peak monthly record — and in the final weeks of their war often flew 'Cab Rank' sorties, a flying artillery at the beck

of army liaison officers on the jungle floor. Its final war sorties 'in anger' were flown on 12 May 1945, though all crews were to remain on war-status 'Readiness' for several months thereafter during the Allied 'mopping-up' operations of a scattered and defeated Japanese army. The Squadron was then disbanded at St Thomas Mount (Madras) on 15 March 1946.

Main bases

Kolar, India	July 1944
Ranchi	October 1944
Chharra, India	December 1944
Kumbhirgram	December 1944
Cholavaram	May 1945
St Thomas Mount	October 1945

Aircraft examples flown

HR238, 'R'; HR334, 'S'; HR400, 'L'; HR402; HR415, 'B'; HR493, 'C'; HR497; HR545, 'S'; HR665, 'C'; LR449, 'R'; RF717, 'B'.

Commanding Officers

Wg Cdr L. V. Hudson	July 1944
Wg Cdr F. W. Snell DFC	December 1944

No 84 Squadron

In July 1944 No 84 Squadron, a Vengeance bomber unit operating over Burma, was stood down from operations to convert to Mosquito

Below:
HR493, 'C' of 82 Squadron in Burma, 1945.
via S. Howe

Right:
No 84 Squadron's Mosquitos flying over Batavia Harbour, near Jakarta in Java, 1945.

FBVIs, but the Command order grounding all Mosquito aircraft for major structural inspection delayed conversion until March 1945, and in the event No 84 Squadron's Mosquito crews took no part in operations against the Japanese. After Japan's surrender, however, No 84 Squadron was detached to Java in November 1945 and flew several 'war' sorties in the Indonesian insurrection campaign. By December 1946 the Squadron had phased out Mosquito aircraft in favour of Beaufighter Xs.

Main bases

Quetta, India	July 1944
Yelahanka	October 1944
Chharra	April 1945
St Thomas Mount	June 1945
Guindy, India	September 1945
Seletar, Singapore	September 1945
Kemajoran, Java	January 1946
Kuala Lumpur, Malaya	May 1946
Seletar	September 1946

Aircraft examples flown

HR561, 'R'; RF493, 'H'; RF698, 'C'; TA447, 'J'; TA478, 'K'; TE601, 'Q'.

Commanding Officers

Wg Cdr R. E. Jay	November 1944
Sqn Ldr M. H. Constable Maxwell DSO, DFC	June 1945

No 85 Squadron

Re-formed as a fighter squadron at Debden on 1 June 1938, No 85 Squadron saw fierce active operations almost from the outset of World War 2, fighting throughout the battles of France and Britain in 1940, and claiming over 200 combat victories in the first 12 months of operations. By the end of November 1940 the Squadron changed from its day fighter role to night interception, initially flying existing Hurricanes, then Boulton Paul Defiants. The latter began being replaced by Douglas Havocs (the first example arriving on 15 February 1941) with which the unit remained a nightfighter squadron for more than a year. On 29 July 1942, however, No 85 Squadron received its first Mosquito, a T3 dual control trainer for crew con-

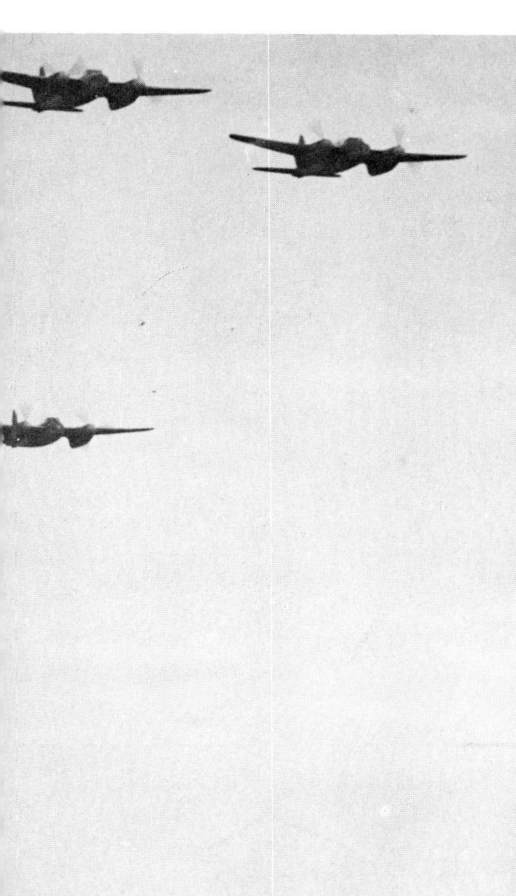

Left:

Morale-boosting. Wg Cdr G. L. Raphael, DFC leading 12 of No 85 Squadron's Mosquitos over the de Havilland airfield at Hatfield on 2 November 1942 as a gesture to the 'Mosquito-makers'. *de Havilland*

Below left:

NF36s of 85 Squadron at Coltishall on 28 September 1951, including (nearest) RL174, 'E'. *M. C. Gray*

Below:

Mk XXX of 85 Squadron about to leave on a night intrusion sortie. *IWM*

version, though this crashlanded on the same day. Further Mosquitos arrived in August and September, and the first Mosquito operational combats took place in the morning of 19 October when two 'sneak raiders', a Ju88 and a Do217, were claimed as damaged or probably destroyed. Over the following months engagements with the Luftwaffe were relatively few, but from March 1943 these increased and the Squadron's victory tally steadily mounted, led by its latest commander, Wg Cdr John Cunningham. Until March 1943 it flew Mosquito NFIIs, but on 28 February the first Mk XII (HK107) arrived, and on 24 March the unit flew its first sorties with the new version scoring its first 'kills' in Mk XIIs on the night of 14/15 April. On 16/17 May No 85 Squadron claimed no less than five Focke Wulf Fw190s — the first to be shot down at night over Britain — this being the most successful night's work in that month which saw No 85 Squadron fly a total of 264 hours on operations. The Squadron recorded another 'first' on 13/14 July by destroying the first Messerschmitt Me410 shot down over Britain, while on 8/9 October it claimed its first Junkers Ju188. On 1 May 1944, No 85 Squadron was transferred from No 11 Group, Fighter Command to No 100 (Special Duties) Group for bomber support duties, though from 25 June to 29 August 1944 it was switched to defensive interception of the V1 'flying bombs' being launched against southeast England. The unit's first night victory with 100 Group came on 11/12 June when Wg Cdr C. M. Miller DFC intruded over Melun airfield and destroyed an Me110; and a V1 victim was destroyed by Captain Weisteen on 26 June, the first of 33 'buzz-bombs' destroyed by No 85 Squadron by the end of August 1944 when it returned to its prime role of bomber support. From 5/6 June the Squadron had been flying Mosquito XIXs, but from November 1944 had re-equipped with Mk XXXs, and by mid-February 1945 was celebrating its 250th claimed victory of the war. The Squadron continued flying operations until the end of April 1945, and when peace was officially declared on 8 May No 85 Squadron's war tally stood at 278 enemy aircraft destroyed, a further 120 probably destroyed or at least seriously damaged, plus 33 V1 flying bombs destroyed. Its own losses amounted to 28 men killed or missing on operations. Returning to the aegis of Fighter Command, No 85 Squadron

remained a night interceptor unit within No 11 Group, and in 1947 was re-equipped with Mosquito NF36s. Then, in October 1951, Mosquitos began being replaced by Meteor NF11s, with which the Squadron was fully operational by February 1952.

Main bases

Hunsdon	May 1941
West Malling	May 1943
Swannington	May 1944
West Malling	July 1944
Swannington	August 1944
Castle Camps	June 1945
Tangmere	October 1945
West Malling	April 1947

Aircraft examples flown

W4087; DD714; DD718; DD731; DD741; DD720; DZ366; DZ385; DZ417; DZ469; HJ864; HK107; HK111, 'T'; HK119, 'S'; HK120, 'P'; HK218, 'U'; HK245, 'X'; HK282, 'D'; HK299, 'C'; HK374, 'L'; KA117; MM625; MP469; MV525; MV533, 'G'; MV546, 'P'; MV565; NS998; NT252, 'Y'; NT324; RK982, 'B'; RK991, 'K'; RL128, 'D'; RL148, 'H'; RL174, 'L'; RL198; RL199, 'L'; RL203; RL205, 'M'; RL213, 'F'; RL232; RL246, 'C'.

Commanding Officers

Wg Cdr G. L. Raphael DFC	May 1942
Wg Cdr J. Cunningham DSO, DFC	January 1943
Wg Cdr C. M. Miller DFC	March 1944
Wg Cdr F. S. Gonsalves DFC	October 1944
Wg Cdr W. K. Davison	January 1945

No 89 Squadron

A Beaufighter nightfighter unit, No 89 Squadron saw operational service in the Middle East from January 1942 until November 1942, when it moved to Ceylon (now Sri Lanka) to continue its night interception role. In February 1945 the Squadron began re-equipment with Mosquito FBVIs but saw no further operations during the war. On 1 May 1946 the unit was renumbered as No 22 Squadron.

Main bases

Baigachi	August 1944
Hmawbi	September 1945
Seletar	September 1945

Aircraft examples flown
TA178.

Commanding Officers

Wg Cdr F. Collingridge	November 1944
Sqn Ldr A. E. Browne	July 1945
Sqn Ldr A. G. A. Good	September 1945

No 96 Squadron

A nightfighter Beaufighter unit, originally formed on 18 December 1940 from the expansion of No 422 Flight at Cranage, No 96 Squadron began re-equipping with Mosquito NFXIIs from June 1943, and its first Mosquito victory was registered on 2 January 1944. In June 1944 the unit was 'diverted' to combat the V1 flying bomb menace, and its first V1 was destroyed on 17 June by HK415 — the first of 24 shot down within seven days. By 17 July the unit had claimed 88 V1s destroyed. On 12 December 1944 the Squadron was disbanded at Odiham.

Main bases

Honiley	October 1942
Church Fenton	August 1943
Drem	September 1943
West Malling	November 1943
Ford	June 1944
Odiham	September 1944

Aircraft examples flown
HK306, 'P'; HK370; HK372; HK373; HK379, 'F'; HK396; HK397; HK404; HK405; HK407; HK414; HK415, 'R'; HK425; HK426; HK499; MM446; MM452; MM494; MM499, 'V'; MM562; MM575, 'X'; MM577.

Commanding Officer

Wg Cdr E. D. Crew DFC	June 1943

No 98 Squadron

A bomber unit, flying Battles then Mitchells throughout World War 2, No 98 Squadron only converted to Mosquitos at the end of September 1945 when Mk XVIs began arriving on the unit. From then to 1947 the Squadron carried out routine 'peacetime' duties and training, and on 1 May 1947 was transferred from No 2 Group to

HK419, 'B-Beer' of 96 Squadron at West Malling, 1943. *via S. Howe*

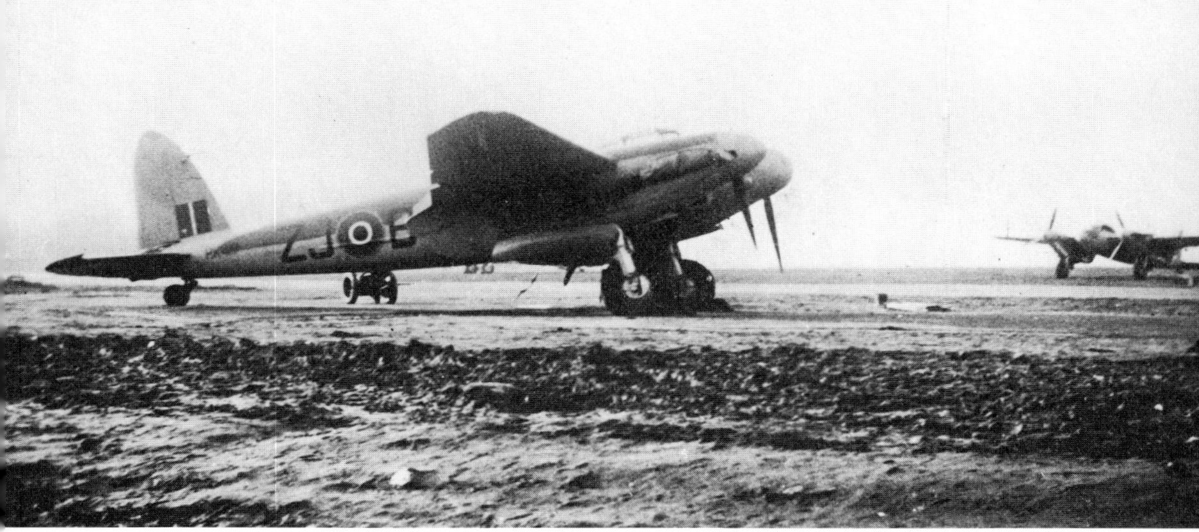

No 84 Group. In August 1948 the Mk XVIs
began being replaced by Mosquito B35s, but in
February 1951 these too began being phased out
to be replaced by Vampire FB5s.

Main bases

Melsbroek	September 1945
Wahn	March 1946
Celle	September 1949
Fassberg	November 1950

Aircraft examples flown

MM185, 'E'; PF545, 'Z'; PF607; RS718, 'W';
RV340, 'M'; RV362, 'C'; TA696; TH995, 'Y';
TJ120, 'Z'; TJ138; VP181, 'B'.

Commanding Officers

Wg Cdr V. E. Marshal	February 1945
Wg Cdr E. W. Thornewill	February 1946
Wg Cdr D. B. Gericke	February 1947
Sqn Ldr P. W. Cook	November 1947
Sqn Ldr D. R. M. Frostick	July 1949
Sqn Ldr J. M. Rumsey	August 1950

No 105 Squadron

To No 105 Squadron fell the distinction of
becoming the first squadron (though not the first
unit) to receive the Mosquito for operations.
Having flown Fairey Battles and Bristol
Blenheims on operations from September 1939,
No 105 Squadron received its first Mosquito,
W4064, on 15 November 1941 at Swanton
Morley, and by 7 April 1942 had seven aircraft
and 20 'converted' crews. By 31 May this complement had increased to eight aircraft, and that
morning the Squadron flew its first operational
sorties, to Cologne. On 8 June the second Mosquito squadron to be formed, No 139, came into
existence, but had to use No 105 Squadron's aircraft for its initial sorties. During the early
months No 105 Squadron flew daylight sorties
over a wide range of enemy objectives, bombing
targets in Norway, Denmark and Germany, and
at the same time was virtually 'proving' the
Mosquito in operational conditions, thereby
originating various tactics later to become
standard, as well as initiating various technical
modifications in the light of hard experience. On

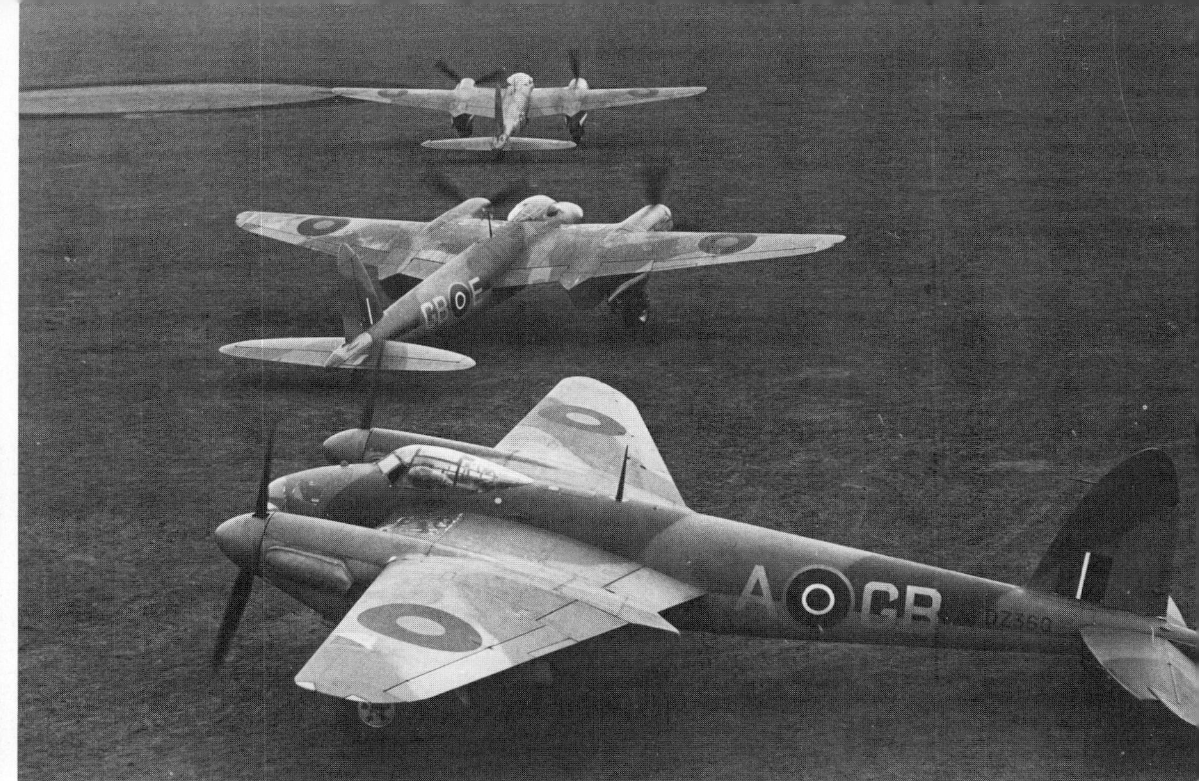

19 September 1942 No 105 Squadron attempted the RAF's first daylight bombing attack on Berlin, though not with any great success; but on 30 January 1943 it despatched six Mosquitos again to Berlin in the morning and achieved world headlines for bombing the enemy capital just as the Luftwaffe supremo, Göring, was about to broadcast to the German nation. In the interim, often led by Wg Cdr Hughie Edwards VC, the Squadron developed high and low-level operational techniques in conjunction with No 139 Squadron* with increasing accuracy in bombing. On 27 May 1943 it flew its last daylight sorties, to Jena, having despatched a total of 524 sorties during its first year of Mosquito operations, and lost 35 Mosquitos which 'failed to return'. A policy change effective from July 1943 saw 105 Squadron transferred to the aegis of No 8 Group, Path Finder Force (PFF) for future night operations, and on 5 July five *Oboe*-equipped Mosquito Mk IXs were assigned to the unit from No 109 Squadron. The first Mk IX sorties were mounted on 13 July when two aircraft (LR506 and LR507) attempted to

*For details of these raids see *Low Attack* by J. Wooldridge.

The first Mosquito bomber unit was No 105 Squadron, three of whom's initial batch are seen here at Marham in December 1942, including DZ360 ('A') and DZ353 ('E')
Flight International

mark Cologne for a main bomber raid. *Oboe*-marking sorties continued until September 1943, from when the Squadron commenced particularly daring and accurate precision bombing sorties against pinpoint targets in western Germany; usually carrying some 3,000lb of bombs per aircraft in bomb bays and on wing racks. Such attacks were now delivered from high levels, and in December that year No 105 Squadron began receiving pressurised Mosquito BXVIs, flying its first sorties in these on 2/3 March 1944. Targets by then included precision attacks against identified V1 sites, Luftwaffe airfields in the Low Countries, and rail communication centres. On the eve of D-Day (5/6 June 1944) 105 Squadron despatched 25 Mosquitos to mark heavy gun sites along the Normandy coast in aid of the initial Allied invasion forces, then concentrated over the following weeks on enemy rail and road communication systems in the areas adjacent to

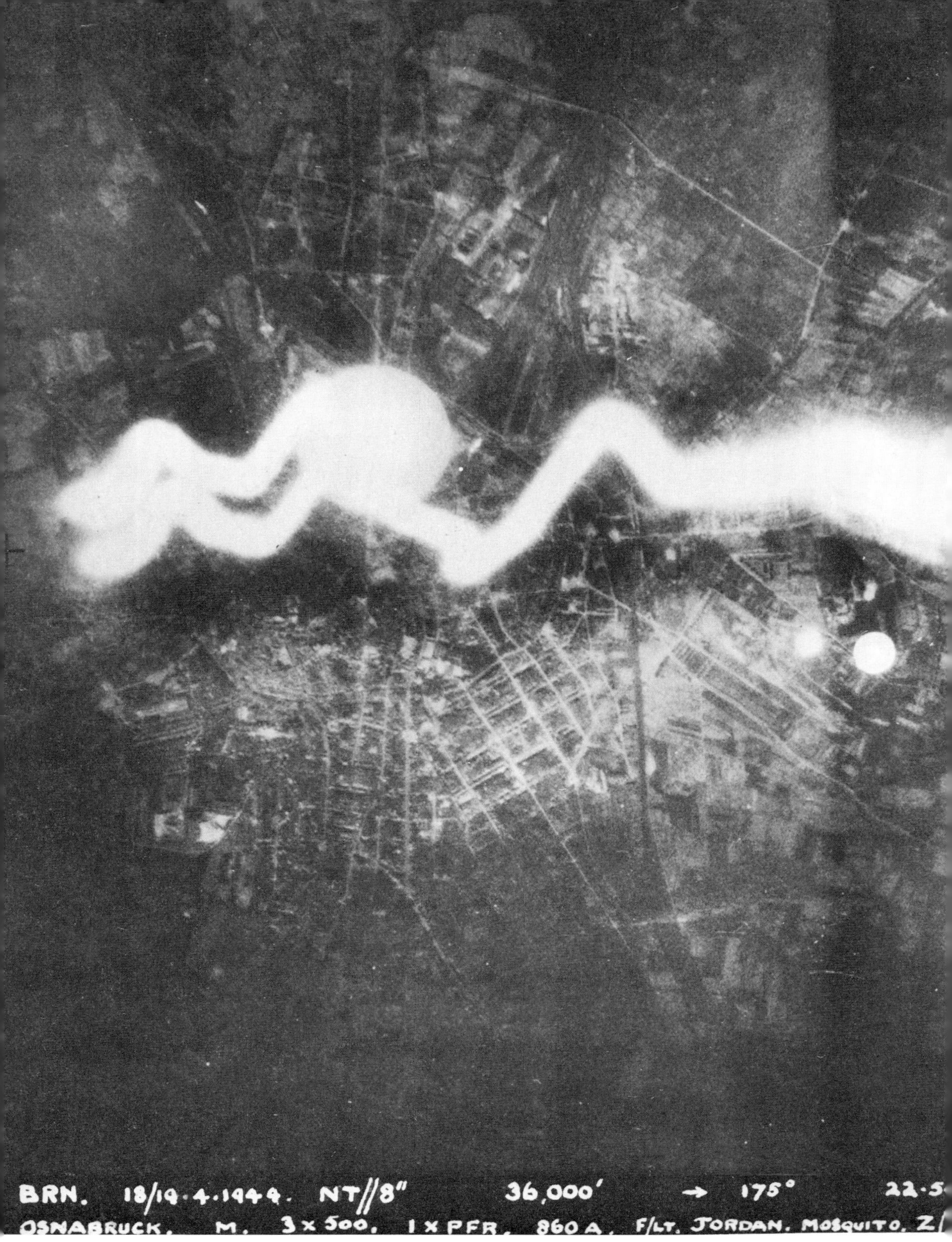

BRN. 18/19.4.1944. NT//8" 36,000' → 175° 22·5
OSNABRUCK. M. 3 x 500. 1 x PFR. 860 A. F/LT. JORDAN. MOSQUITO. Z/

the Allied beach-head, or marking troop and armour concentrations prior to main force bomber raids in daylight. With the onset of winter the pace of operations inevitably slackened; in September, November and December the Squadron flew 397, 302 and 258 sorties respectively. With the new year opening No 105 Squadron became steadily employed in marking targets deep into Germany for the RAF's night bomber streams, intermingled with daylight assaults on their own account. By April 1945 these targets included Berlin again, with No 105 Squadron despatching 46 sorties to the 'Big City' between 8 and 21 April, but also ranged as far afield as Gotha and Jena, Munich and Potsdam. The Squadron's final war sorties were flown on 2/3 May 1945, when four Mosquitos bombed Eggebeck. For the remainder of the year 105 Squadron undertook various peace-time duties, including marking areas for the dropping of food supplies to former German-occupied towns (Operation 'Manna'), then on 1 February 1946 it was disbanded at Upwood.

Main bases

Swanton Morley	October 1940
Horsham St Faiths	December 1941
Marham	September 1942
Bourn	March 1944
Upwood	June 1945

Aircraft examples flown*

W4065, 'N'; W4066, 'A'; W4069, 'M'; W4070, 'C'; W4071, 'L'; W4072, 'D'; DK288; DK295, 'P'; DK297, 'O'; DK299, 'S'; DK300; DK308, 'J'; DK316, 'J'; DK322, 'P'; DZ311; DZ313, 'E'; DZ340; DZ341, 'A'; DZ360, 'A'; DZ367, 'J'; DZ374, 'X'; DZ408, 'F'; DZ414, 'O'; DZ441; DZ460; DZ467, 'P'; DZ483; DZ489, 'B'; DZ518, 'A'; DZ536, 'E'; DZ548, 'D'; DZ550, 'A'; DZ591, 'O'; DZ595, 'C'; LR476; LR500; LR507, 'F'; LR510; LR512; ML896; ML913, 'F'; ML920; ML922, 'Y'; ML938, 'D'; ML956; ML973; ML981; ML993; ML999; MM132; MM151; MM170; MM194; MM225; MM234; MM237, 'Q'; MM241; MM297; PF385; PF404; PF460; PF484; PF497; RV298; RV304; RV322.

The highest night photo of the war. Osnabruck viewed from 36,000ft by Mosquito 'Z' of 105 Squadron (Flt Lt Jordan) on the night of 18/19 April 1944. *Sqn Ldr H. Lees*

Commanding Officers

Wg Cdr P. H. A. Simmons DFC	October 1941
Wg Cdr H. I. Edwards VC, DFC	August 1942
Wg Cdr G. P. Longfield	February 1943
Wg Cdr J. de L. Wooldridge DFC, DFM	March 1943
Gp Capt H. J. Cundall DFC, AFC	July 1943
Gp Capt K. J. Somerville DSO, DFC, AFC	September 1944
Wg Cdr T. W. Horton DSO, DFC	June 1945
Wg Cdr C. N. Collard DSO, DFC	October 1945
Sqn Ldr G. O. Lister	November 1945
Wg Cdr D. G. Stokes	December 1945

No 107 Squadron

At the outbreak of World War 2 No 107 Squadron was based at Wattisham, flying Blenheim bombers under the control of No 2 Group. In January 1942 the Blenheims were replaced by Douglas Bostons. On 1 February 1944 the Squadron moved base to Lasham where it began re-equipping with Mosquito FBVIs, and recommenced operations on 15 March when a V1 site was attacked; this was the first of seven such raids by the end of that month during which the Squadron's first loss (NS856, 'T') was the victim of a 'friendly' USAAF P-51 Mustang†. After a few weeks of (mainly) daylight sorties, No 107 Squadron began night intruder operations by the end of April 1944, mainly against enemy airfields, as part of the build-up to the Allied invasion of France. From 4 June the Squadron changed to direct tactical strikes against German rail, road and river transports in the invasion back areas of France. By 18 August the Squadron was concentrating on the River Seine crossings, rail lines and other 'opportunity' targets, then generally followed the advancing Allied armies towards Germany by attacking retreating enemy troops and transport. On 17 September the Squadron despatched 16 crews to bomb specific buildings in Arnhem, in support of the Allied airborne venture there, and scored direct hits,

*At least 150 different Mosquitos were flown by No 105 Squadron during the war

†Ironically, the Mosquito crew was American too. . .

Above:
TA118 of 107 Squadron.   *J. E. Bilbrough*

Below:
FBVIs of Nos 107 and 21 Squadrons at Gu+ersloh, 1947, including HR358 ('OM-B').
via A. Thomas

though two Mosquitos were lost and a third returned on one engine. Operating mainly along the Rhine from the Ruhr to the Dutch border, the Squadron's purpose was to isolate enemy forces west of the Rhine from supplies and reinforcements; an example being the night of 1 October when 12 crews claimed successful attacks on 27 trains and a string of river barges, without any Mosquito losses. A period of foul weather prevented many sorties in mid-October and on the 30th the Squadron moved base to Hartford. Next night, despite continuing bad weather, eight of the crews joined in the aerial 'softening' of German defences on Walcheren Island prior to the Canadian Army's assault there. On 19 November the Squadron moved base again, this time to the Continent, taking up 'residence' at Epinoy on 21 November. From here it continued its harassment of enemy troops and transport almost nightly, a particularly successful strike being recorded on the night of 6/7 December when 16 crews attacked enemy troops and tanks concentrated near Heinsburg. This constant offensive against German transportation in all forms was to remain No 107 Squadron's prime task until the close of the European conflict, and the Squadron's final war sorties were flown on the night of 26 April 1945, when 12 Mosquito crews set out to strafe all or any German troops or transport they could find. Three further scheduled operations were subsequently cancelled for various reasons. On 7 May the Squadron formally adopted a routine day flying schedule, with emphasis on formation practice, and took part in many of the celebratory ceremonial fly-pasts mounted over the following months in Europe. At the end of 1945 the Squadron moved to Guterslöh in Germany, where it remained for two years, then moved Wahn, but on 4 October 1948 was effectively disbanded when it was officially renumbered as No 11 Squadron.

Main bases

Lasham	February 1944
Hartford Bridge	October 1944
Epinoy	November 1944
Melsbroek	July 1945
Guterslöh	November 1945
Wahn	December 1947

Aircraft examples flown
HJ771, 'J'; HR145; HR198, 'D'; HR350; HX832, 'D'; LR257, 'F'; LR264, 'X'; LR336, 'W'; LR384, 'B'; MM411, 'V'; NS820, 'P'; NS831, 'O'; NS833, 'V'; NS836, 'G'; NS853; NS855, 'Q'; NS905, 'D'; NS908, 'N'; NS910, 'T'; NS912, 'C'; NS952, 'S'; NS958, 'R'; NT115, 'D'; NT128; NT136, 'A'; NT207, 'B'; NT226, 'G'; PZ169, 'R'; PZ222; PZ225, 'B'; PZ258; PZ376; PZ392, 'D'; RS533, 'P'.

Commanding Officers

Wg Cdr M. E. Pollard	November 1943
Wg Cdr W. J. Scott AFC	July 1944
Wg Cdr W. C. Maher DFC, AFM	April 1945
Wg Cdr D. P. Hanafin	August 1946
Wg Cdr B. Kemp	December 1946
Wg Cdr Banning-Lover	June 1947

No 108 Squadron

In February 1944 No 108 Squadron was based at Luqa, Malta, flying Beaufighter VIFs, and on 16 February received its first Mosquito XII. In the following weeks a few more arrived, all to be flown by 'B' Flight only, and the first Mosquito operation was flown on 5 April. In May, June and July the few Mosquitos flew night convoy patrols and some intruder sorties, but by the end of July all had been replaced by more Beaufighters.

Aircraft examples flown
HK127; HK178, 'S'; HK507, 'U'; MM442, 'M'; MM471, 'S'; MM504, 'U'; MM534, 'W'; MM581, 'Q'.

Commanding Officer

Wg Cdr A. J. Banham	December 1943

No 109 Squadron

Apart from a brief non-operational existence in 1918-19, No 109 Squadron came into RAF firstline being via the Wireless Intelligence Development Unit (WIDU) which was based at Boscombe Down investigating various airborne scientific radio devices, etc. The WIDU was retitled as No 109 Squadron from 10 December 1940, equipped with a variety of aircraft types, and continued the research of its predecessor. On 21 July 1942 the Squadron received a Mosquito (DK300) for experiments with radar installations, but on moving base to Wyton in 1942 to be 'attached' to the newly-formed Path Finder Force it received eight more Mosquitos, specifically for use in trials of *Oboe*. On 20 December that year Squadron strength stood at eight aircraft and six crews, and that day saw No 109 Squadron fly its first *Oboe* sorties, when six Mosquitos attacked a coking plant at Lutterade in east Holland. Fifteen more sorties were mounted in the following 10 days. By January 1943 four more crews had been trained, and in June 1943 the Squadron could boast 20 trained crews. On 31 December 1942 it made its first operational sorties as sky-markers for the main bomber force; on 28 February 1943 the unit initiated its ground-marking technique during a raid on St Nazaire, then followed this with its first ground-marking of a German target against Essen on 5 March 1943. For the next year No 109 Squadron's *Oboe*-Mosquitos were mainly employed marking for main force bomber attacks against targets in the Ruhr. On 21 April 1943 it began receiving the much-improved Mosquito IX, and its first sortie with this version took place on 11 June when Sqn Ldr F. A Green flew LR497, 'Z' to Dusseldorf, one of eight Mk IXs on Squadron strength by then. The relatively few *Oboe*-equipped Mosquitos with trained crews available led to No 109 Squadron being employed sparingly, marking for particularly heavy raids only, but once such targets became beyond *Oboe* range the Mosquitos began to raid special targets in western Germany, including power stations, factories and foundries, bombing these with remarkable precision. On 19 December 1943 pressurised Mosquito BXVIs began arriving on the Squadron, the first pair being ML928 and ML930, and No 109's first sortie with this Mark was flown on 1/2 March 1944, to Deelen. From that date too No 109 Squadron's *Oboe*-Mosquitos commenced daylight sorties, attacking V1 sites, airfields and communications targets, while on 8 May the Squadron's veteran aircraft, DZ319, flew its 100th operational sortie marking the V1 site at Bruneval. Prior and subsequent to 6 June (D-Day), No 109's crews were kept busy in direct support of the Allied invasion forces in Normandy, both by night and, later, by day; marking for Bomber Command's 'heavies' as these blasted a path forward for the ground armies. From then until the eventual surrender of German forces 109's crews pursued an unrelenting offensive at the spearhead of huge bomber formations, marking mainly for the bomber streams with pinpoint accuracy, but occasionally undertaking pure 'solo' sorties. An example of the pace of operations was September 1944, when No 109 Squadron despatched a total of 426 individual sorties in that month alone. By April 1945, with improved radar installations, the Squadron's aircraft could reach Berlin; the final war sorties were flown on 2/3 May 1945, either marking Kiel or attacking airfields at Husum and Eggebeck. On 30 September 1945 the Squadron was officially disbanded at Little Staughton, but the following day saw No 627 Squadron at Woodhall Spa renumbered as No 109 Squadron and continue to serve in Bomber Command. In 1948 Mosquito B35s replaced the Mk XVIs, but in July 1952 these too were phased out when No 109 Squadron began receiving Canberra B2 jet bombers.

Main bases

Wyton	December 1942
Marham	July 1943
Little Staughton	April 1944
Woodhall Spa	October 1945
Wickenby	October 1945
Hemswell	November 1945
Coningsby	November 1946
Hemswell	March 1950

Aircraft examples flown

DK318, 'B'; DK319, 'H'; DK321, 'C'; DK331, 'D'; DK333, 'F'; DZ319, 'H'; DZ356, 'J'; DZ245, 'K'; DZ429, 'L'; DZ432; DZ433, 'O'; DZ436, 'T'; DZ525; LR497, 'Z'; LR498, 'O'; LR499; LR500; LR507; LR511, 'Q'; ML905; ML927; ML956; ML957, 'D'; ML991, 'P'; ML992, 'U'; MM117, 'U'; MM123, 'A'; MM222, 'X'; PF382; PF396, 'S'; PF408, 'B' and 'J'; PF429; PF446; PF574; PF592; RV295, 'K'; RV308; RV318; TA617; VP199; VR798.

Commanding Officers

Wg Cdr H. E. Bufton DFC, AFC	July 1942
Wg Cdr R. M. Cox AFC	March 1944

Above:
Mosquito XVI, ML991, 'P' of 109 Squadron on 25 April 1944. Note bulged ('Fat-belly') bomb bay.

Below:
Mk IV, DK333, 'F' (*The Grim Reaper*) of 109 Squadron. Left to right: Frank Ruskell, DFC (Navigator), Harry B. Stephens (Pilot), and groundcrew. *Wg Cdr F. Ruskell, DFC*

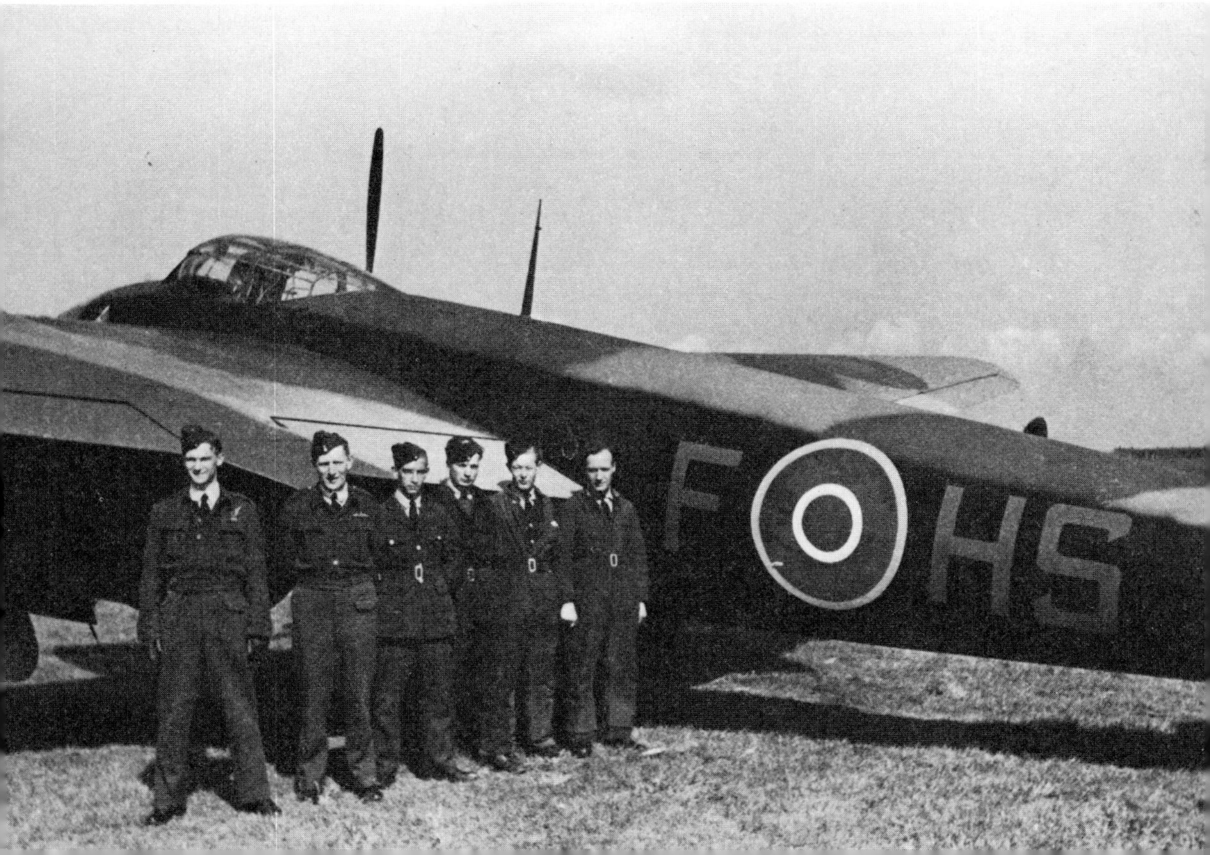

Wg Cdr T. F. Grant DSO, DFC   May 1944
Wg Cdr R. C. F. Law DFC   December 1944
Wg Cdr C. W. Scott DFC   September 1945

No 110 Squadron

A former Blenheim unit of No 2 Group, Bomber Command which had taken part in the RAF's first bombing raid of World War 2, No 110 Squadron re-equipped with Vengeance dive-bombers in early 1943 after moving to India. On 1 November 1944, having disposed of most of its Vengeance aircraft, the Squadron began re-equipping with Mosquito FBVIs, and by 6 November possessed 14 of these, only to receive orders on 21 November grounding all Mosquito aircraft due to faulty casein glue joints in their structure. However, from 28 January 1945 new Mosquitos with formaldehyde glued joints began arriving on the Squadron and crews began working up for operations again, making their first Mosquito sorties 'in anger' on 31 March. In support of the Allied armies' advance the Squadron flew daily strikes against Japanese road, rail and river transportations during April 1945, then provided close support for Operation 'Dracula' — a seaborne assault on Rangoon — when this was launched on 1 May. From then until the announcement of Japan's surrender on 14 August, the Squadron continued its direct tactical support role to the Allied armies, and indeed flew its final war sorties on 20 August against Japanese troops still fighting at Tikedo, east of the Sittang river — thus No 110 Squadron had participated in both the first and the last RAF operational war sorties of World War 2. Moving to Singapore, the Squadron detached six aircraft to Djakarta (Batavia) on 31 September in support of Dutch authorities faced with Indonesian insurrection. This chore was over by the end of November, when the Squadron moved to Labuan where it was officially disbanded on 15 April 1946, only to be re-formed on 15 June when No 96 Squadron at Kai Tak (Dakotas) was renumbered.

Main bases
Yelahanka	October 1944
Joari	March 1945
Kinmagan	May 1945
Hmawbi	August 1945
Seletar	October 1945
Labuan	December 1945

Aircraft examples flown
HR292, 'Y'; HR308, 'W'; HR387, 'H' and 'L'; HR438, 'A'; HR446, 'Z'; HR456, 'G'; HR498, 'H'; HR512, 'R' and 'F'; HR540, 'B'; HR546, 'G'; HR547, 'G'; HR548, 'D'; HR555, 'R'; HR556, 'G'; HR561, 'T'; HR562, 'T'; HR604, 'A' and 'S'; HR605, 'A'; HR620, 'P'; HR622, 'J'; HR625, 'Z'; HR629, 'W'; HR631, 'S'; HR637, 'H'; RF582, 'K'; RF586, 'C'; RF589, 'P'; RF594, 'C'; RF600, 'K'; RF663, 'P'; RF664, 'Y'; RF672, 'V'; RF673, 'Q'; RF702, 'V'; RF704, 'B'; RF731, 'Z'; RF954, 'Y'; TE606.

Commanding Officers
Wg Cdr A. E. Saunders	September 1944
Sqn Ldr P. C. Joel	May 1945
Wg Cdr A. F. Binks DFC	November 1945

TA230, 'N' of 110 Squadron at Singapore.
via RAF Museum

Mozzie Men

Right:
No 29 Squadron crews at 'Readiness',
Hunsdon, September 1944.

Below:
Flt Sgts I. Kenway and T. H. Gibbons entering
'SB-O' (believed to be HX914) of 464 Squadron
RAAF on 9 December 1943 at Hunsdon. Insigne
below cockpit was a stylised Kiwi and
Kangaroo, with a boomerang, on which was a
'motto', *Per Ardua ad Australia.*   *RAAF Official*

48

Above left:
A 613 Squadron Mosquito crew 'in situ' at Lasham, 1944. *Flight International*

Far left:
Gp Capt H. E. — 'Hal' — Bufton, DSO, OBE, DFC, AFC, the *Oboe* pioneer pilot with 109 Squadron. *IWM*

Above right:
Wg Cdr John de L. Wooldridge and his 105 Squadron crews on 28 June 1943. *de Havilland*

Left:
Wg Cdr J. R. G. Ralston, DSO, AFC, DFM (right) and Flt Lt (later Sqn Ldr) S. Clayton, DSO, DFC, DFM, a veteran Mosquito crew with 105 Squadron.

Above left:
Gp Capt (later, ACM Sir) Basil Embry (left) and
his usual navigator, Flt Lt Peter Clapham, DFC,
at Wittering in 1942.

Below left:
Sqn Ldr R. Bannock, DFC (left) and Flg Off R.
Bruce of 418 Squadron RCAF, a crew which
destroyed nine enemy aircraft and 19 V1 'buzz
bombs'. *Public Archives of Canada*

Top:
Wg Cdr B. R. O'B. — 'Sam' — Hoare, DSO,
DFC and his navigator, Flg Off Potter, DFC
receiving a silver model Mosquito at the
Dorchester Hotel reception for 605 Squadron
AAF on 15 April 1944, to mark the Squadron's
100th claimed victory (scored by Hoare).

Above:
FBVI, PZ338 of 515 Squadron at Little Snoring
on 4 November 1944, with (left to right) Wg Cdr
F. F. Lambert, DSO, DFC (OC Squadron),
Sqn Ldr Farrell, Flg Off Lake, DFC, AFC, and
Plt Off Groves, DFC. *Topix Agency*

Right:
Gp Capt Hon Max Aitken, DSO, DFC, OC Banff Wing, Coastal Command. *IWM*

Left:
Briefing. Navigators of the Banff Wing preparing for a sortie to Norway, early 1945.
Hawker Siddeley Aviation

Below:
Markers. Flt Lt (later, Gp Capt) J. R. Goodman, DFC (right) and Flt Lt W. Hickox, DFC of 627 Squadron, with Mosquito DZ484, 'AZ-G'.
Gp Capt J. R. Goodman DFC, AFC

Left:
Wg Cdr (later AVM) Desmond Hughes, OC 604 Squadron AAF in 1944, who was credited with at least 18 combat victories. *Keystone Agency*

Below left:
Gp Capt Paul Y. Davoud, RCAF who successively commanded Nos 409, 410 and 418 Squadrons RCAF. *Public Archives of Canada*

Below:
Wg Cdr Hope, Gp Capt P. C. Pickard, DSO, DFC with his dog 'Ming', and Flt Lt Johnson. *IWM*

Right:
Sqn Ldr M. Constable Maxwell, DSO, DFC (on wing) and Flt Lt John Quinton, DFC of 264 Squadron, Colerne. On 13 August 1951 Quinton sacrificed his own life to save an ATC cadet's when serving at 228 OCU, (Wellingtons), during an air collision, and his name is perpetuated in Halton's Quinton Trophy, awarded to the best ex-ATC cadet graduating from the Aircraft Apprentice School.

Mosquito 'D-Dorothy', a PRIX, ML897, which flew 161 sorties, with (at left) Flg Off J. Baker DFC (Navigator) and Flt Lt M. Briggs, DSO, DFC, DFM. Briggs, who started the war as an LAC air gunner with 77 Squadron (Whitleys), died with Baker in Mosquito LR503 on 10 May 1945 during a display at Calgary airport, Canada.

Wg Cdr J. R. H. Merifield, DSO, DFC (left) & Flt Lt J. H. Spires, DFC, DFM, who flew from Gander to St Mawgan in five hours 10mins on 23 October 1945, at an average speed of 445mph. *Hawker Siddeley Aviation*

Erks. Ground crews at Hunsdon giving the 'once-over' to a 464 Squadron RAAF Mosquito. *Hawker Siddeley Aviation*

Above:
PRIX *Lovely Lady* **of 60 Squadron SAAF undergoing maintenance at San Severo.**
Lt-Col O. G. Davies DFC

Right:
Armourer checking ammunition boxes for the .303in Browning guns of LR366, 'SY-L' of 613 Squadron, at Lasham in early 1944. In the background is LR370, 'Y'. *Keystone Agency*

Far right:
Lapping in belts of .303in calibre ammunition for a 613 Squadron Mosquito FBVI, Lasham, early 1944. *Flight International*

Below:
Big Stuff. Loading a 4,000lb HC 'Cookie' into PF432, 'W' of 128 Squadron at Wyton on 21 March 1945 for that night's raid on Berlin.

Squadrons Nos 114-334

No 114 Squadron

Reformed at Wyton on 1 December 1936, No 114 Squadron was the first RAF squadron to be equipped with Bristol Blenheim bombers, with which it saw operational service in France and England from 1939 to 1942, then North Africa. In April 1943 Blenheims were replaced by Bostons and No 114 Squadron retained these until the end of the war. When the Squadron moved to Khormaksar, Aden in September 1945 it exchanged its Bostons for Mosquito FBVIs and for a few months flew routine local 'security' patrols. On 1 May 1946 the Squadron was reduced to cadre only, and on 1 September that year was renumbered No 8 Squadron.

Aircraft examples flown
TE659, 'B'; TE702; TE770, 'D'.

No 125 Squadron at Church Fenton, 1945.
via S. Howe

No 125 Squadron

A former Beaufighter unit from February 1942, No 125 Squadron began exchanging these for Mosquito XVIIs from February 1944 and became heavily involved in the night defence of Britain over the ensuing months, claiming six victories in April 1944, and four in May. In June 1944 the Squadron flew patrols over the Normandy invasion beach head, then participated in the anti-V1 'buzz-bomb' campaign. Its final claim came on 20 March 1945, thus bringing its wartime tally to 44 destroyed and a further 25 probably destroyed or damaged. In March 1945 it received Mosquito Mk XXXs which it retained until being disbanded at Church Fenton on 20 November 1945, when the unit was renumbered as No 264 Squadron

Main bases

Valley	November 1943
Hurn	March 1944
Middle Wallop	July 1944

Mk XXX, NT245 of 125 Squadron shortly before the unit was renumbered as No 264 Squadron on 20 November 1945. *via S. Howe*

Coltishall   October 1944
Church Fenton   April 1945

Aircraft examples flown

HK238; HK245,'V'; HK249; HK259; HK261; HK262; HK263, 'M'; HK283; HK287, 'S'; HK291; HK299, 'C'; HK301; HK310, 'J'; HK318; HK325; HK346; HK355, 'T'; HK356; NT367, 'T'; NT376, 'K'; NT393, 'L'; NT415; NT426, 'A'; NT435, 'S'; NT436, 'Q'; NT450, 'B'; NT585, 'H'.

Commanding Officers

Wg Cdr J. G. Topham
   DSO, DFC   October 1943
Wg Cdr G. L. Howitt
   DFC   December 1944
Wg Cdr V. R. Snell   October 1945

No 128 Squadron

Disbanded in West Africa on 8 March 1943, No 128 Squadron was re-formed *officially* on 15 September 1944 at Wyton, as part of No 8 (PFF) Group's Fast Night Striking Force. In fact, its first two Mosquito XXs arrived on 8 September (KB210 & KB353), and KB353 actually bombed Berlin two nights later. On 11 September both raided Berlin; on the 12th KB210 attacked Frankfurt, then returned to Berlin on the 13th and 15th — the day its Squadron came into existence! By the end of September the Squadron possessed just four Mosquitos (KB210 had been lost over Brunswick on 15 September) which had flown 22 sorties. In October 1944 it also received a mixture of Mosquito XXVs and XVIs, flying the first sorties in these on 18 and 23 October respectively. By the close of the year No 128 Squadron's crews had flown a total of 551 sorties, attacking most of the German major

BXVI, RV297 of 128 Squadron leaving Wyton to attack Berlin on 21 March 1945.

cities. On New Year's Day, 1945 its crews took part in a novel operation, ie 'skip-bombing' rail tunnels in the Coblenz area, but soon returned to their prime role of attacking targets in Hitler's Reich. In March 1945 the Squadron totted up a total of 271 sorties, of which 23 raids had been on Berlin; a target which it was eventually to 'visit' no less than 65 nights. The Squadron's final war sorties were flown by 16 Mosquitos attacking Kiel on the night of 2/3 May 1945, these bringing No 128s Mosquito sorties total to 1,416. On 20 September 1945 the Squadron was posted from No 8 Group to No 2 Group in Europe and became a Mosquito courier and communications unit virtually until its disbandment on 1 April 1946 when the unit was retitled as No 14 Squadron.

Main bases

Wyton	September 1944
Warboys	June 1945
Melsbroek	October 1945
Wahn	March 1946

Aircraft examples flown
KB199, 'A'; KB210; KB221, 'B'; KB353; KB443, 'D'; KB449, 'V'; MM192, 'R'; MM194; MM195, 'A'; MM197; MM198; MM202, 'V'; MM203; MM204, 'X' and 'A'; MM223, 'S'; PF403; PF406; PF405, 'J'; PF405, 'E'; PF411, 'B'; PF413, 'Y'; PF415, 'B'; PF428, 'D';
PF432, 'W'; PF440, 'H'; PF443, 'A'; PF449, 'T'; PF451; PF457, 'U'; PF458, 'Z'; PF461, 'C'; RV297, 'F'; RV307, 'K'; RV319, 'B'.

Commanding Officer

Wg Cdr K. J. Burrough DFC	September 1944

No 139 Squadron

No 139 Squadron became the second RAF squadron to operate Mosquitos when it was re-formed at Horsham St Faiths (now Norwich Airport) on 8 June 1942, though it was not to receive its 'own' aircraft until some four months later, and its crews flew 105 Squadron's Mosquitos in the interim. The first Squadron sortie by a No 139 crew came on 25/26 June when Sqn Ldr Houlston AFC took DK296 to Stade airfield for a low-level strafe. The first occasion on which No 139 operated its own aircraft was on 6 December, when the Squadron despatched three of 11 Mosquitos, led by Wg Cdr Hughie Edwards, VC, to bomb the Philips radio factory

B35s TK620 ('L'), VP194 and VP185 ('N') of 139 Squadron at Hemswell, May 1950. The spinners were painted red. *Flight International*

at Eindhoven; the start of a combined offensive by Nos 105 and 139 Squadrons by day, flying high and low-level sorties deep into Germany and across enemy-occupied countries. The Squadron's first raid on Berlin on 30 January 1943 was made by three of its crews, one of which was shot down, but over the following four months No 139 undertook a wide variety of daring daylight assaults on factories, railway depots and workshops in France and the Low Countries. One particularly successful raid was flown on 3 March when nine Mosquitos from No 139 Squadron, led by Wg Cdr Peter Shand DFC, bombed the Knaben molybdenum mine and plant in Norway, losing one Mosquito to Luftwaffe fighters. The last daylight attacks by No 139 Squadron were flown on 27 May when Wg Cdr R. W. Reynolds, DSO, DFC led six of the unit's aircraft to bomb the Schott glass works at Jena. From June 1943 the two Mosquito 'partner' Squadrons (Nos 105 and 139) joined No 8 (PFF) Group, with No 139 now spearheading main force bomber raids dropping *Window* (anti-radar foil strips) of flying feint attacks on other targets to diversify enemy nightfighter opposition to main raids. From August the Squadron added its own 'nuisance'

bombing raids, despatching 145 sorties in that month; while on 3 October it sent two Mosquito IXs (ML908 and ML909) to Hanover — the first unit use of this Mark. In November No 139's crews made eight night visits to Berlin (some 60 sorties) of the 23 nights it operated. In the same month No 139 Squadron provided the nucleus of a new Mosquito unit, No 627 Squadron, which officially formed in 12 November, and immediately became No 139's latest 'partner' for raiding Germany. Throughout 1943 the Squadron had mounted 730 *effective* sorties* (including 41 attacks on Berlin), but in the new year No 139 Squadron became the principal marker force for the bomber 'heavies' over Germany, as well as the prime marking element for other Mosquito operations. From early 1944 the Squadron began using the *H2S* radar and introduced it to Mosquito operations in March, and by the end of the year had completed a total of 2,443 sorties for 1944 alone. In early 1945 the Squadron operated almost every possible night, including leading 33 consecutive night raids against Berlin from the beginning of February. The Squadron's final war operations came on 2 May 1945 when 16 Mosquitos attacked Kiel; bringing its total Mosquito sorties' tally up to 4,306 in almost exactly two years of operating the 'Wooden Wonder'. In

---

*Of 302 sorties actually despatched.

Above:
DZ515 of 139 Squadron. *R. C. B. Ashworth*

Below:
Line-up of 139 Squadron at Marham, early 1943, with unit commander, Wg Cdr P. Shand, DFC nearest in shirtsleeves. Aircraft (left to right) included DZ421, 'G'; DZ423, 'T'; and DZ428, 'K'. Shand was killed on a Berlin raid on 20/21 April 1943. *Topical Press Agency*

peace the Squadron remained in its specialised marker role for low-level sorties, and from 1948 flew Mosquito B35s. In November 1953 it finally exchanged its Mosquitos for Canberra B2 jet bombers.

Main bases

Horsham St Faiths	June 1942
Oulton	June 1942
Horsham St Faiths	June 1942
Marham	September 1942
Wyton	July 1943
Upwood	February 1944
Hemswell	February 1946
Coningsby	November 1946
Hemswell	March 1950

Aircraft examples flown

W4072; DK296; DK324, 'R'; DK330, 'A'; DZ348, 'O'; DZ371, 'A'; DZ373, 'B'; DZ423, 'T'; DZ463, 'O'; DZ464, 'G'; DZ465, 'E'; DZ470, 'N'; DZ476, 'S'; DZ477, 'D'; DZ478, 'V'; DZ482, 'P'; DZ491, 'F'; DZ497, 'Q'; DZ515, 'M'; DZ518, 'D'; DZ609, 'O'; DZ612, 'C', DZ644, 'V'; KB161, 'H'; KB162, 'J'; KB184, 'V'; KB192, 'S', KB205; KB208, 'V'; KB210, 'P'; KB217; KB225, 'C'; KB263; KB354, 'C'; KB390, 'B'; KB434, 'V'; LR475, 'W'; ML908, 'Y'; ML909, 'Z' and 'S'; ML934, 'C'; MM200, 'E'; PF383, 'P'; PF514; PF573; PZ445; RS699; RV310; RV313, 'V'; TA640; TK620, 'L'; TK628; TK630; TK633; VA887; VP184; VP194; VR792.

Commanding Officers

Wg Cdr P. Shand DFC	July 1942
Wg Cdr. R. W. Reynolds, DSO, DFC	May 1943
Wg Cdr G. H. Womersley, DSO, DFC	April 1944
Wg Cdr J. R. G. Ralston, DSO, AFC, DFM	March 1945

No 140 Squadron

Re-formed at Benson on 17 September 1941, when No 1416 Flight was re-titled, No 140 Squadron initially flew Spitfires and a few Blenheim IVs in the photo-reconnaissance role. When, in November 1943, the 2nd Tactical Air Force (TAF) was formed preparatory to the intended 1944 invasion of Normandy, No 140 Squadron joined No 16 Squadron to form No 34 Wing of 2nd TAF, both units based at Hartford Bridge. In that month No 140 Squadron transferred eight of its Spitfires to No 16 Squadron and began receiving Mosquito IXs in their place. Operations over the following months mainly comprised photo-reconnaissance over western Europe for the preparation of mosaic maps for use by the invasion forces. In December 1943 the Squadron's Mk IXs were supplemented by some Mk XVIs, while in the early months of 1944 its crews commenced training with *Gee* and *Rebecca-H* radar aids (for night and/or bad weather photography). On 7 April 1944 No 140 Squadron, with No 16 Squadron, moved base to Northolt, from where No 140 Squadron flew its final Spitfire sorties and, by mid-month, became an all-Mosquito unit. On the eve of D-Day No 140's Mosquitos flew several sorties, losing two of these to enemy opposition, and flew a total of 177 sorties throughout June. On 3 September the Squadron moved to Balleroy (A12) airstrip in Normandy, then again moved within days to Amiens/Glisy (B48), and finally to Melsbroek on the 26th where it remained based for almost the rest of the war. The loss of several Mosquitos to Luftwaffe opposition over the next few months led No 140 Squadron to concentrate mainly on night PR sorties in early 1945, and on 15 February the unit moved to Eindhoven (B78). In March 1945 the Squadron flew 180 sorties, all but 17 of these by night, but as the war came to a close the crews began flying shipping recces over Norwegian and Baltic waters, flying the unit's final war sortie on 7 May 1945. In July No 140 Squadron returned to England, and was disbanded at Fersfield on 10 November 1945.

Main bases

Hartford Bridge	March 1943
Northolt	April 1944
Balleroy	September 1944
Amiens/Glisy	September 1944
Melsbroek	September 1944
Eindhoven	February 1945
Acklington	July 1945
Fersfield	September 1945

Aircraft examples flown
LR416; LR435; LR479; MM243; MM248;
MM249; MM250; MM251; MM271; MM279;
MM280; MM282; MM294; MM301; MM305;
MM307; MM356; MM395; NS507; NS517;
NS522; NS563; NS575; NS578; NS580;
NS777; NS798; RF993.

Commanding Officers
Wg Cdr R. I. Mallafont-Bowen   November 1943
Wg Cdr C. F. M Chapman   September 1944
Wg Cdr F. O. S. Dobell   October 1944
Wg Cdr D. R. M. Frostick   April 1945

No 141 Squadron

After four years of operating Defiants and
(mainly) Beaufighters as a night interceptor unit,
No 141 Squadron began re-equipping with Mosquito NFIIs, receiving its first example on
16 October 1943. These were fitted with *Serrate*
radar but the Squadron's intruder sorties of that
period produced few victories. On 4 December
1943 it transferred to No 100 (SD) Group for
bomber support duties, and a No 141 Squadron

**PRXVI, NS777 of 140 Squadron, winter
1944-45.** *C. E. Brown/RAF Museum*

Mosquito claimed 100 Group's first 'victims' on
17 December, an Me110 damaged and a Bf109
destroyed on 28 January 1944. From August
1944 the Squadron began flying Mosquito VIs,
but victories remained mainly elusive, and the
Squadron's last Mk II sorties were flown on
29 August. Improved radar came into use on the
Mk VIs, including the American AI Mk XV,
known as *Ash*, and on 21 December the
Squadron became the first to operate with *Ash*
— claiming its first *Ash* victim, a Ju88, on
1 January 1945. In the interim No 141's crews
had diverted from their normal role by undertaking the occasional 'spoof' bombing raid
during November and December 1944. From
15 March until 3 April 1945 the Squadron was
non-operational while its crews converted to
Mosquito XXXs, flying its last Mk VI patrol on
8 March, then resumed operations with their
Mk XXXs on 4 April. For the final weeks of the
war No 141 participated in various bombing
raids over Germany; one unusual form of attack
taking place on 18 April when seven of No 141's
Mosquitos dropped 100gal drop-tanks filled

RL239, 'TW-D' of 141 Squadron at Coltishall on 3 January 1951. *R. A. Brown*

with napalm gel on an airfield near Munich. They repeated this form of 'firebomb' raid on 2/3 May when 13 of the Squadron's Mosquitos dropped napalm 'bombs' on Hohn and Flensburg. Disbanded at Little Snoring on 7 September 1945, No 141 Squadron was re-formed at Coltishall on 17 June 1946, equipped with Mosquito NF36s and flew these until September 1951 when re-equipment with Meteor NF11s commenced.

Main bases

Wittering	April 1943
West Raynham	December 1943
Little Snoring	July 1945
Coltishall	June 1946
Church Fenton	November 1949
Coltishall	September 1950

Aircraft examples flown

W4089, 'W'; DD615; DD672, 'P'; DD712, 'E'; DD717; DD725; DD755; DD758, 'N'; DZ240, 'H'; DZ266; DZ296; DZ303, 'E'; DZ761, 'C'; HJ659, 'B'; HJ701, 'U'; HJ707; HJ911, 'A'; HJ941; HR180, 'B'; HR203, 'C'; HR213; HR250, 'Y'; NS961, 'H'; NT234, 'W'; NT371, 'D'; NT456; NT472, 'H'; NT500, 'K'; NT507, 'F'; NT554,'R'; PZ165, 'S'; PZ171, 'R'; PZ234; PZ235; PZ244, 'M'; PZ252, 'Z'; RK956; RK981, 'F'; RK990, 'B'; RK995; RL118, 'D'; RL147, 'H'; RL154, 'E'; RL182, 'M'; RL209, 'E'; RL230, 'F'; RL252, 'C'; RL263, 'E'; RV302; VT614.

Commanding Officers

Wg Cdr K. C. Roberts AFC	October 1943
Wg Cdr F. P. Davies DFC	February 1944
Wg Cdr C. V. Winn DSO, DFC	June 1944

No 142 Squadron

No 142 Squadron re-formed at Gransden Lodge on 25 October 1944, and received its first two Mosquito XXVs, KB430 and KB460, two days later. On 29 October both aircraft made the unit's initial sorties, to Cologne. Its prime role was as part of No 8 Group's Light Night Striking Force, in which its crews spearheaded main bomber raids, made mock marking sorties to confuse enemy defences, or bombed specified targets. The Squadron usually participated in the increasingly large all-Mosquito attacks on Germany; the largest of which took place on 21/22 March 1945, when No 142 Squadron contributed 14 Mosquitos of the total of 103 in Phase 1 of an attack on Berlin, and further one of the 35 which returned for Phase 2 of the same raid. The Squadron's last war sorties were flown on 2/3 May 1945 when 16 Mosquitos raided Kiel, thus completing an overall total of 1,221 sorties in some six months of operations. On 28 September 1945 the Squadron was disbanded at Gransden Lodge.

Aircraft examples flown

KB397, 'P'; KB400, 'V'; KB408; KB421;
KB423, 'V'; KB430; KB432, 'M'; KB435, 'C';
KB436, 'A'; KB439, 'G'; KB444, 'B'; KB449, 'S'
and 'V'; KB450, 'E'; KB457, 'R'; KB460;
KB466, 'U'; KB468, 'B'; KB470, 'O';
KB473, 'D'; KB487, 'J'; KB519, 'K'; KB613;
KB655, 'L'.

Commanding Officer

Wg Cdr B. G. D. Nathan   October 1944

No 143 Squadron

After a varied existence in Coastal Command as a strike unit and virtual OTU, No 143 Squadron was based at North Coates operating Beaufighters over Dutch waters in late 1944. In October, however, the Squadron was transferred to Banff, there to convert to Mosquitos as part of the Banff Strike Wing, commanded by Gp Capt Max Aitken DSO, DFC. Its first Mosquito sorties were flown on 7 November when HR141 and PZ419 patrolled off the Norwegian coastline. This area became the Banff Wing's prime operational zone for the remaining months of the war, mostly in an anti-shipping strike role, though occasionally attacking land targets. Armed with cannons and RP, No 143's Mosquitos contributed a large part to the Wing's many successes; in particular sharing in the destruction of the *U804* and *U1065* on 9 April 1945, the *U251* on 19 April, and the *U2359* on 2 May. In air combat too it scored occasional victories, and on 21 April the

Two views of RS625, 'D' of 143 Squadron, Banff Wing, Coastal Command on 6 April 1945.
Both: Hawker Siddeley Aviation

Squadron claimed many of the nine German bombers shot down in a single engagement over the North Sea. The final major sorties were flown on 3 May 1945 when the Wing flew an anti-shipping sweep off Kiel Bay. The last 'operations' by No 143 Squadron were by two aircraft on an anti-submarine patrol on 21 May. Four days later the Squadron was 'disbanded' at Banff by being renumbered as No 14 Squadron.

Aircraft examples flown

HR141; HR373, 'N'; HR414, 'L'; PZ379, 'R';
PZ413, 'Y'; PZ418; PZ419; PZ446; PZ466, 'Q';
RF622, 'K'; RF624; RS625, 'D' and 'A'; RS627.

Commanding Officers

Wg Cdr E. H. McHardy
   DSO, DFC   November 1943
Wg Cdr J. M. Maurice
   DSO, DFC*   December 1944
Wg Cdr C. N. Foxley-Norris
   DSO   February 1945

*Pseudonym for the Frenchman, Wg Cdr M. Guedj DSO, DFC.

NORGE

No 151 Squadron

With the distinction of being the RAF's first-ever night 'intruder' and 'bomber support' fighter squadron — in France, flying Sopwith F1 Camels in 1918 — No 151 Squadron began its second world war as a Hurricane I unit in Fighter Command, and fought the Luftwaffe over France and Britain throughout 1939-40. In November 1940 the Squadron reverted to its original pioneering role as 'night fighters', initially flying Defiants and Hurricane IICs, until 6 April 1942 when it received its first Mosquito NFII (DD608). By the end of the month the Squadron possessed 16 Mosquitos and flew its first operational patrols on 30 April. A month later its first successful interception was made on 29 May by DD628, but it was not until 24/25 June when two Dornier 217s were shot down that No 151 could claim definite victories. Two more German bombers were destroyed in June, followed by six more in July. Thereafter 'trade' slackened for the nightfighters, so in February 1943 No 151 Squadron began flying 'Night Ranger' sorties — night-intruder roving commission patrols of specified areas of enemy-occupied territories — flying the first such sorties on 16/17 February alongside Mosquitos of No 25 Squadron; it then added 'Instep' sorties — patrols over the Atlantic seaboard along Biscay, etc — to its chores. On 13 June during an 'Instep' patrol two of No 151's Mosquitos destroyed a Focke Wulf Fw200 — the first to fall to any Mosquito — and four days later accounted for two Ju88s. In July 1943 the Squadron began flying Mosquito NFXIIs,

Above:
Mk XII, HK183 of 151 Squadron, c1944.
Z. Hurt

Below:
HR350, 'P' and crew, 151 Squadron.
M. N. Austin via D. Vincent

mixed with a few Mk VIs, with which it tackled some of the Luftwaffe's night intruders preying around East Anglian bomber bases at that period. On the night of 21/22 January 1944 a No 151 crew registered another 'first' by shooting down a Heinkel He177 — the first to be brought down on British soil. By October that year the Squadron had received its latest equipment, Mk XXXs, flying its first sorties in these on 11 October, but few victories were obtained. During the closing months of the war No 151 Squadron mainly provided night bomber support sorties. On 10 October 1946 the Squadron was disbanded at Weston Zoyland.

Main bases

Wittering	December 1940
Colerne	April 1943
Middle Wallop	August 1943
Colerne	November 1943
Predannack	March 1944
Castle Camps	October 1944
Hunsdon	November 1944
Bradwell Bay	March 1945
Predannack	May 1945
Exeter	June 1946
Colerne	September 1946
Weston Zoyland	October 1946

Aircraft examples flown

W4087; W4095; W4097, 'N'; DD601; DD606; DD608; DD613; DD617; DD624; DD660; DD663; DD669; DD707; DD732; DD749; DD787; DZ241; DZ245; DZ300; DZ787; HJ642; HJ655; HJ931; HK177; HK183; HK190; HK193; HK199; HK222; HK225; HK232; HK235; HK362; HK377; HK503; HR190; HR240; HX829; MM436; MM437, 'F'; MM438; MM445; MM446; MM448, 'E'; MM469; MM726; MM791; MM796; MM800, 'V'; MM802, 'C'; MM814; MV559; NS982; NT253; NT304, 'T'; NT306; NT474; NT489; NT500, 'J'; NT536, 'F'; NT547; NT553, 'W'; NT595, 'L'; PZ191; PZ201; PZ224.

Commanding Officers

Wg Cdr I. S. Smith DFC	February 1942
Wg Cdr D. V. Ivins	March 1943
Wg Cdr S. P. Richards AFC	May 1943
Wg Cdr G. H. Goodman DSO, DFC	October 1943
Wg Cdr W. R. L. Beaumont DFC	December 1944

No 157 Squadron

To No 157 Squadron fell the honour of becoming the first Mosquito fighter squadron when it was re-formed at Debden on 13 December 1941. Moving to Castle Camps in the same month, it received its first Mosquito, W4073, a dual control aircraft, on 17 January 1942, but initial deliveries of NFIIs to the Squadron were slow, and by 28 March Squadron strength was merely 14 aircraft. Six more arrived by mid-April, though not all had complete operational radar installed as yet. The first patrol was flown on 27 April by night, while the first day sortie came on 12 May, but the first successful intercept did not happen until 30 May when Sqn Ldr G. Ashfield in W4099 destroyed a Do217, albeit only claiming it as a 'probable'. The first victim to be actually confirmed as destroyed was a Do217 shot down on 22 August, while the first day combat victory was claimed on 30 September by DD607 (Wg Cdr R. F. H. Clerke). Though occasional victories followed, night activity lessened by the Luftwaffe and No 157's crews began flying intruder ('Ranger') sorties from early 1943, the first 'Ranger' being flown on 23 March. By June 1943 the Squadron was also flying 'Instep' sweeps over the Western Approaches, seeking out the Luftwaffe and any German shipping; a form of operation which it was to continue until April 1944. In August 1943 Mosquito VIs began to be flown by the Squadron with a view to undertaking bomber support roles, and in August 1944 the unit was transferred to No 100 (SD) Group accordingly. By then its crews had worked up on Mosquito XIXs, the first sorties of which were flown on 5/6 June 1944, and the first Mk XIX victory was a Ju188 destroyed by MM630 on 12/13 June. From 27 June the Squadron was diverted to exclusive offensive against the V1 menace, and its crews destroyed two 'buzz-bombs' that day. On 2 March 1945 the Squadron flew its first sorties with the Mosquito XXXs which had recently begun to replace its XIXs and continued its night intruder sorties, mainly selecting Luftwaffe airfields for targets. The unit continued in this role until the end of the war in Europe, and was then disbanded at Swannington on 16 August 1945.

Above:
Black Beauty. NFII, DD750, which served in Nos 157, 25, 239 and 264 Squadrons.

Below:
NFXIX, MM652 which served as 'S' with 157 Squadron, later serving on 169 Squadron.
Crown copyright

Main bases

Debden	December 1941
Castle Camps	December 1941
Bradwell Bay	March 1943
Hunsdon	May 1943
Predannack	November 1943
Valley	March 1944
West Malling	July 1944
Swannington	August 1944

Aircraft examples flown

W4079, 'F'; W4082, 'W'; W4084; W4087;
W4094; W4096; W4098, 'M'; W4099; DD601;
DD602; DD603; DD604; DD607; DD611;
DD627; DD636; DD640; DD716; DD730;
DD750; DD777; DZ243; DZ248; DZ260, 'B';
DZ654, 'A'; DZ687, 'V'; DZ707; DZ739;
DZ740; DZ749; HJ911, 'H'; HP850;
MM369, 'A'; MM629; MM630, 'E';
MM643, 'F'; MM652, 'S'; MM654; MM655;
MM671, 'C'; MM677, 'U'; MV534, 'F';
MV551, 'W'; NT242, 'F'; NT319, 'V'; NT330;
NT364, 'K'; NT382, 'T'; TA391, 'N';
TA392, 'K'; TA398; TA404, 'K' and 'M';
TA446, 'Q'; TA487, 'M'; TA493, 'H'.

Commanding Officers

Wg Cdr R. G. Slade	December 1941
Wg Cdr V. J. Wheeler MC, DFC	January 1943
Wg Cdr J. A. Mackie	August 1943
Wg Cdr H. D. U. Denison	March 1944
Wg Cdr W. K. Davison	June 1944
Wg Cdr K. H. P. Beauchamp DSO, DFC	September 1944

No 162 Squadron

Formed at Kabrit, Egypt, on 4 January 1942 for
signals calibration and anti-enemy radio
jamming duties, No 162 Squadron initially flew
Blenheims and Wellingtons, but in January 1944
it received a Mosquito VI, HJ671, which flew a
few patrols investigating enemy radar defences.
However, the Squadron was disbanded on
25 September 1944. The Squadron was next
re-formed in England at Bourn on 18 December
1944 as a Mosquito BXXV unit of No 8 (PFF)
Group's Light Night Striking Force. Though
nominally a bomber unit the Squadron quickly
assumed marker duties alongside No 139
Squadron, and from March 1945 began operating as an *H2S* Squadron in part, though the
bulk of its operations remained pure bombing on
'Siren tours' (nuisance raids designed to keep
enemy defences fully stretched). By the end of
the European war No 162 Squadron had logged
a total of 913 operational sorties (15 of these
abortive) and dropped almost 800 tons of bombs
on enemy objectives. In June 1945 the Squadron
was transferred to Transport Command as a
fast courier unit in Europe, but on 14 July 1946
it was disbanded.

Aircraft examples flown

HJ671; KB189, 'B'; KB407, 'R'; KB415, 'C';
KB445, 'E'; KB452, 'Q'; KB453, 'G';
KB454, 'T'; KB458, 'U'; KB459; KB461, 'V';
KB462 'B'; KB465, 'F'; BK477, 'A';
KB483, 'D'; KB492, 'S'; KB497, 'J';
KB509, 'Z'; KB520, 'L'; KB534; KB547, 'Q'.

Commanding Officers

Wg Cdr J. D. Bolton DFC	December 1944
Wg Cdr M. K. Sewell DFC	April 1945

No 163 Squadron

Re-formed at Wyton on 25 January 1945, No 163 Squadron received its first Mosquito XXVs (six) on 26 January, and on the night of 28/29 January despatched four of these on the Squadron's first sorties — dropping *Window* ahead of a PFF force. Thereafter the Squadron operated almost nightly, particularly against industrial targets and its 'favourite' objective Berlin, which it visited no less than 24 times in a single month, March. By May 1945 — its final sorties were to Kiel on 2/3 May — the Squadron had flown nearly 500 sorties. It then exchanged its Mk XXVs for BXVIs but was disbanded at Wyton on 10 August 1945.

Aircraft examples flown
KB403, 'Z'; KB425, 'V'; KB427, 'X'; KB464, 'T'; KB488, 'D'; KB502, 'U'; KB510, 'B'; KB511, 'E'; KB518, 'J'; KB526, 'F'; KB541, 'Y'; KB555, 'R'; KB568, 'V'; KB619, 'T'; KB623, 'S'; KB624, 'G'; PF405; PF517, RV310.

Commanding Officer

Wg Cdr I. G. Broom DFC	January 1945

No 169 Squadron

Disbanded as a Mustang fighter-reconnaissance unit at Middle Wallop on 1 October 1943, No 169 Squadron was 'reborn' on the same date at Ayr as a nightfighter unit equipped initially with Mosquito NFIIs. Moving to its operational base at Little Snoring on 8 December the Squadron flew its first operational sortie on 20 January 1944, under the aegis of No 100 (SD) Group. Crews quickly began claiming victories, a particularly successful night being 15 May when the crew of DZ478 claimed three victims near Kiel. In early June 1944 the Squadron began receiving *Serrate*-equipped Mk VIs, flying its first patrols with these on 18 June, and on 20/21 July NT113 (Wg Cdr N. B. R. Bromley, OBE) claimed 100 Group's 100th claimed victory. By the end of 1944 the Squadron was flying a mixture of Mosquito VI, XIX, and XXXs and was undertaking varied roles, including marking, high-level patrols, intruders, and low-level 'Rangers', apart from occasional 'Spoof' bombing raids. The Squadron's ultimate war sorties were flown on 2/3 May when it attacked Schleswig and Westerland with napalm 'tanks'. On 10 August 1945 No 169 Squadron was again disbanded, at Great Massingham.

Main bases

Ayr	October 1943
Little Snoring	December 1943
Great Massingham	June 1944

Aircraft examples flown
W4076, 'F'; DD629; DD631, 'G'; DD783; DD799; DZ231; DZ241; DZ310, 'B'; DZ607; DZ748; HJ707, 'B'; HJ711, 'C'; HJ917, 'N'; HJ944, 'C'; MM626; MM644, 'V' and 'G'; MM652; MM670, 'G'; MM685; MT148; MT376; NS997, 'C'; NS998; NT110, 'T'; NT113; NT121; NT150; NT169, 'T'; NT176; NT238; PZ247, 'M'; TA263; TA394.

Commanding Officers

Wg Cdr E. J. Gracie DFC	October 1943
Wg Cdr R. G. Slade	February 1944
Wg Cdr N. B. R. Bromley, OBE	April 1944
Wg Cdr T. A. Heath, DFC, AFC	September 1944
Wg Cdr N. E. Reeves, DSO, DFC	January 1945

No 176 Squadron

Formed as a Beaufighter squadron in India in January 1943, No 176 Squadron flew these and, later, Hurricane IICs throughout the war. On 14 July 1945 the Squadron began converting to Mosquito NFXIXs, and by 1 August had eight aircraft on strength, though still being listed as non-operational. It remained non-operational until its disbandment at Baigachi on 1 June 1946.

Aircraft examples flown
TA155; TA176; TA225; TA246; TA264;

TA273; TA280.

Commanding Officers

Wg Cdr G. M. Merrifield AFC	January 1945
Sqn Ldr L. W. H. Welch DFC	September 1945

No 180 Squadron

Although No 180 Squadron had served from 1942-45 as a Mitchell bomber unit, it was not until September 1945 that it re-equipped with Mosquito BXVIs. Then, on 1 April 1946, while based at Wahn, Germany, the unit was retitled as No 69 Squadron.

Aircraft examples flown
ML970; PF448, 'C'; PF455.

No 192 Squadron

On 4 January 1943 at Gransden Lodge No 1474 Flight, equipped then with Wellingtons and three Mosquito IVs, was retitled as No 192 Squadron. Its initial primary role was investigation and identification of enemy radar units and wavelengths, and its aircraft ranged from Norway to France when Squadron operations commenced from 11 June 1943. By then a detachment had passed to temporary Coastal Command control to cover the Biscay zones too. In November 1943 control of No 192 Squadron was transferred to No 100(SD) Group, while in February 1944 No 1473 Flight was merged with the Squadron. It continued its former 'detective' patrols over Germany, logging nearly 60 sorties by April 1944, then concentrating on enemy locations in France during the pre-invasion weeks recording 136 sorties in June and 153 in July 1944. This pace of operations increased in September when 196 sorties were completed. In April 1945 Mosquito PRXVIs replaced the Squadron's Mk IVs, though the first PRXVI sortie had been flown in February, and the ultimate Mk IV sortie on 9 April. The Squadron was disbanded at Foulsham on 22 August 1945

but immediately became the virtual nucleus of the recently formed Central Signals Establishment.

Main bases

Gransden Lodge	January 1943
Feltwell	April 1943
Foulsham	November 1943

Aircraft examples flown
W4071; DK292; DK327; DK357; DZ292; DZ375; DZ376; DZ377; DZ410, 'K'; DZ491; DZ535; DZ590; DZ617; NS776, 'I'; NS797, 'N'; NS816, 'O'; RF974, 'J';

Commanding Officers

Wg Cdr C. D. V. Willis DFC	January 1943
Wg Cdr E. P. M. Fernbank DFC	March 1944
Wg Cdr E. W. Donaldson, DSO, DFC	June 1944

No 199 Squadron

A former Radio Counter-Measures (RCM) squadron within No 100 (SD) Group 1944-45, No 199 Squadron was re-formed on 15 July 1951 at Watton as a unit of No 90 Signals Group, and was mainly equipped with Avro Lincolns. Its role remained RCM, for which it was also issued with a few Mosquito NF36s that were phased out in 1953.

Main bases

Watton	July 1951
Hemswell	April 1952

Aircraft examples flown
RK958; RL189.

No 211 Squadron

In May 1945 No 211 Squadron, based then at Yelahanka with Beaufighters, became non-operational in order to convert to Mosquito FBVIs as part of a force intended to cover the

Above:
NF36, RL239 of 199 Squadron
R. C. B. Ashworth

Below:
FBVIs of 211 Squadron at Bangkok, November 1945, including RF751, 'B', and RF711, 'A'.
via RAF Museum

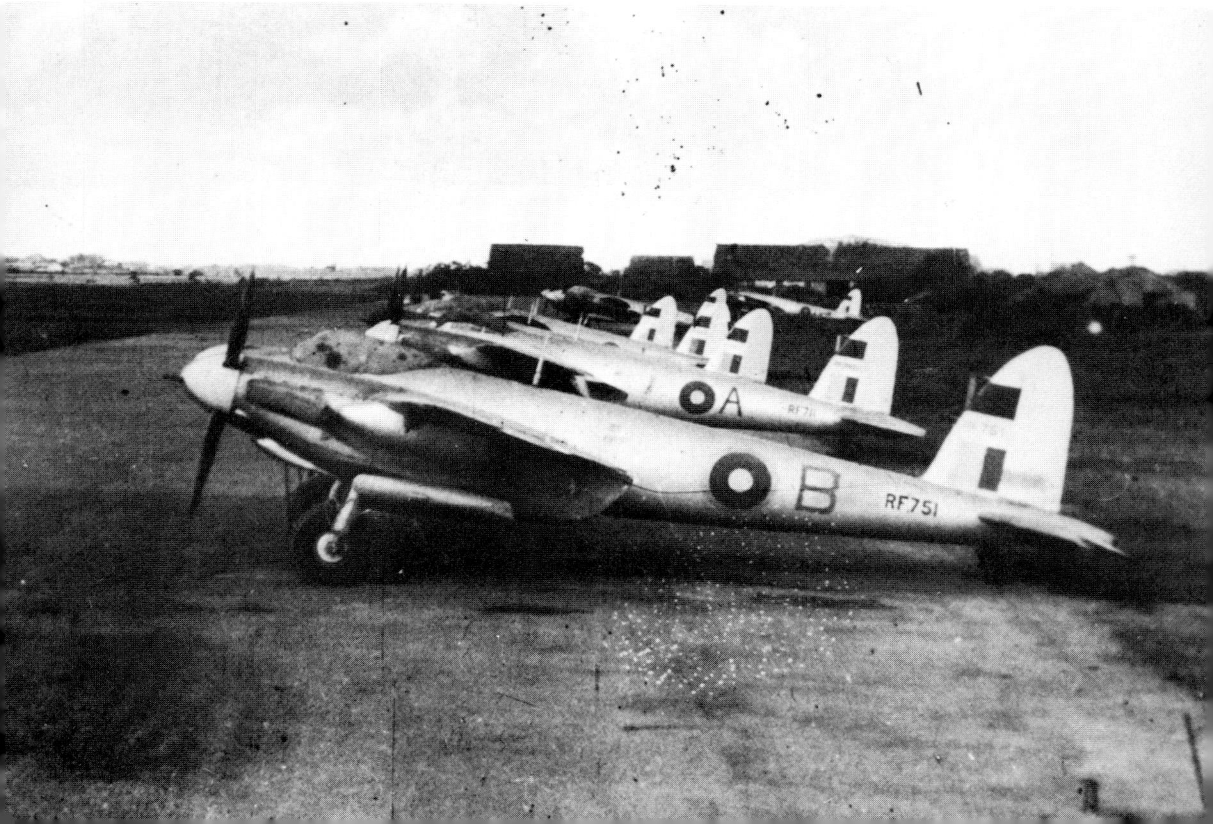

projected Allied invasion of Malaya. By 1 August Squadron strength stood at 16 aircraft but the Japanese surrender occurred before the Squadron could recommence operations. A series of structural failures resulted in all Mosquitos being grounded in January 1946, and the Squadron disbanded at Don Muang on 28 February 1946.

No 219 Squadron

Re-formed at Catterick on 4 October 1939 as a nightfighter unit, equipped initially with Blenheim IFs, No 219 Squadron continued in that role until the end of the war, exchanging its Blenheims for Beaufighters from September 1940. By September 1942 its crews had claimed at least 44 victories in combat, but the following nine months brought few claims. A move to North Africa in May-June 1943 gave the Squadron renewed success, still in the night defence role, and in January 1944 it returned to England for re-equipment with Mosquito XVIIs, claiming its first victim with these on 27 March. Not content with purely defensive tactics, the Squadron soon began offensive sorties across the Channel seeking out the Luftwaffe. In June 1944 it was diverted to combat the V1 assaults, but continued to fly patrols over the Allied beach-head in Normandy. By October, with the Allied armies now advancing to German frontiers, No 219 Squadron moved base to Amiens to continue its support, and remained on the Continent until Germany's surrender. In its last year of operations the Squadron added at least 33 more victories to its combat tally, its final victim being a Heinkel He177 destroyed on 9 April 1945. Returning to England in August 1945, the Squadron remained part of Fighter Command's night defences, flying Mosquito NFXXXs, but was disbanded at Acklington on 1 September 1946.

Main bases

Woodvale	February 1944
Honiley	February 1944
Bradwell Bay	May 1944
Hunsdon	August 1944
Amiens/Glisy	October 1944
Gilze/Rijen	March 1945

Mosquito TIII, TV970, 'FK-V' of 219 Squadron, 1950.

Enschede	June 1945
Twente	July 1945
Acklington	August 1945
Wittering	April 1946
Acklington	August 1946

Aircraft examples flown

HK248; HK260; HK279; HK314; HK315, 'N';
HK319; HK320; HK344; HK362; KA120;
MM690; MM696; MM698; MM702; MM703;
MM706; MM790; MM792; MM796;
MM756, 'A'; MM813, 'H'; MV522, 'F';
NT251,'O'; NT270; NT297; NT336, 'P';
NT457, 'K'; NT501, 'D'; NT538, 'Y'.

Commanding Officers

Wg Cdr A. D. McN. Boyd DFC	March 1943
Wg Cdr W. P. Green DSO, DFC	August 1944
Wg Cdr B. Maitland-Thompson	April 1945
Wg Cdr A. Carlisle	August 1945
Wg Cdr Pain DFC, AFC	October 1945
Sqn Ldr P. G. K. Williamson DFC	February 1946

No 235 Squadron

A fighter strike unit with Coastal Command from February 1940, No 235 Squadron flew Beaufighters 1940-1944, and converted to Mosquito VIs in June 1944, flying its first Mosquito sorties on 16 June. Its role continued to be primarily anti-shipping strikes, although occasional clashes with the Luftwaffe gave the

Squadron several air combat victories. In September 1944 it moved north to join the Banff Wing and thereafter became chiefly involved in Wing strikes against shipping in the North Sea, particularly along the Norwegian coastline. Its shared toll of enemy ships sunk or seriously damaged mounted rapidly, and included the sinking of *U843* on 9 April 1945, and a part in the destruction of four other U-boats in the same month. The Squadron's last strike sorties were flown on 3 May 1945, though the Mosquito crews continued to fly general anti-shipping patrols for several weeks thereafter to ensure that enemy U-boats, etc did not continue war operations. On 10 July 1945 the Squadron was disbanded at Banff.

Main bases

| Portreath | August 1943 |
| Banff | September 1944 |

Aircraft examples flown

HP887, 'R'; HP977, 'J'; HP982; HP989;
HR113, 'V'; HR129, 'D'; HR137, 'S'; HR159,
'Y'; HR287, 'Y'; HR298; HR433, 'L';

LR347, 'T'; PZ450; RF602, 'P'; RS523, 'A';
RS524, 'S'.

Commanding Officers
Wg Cdr R. H. McConnell
   DSO, DFC   July 1943
Wg Cdr J. V. Yonge   May 1944
Wg Cdr R. A. Atkinson
   DSO, DFC   October 1944
Wg Cdr A. H. Simmonds
   DFC   December 1944

No 239 Squadron

After three years operations as an army co-operation unit, No 239 Squadron's role was changed to nightfighting, and it received its first Mosquito NFIIs on 11 December 1943 at West Raynham. Becoming operational again, the Squadron flew its first sorties on 26 January 1944, and claimed its first Mosquito victory two nights later. As a *Serrate* unit of No 100 (SD) Group the Squadron's prime role was bomber support, escorting main force bomber streams over Europe, but occasional long-range intrusion sorties were also flown, resulting in several air combat victories, one of the most successful pilots being Flt Lt D. Welfare who claimed six victims in June-July 1944 while 'roaming' over France and Belgium. On 26/27 October the Squadron flew the ultimate Mosquito NFII sortie (DD789), and continued with its FBVIs until January 1945 when NFXXXs came into use, the first Squadron sorties in XXXs being flown on 21/22 January. During the last winter of the war No 239 Squadron flew occasional day 'Rangers' bombing German airfields, but soon returned to nightfighting in the New Year, and by May 1945 had claimed a total of 55 victories for its Mosquito crews. On 1 July 1945 the Squadron was disbanded at West Raynham.

Aircraft examples flown
W4074; W4084; W4097; DD722; DD750;
DD759; DD789; DZ239; DZ247; DZ256;
DZ263; DZ297; DZ298; DZ654; DZ749;
HJ644; HJ709; HJ934; HJ937; HR213;
MM649; NT309; NT330; NT352; NT354;
NT362, 'S'; NT385; NT437; NT480; PZ170;
PZ179; PZ228; PZ245; PZ340; PZ356; PZ498.

Commanding Officers
Wg Cdr P. M. J. Evans DFC   September 1943
Wg Cdr W. F. Gibb   September 1944

No 248 Squadron

In October 1943 No 248 Squadron was based at Predannack, flying Beaufighter Xs with Coastal Command, when it received a detachment of five Mosquito crews from No 618 Squadron and, two weeks later on 22 October also received two Mosquito XVIIIs. These particular versions were fitted with a single 57mm Molins cannon in place of the more normal four 20mm cannons in the fuselage, and were often referred to as 'Tsetse' Mosquitos. Their purpose was primarily anti-shipping, and the first sorties by the 'loaned' 618 crews in 'Tsetses' were flown on 24 October. On 20 November came the first indication that No 248 Squadron would shortly exchange its Beaufighters for Mosquitos, and conversion commenced in December, reaching a strength of 20 Mosquitos (XVIIIs and VIs) by 1 January 1944. By February 1944 the Mosquitos had commenced operations, attacking all types of enemy shipping met and not uncommonly engaging Lufwaffe aircraft escorting their naval forces. On 10 March, for example, the Mosquitos strafed an enemy naval convoy, damaging several ships, and shot down four escorting German aircraft in the process. On 6 June (D-Day) No 248 Squadron flew non-stop from first light to late evening, sinking a destroyer, firing a second, and shooting down a Ju188. On 10 June the Squadron shared in the sinking of *U821*, and throughout that month despatched a total of 274 sorties. On 22 June No 248 Squadron's aircraft carried 25lb depth charges on an anti-submarine sortie — the first operational use of this 'store' — but more normal bomb loads were reinstated a few weeks later. The Squadron's final sorties in the Biscay area were flown on 7 September 1944, after which the unit moved to Banff to become a unit of the Dallachy Strike Wing of Mosquitos and Beaufighters, flying its first sorties to Norwegian waters on 14 September. The next months saw No 248 Squadron heavily involved in the many large strikes undertaken by the Wing, and on 15 January 1945 the unit's Mosquito XVIIIs

Mk XVIII, 'Tsetse' with 57mm Molins cannon in place of the normal four 20mm Hispano cannons; this was a type which equipped 248 Squadron.

flew their last sorties, leaving the Squadron to operate Mk VIs only. By then most Mosquitos in the Wing had been modified to carry RP armament in addition to their normal guns and the RP was used to good effect against a large variety of shipping. By March 1945 the Mosquitos were attacking not only ships but ports and installations in Norway, usually with deadly effect. On 9 April the Squadron shared the destruction of *U804* and *U1065*, and 10 days later also shared the sinking of *U251*, followed by *U2359* on 2 May. No 248 Squadron's last official patrols took place on 21 May 1945 — an anti-submarine patrol — after which its crews flew some search and rescue sorties. Moving to Chivenor in July 1945, the Squadron took part

in various trials of anti-submarine tactics but was effectively disbanded at Thorney Island on 1 October 1946 when it was renumbered as No 36 Squadron.

Main bases

Predannack	January 1943
Portreath	February 1944
Banff	September 1944
Chivenor	July 1945
Thorney Island	May 1946

Aircraft examples flown

HJ828, 'R'; HP866, 'D'; HP909; HP922, 'U'; HP988, 'R'; HR119; HR120, 'G'; HR261, 'N' HR284; HX902, 'E'; HX903, 'I'; LR330, 'J'; LR344; LR346; LR352; LR378, 'C'; LR413, 'G'; LR828, 'R' and 'Q'; MM399, 'S'; MM413; MM424, 'H'; MM425, 'L'; MM430, 'Q'; MM431, 'Z'; NT224, 'E'; PF612; RF387, 'T'; RF603; RF605; RF615, 'S'; RF826; RF877, 'C'; RS610, 'Y'; RS625; RS629; SZ959.

Commanding Officers

Wg Cdr F. E. Burton DFC	July 1943
Wg Cdr O. J. M. Barron DFC	February 1944
Wg Cdr A. D. Phillips DSO, DFC	April 1944
Wg Cdr D. G. Sise DSO, DFC	July 1944
Wg Cdr R. K. Orrock, DFC	March 1945
Wg Cdr H. N. Jackson-Smith DFC	March 1945
Wg Cdr J. V. Hoggarth	October 1945

No 249 Squadron

As a fighter unit No 249 Squadron served from 1940-45 flying Hurricanes, Spitfires and Mustangs before its disbandment on 16 August 1945. The Squadron was next re-formed at Eastleigh, Kenya on 23 October 1945 when No 500 Squadron there was renumbered, and initially flew Martin Baltimores. In February 1946 the Baltimores were exchanged for Canadian-built Mosquito FB26s for general survey duties, but in June 1946 the Squadron moved to Habbaniya, Iraq where it converted to Hawker Tempests.

Aircraft examples flown
KA134; KA135; KA136; KA140; KA151;
KA160; KA171; KA190; KA200; KA227;
KA248; KA256; KA262; KA273; KA282;
KA294; KA304; KA322; KA333; KA341;
KA351; KA362; KA370; KA389; KA406;
KA412; KA417.

No 254 Squadron

Although primarily a Beaufighter X unit based at North Coates in early 1945, No 254 Squadron received five Mosquito XVIII 'Tsetse' aircraft transferred from No 248 Squadron in March, specifically for attacks on all types of German submarines. These first fired their 57mm cannons 'in anger' on 12 April, flying a total of 18 sorties that month. During May 1945 the 'Tsetses' shared in the sinkings of five U-boats — *U2524, U236, U2503, U2338* and *U393* — apart from sinking two surface ships. The

Squadron's final war sorties were flown on 11 May, and shortly after the Mosquitos were phased out, leaving 254 as an all-Beaufighter squadron again, which disbanded on 1 October 1946 at Thorney Island.

Aircraft examples flown
LR349, 'Y'; NT225; PZ252; PZ300; PZ301;
PZ468, 'D'.

Commanding Officers

Wg Cdr D. L. Cartridge DSO, DFC	September 1944
Wg Cdr C. J. S. Dinsdale DFC	March 1946

Right:
RR289, displaying the GN coding of 249 Squadron, at No 107 MU, Kasfareet, Egypt in 1947. *via RAF Museum*

Below:
Mk XVIII, PZ468, 'QM-D', of 254 Squadron at North Coates, June 1945. It also saw service with 248 Squadron. *Crown Copyright*

No 255 Squadron

At the start of 1945 No 255 Squadron was based at Foggia Main, Italy as a nightfighter unit flying Beaufighter VIFs, but began replacing these with Mosquito XIXs in January when it moved base to Rosignano. The Mk XIXs commenced operations on 26/27 February, but made few contacts with the Luftwaffe until late March. In April the Squadron also received Mosquito XXXs, beginning operations with these on 11/12 April but achieving no successes. In September 1945 No 255 Squadron moved to Malta (where a detachment had been based since June) but on moving again to Egypt in early 1946 it was disbanded at Gianaclis on 31 March 1946.

Main bases

Foggia Main	January 1944
Rosignano	February 1945
Hal Far	September 1945
Gianaclis	January 1946

Aircraft examples flown

NT246; TA127, 'Z'; TA131, 'H'; TA408, 'D'; TA427, 'E'; TA437, 'S'; TA440, 'G'.

Commanding Officers

Wg Cdr J. W. R. Kempe	November 1944
Wg Cdr J. R. H. Lewis DFC	July 1945

No 256 Squadron

A Beaufighter nightfighter squadron based at Ford, No 256 Squadron began receiving Mosquito XIIs in May 1943, and flew its first 'XII' sorties on 21/22 May. Its first Mosquito night victory was claimed on 11 June. Two more claims were made in July, and a further four in August, but in the interim the Squadron had been warned of an imminent move to Malta, and on 2 July the first six Mosquitos left Ford to fly to Luqa, via Gibraltar, where they were temporarily attached to No 108 Squadron for operations. Within the next few weeks No 256 Squadron crews claimed 16 victories (10 of these by Sqn Ldr J. W. Allen), but then 'trade' slackened, and the rest of the Squadron arrived on Malta by the end of October. On 20 November the unit received its first pair of Mosquito XIIIs (HK339 and HK400), and now became Malta's chief night defender, although it continued to provide day operations as convoy escorts. Throughout 1944 the Squadron's Mosquitos operated a variety of operations, with various detachments at Catania and Alghero, but on 1 April the unit base moved from Malta to Algiers for night defence of convoys in that zone. Returning to Alghero in August, the

NFXII, HK128, 'JT-G', of 256 Squadron at Luqa, Malta, 1944.

Squadron next moved to Italy where it continued its intruder and general patrolling across the Balkans, adding weather reconnaissance to its other roles during winter 1944-45. By March 1945 its crews became mainly engaged in attacking land and river transports in Italy in pursuit of the retreating German forces, while from 30 March the crews commenced bomber support sorties after their aircraft had been fitted with *Gee* radar. In April 1945 the Squadron was issued with a few Mosquito VIs for the ground attack role, through the prime role for the unit remained night work. After the war No 256 Squadron received a few Mosquito PRXVIs for meteorological sorties, but by May 1946 had been reduced to cadre strength, and on 12 September 1946 the remaining 'Squadron' was disbanded at Nicosia.

Main bases

Ford	April 1943
Woodvale	August 1943
Luqa	October 1943
La Senia	April 1944
Foggia	September 1944
Forli	February 1945
El Ballah	September 1945
Deversoir	December 1945
Nicosia	July 1946

Aircraft examples flown

HK116, 'F'; HK124, 'T'; HK133; HK187, 'V' and 'B'; HK191, 'F', 'S' and 'W'; HK339; HK399, 'D'; HK400; HK410, 'Q'; HK435; HK436, 'Y'; HK508, 'A'; LR461; MM470, 'T'; MM531, 'E'; MM534, 'C'; MM580' MM583, 'D'; MM615, 'R'; RF670, 'B'; RF680, 'S'; RF709, 'R' and 'X'; TA426.

Commanding Officers

Wg Cdr T. N. Hayes	October 1942
Wg Cdr G. R. Park DFC	June 1943
Wg Cdr P. M. Dobree-Bell	February 1944
Wg Cdr H. W. Elliot DSO, DFC	October 1944
Wg Cdr H. E. Tappin DFC	March 1945
Wg Cdr D. Giles DFC	December 1945
Wg Cdr A. P. Dottridge DFC	January 1946

No 264 Squadron

No 264 Squadron was one of the relatively few units to operate Mosquitos for almost 10 years in war and peace. A Defiant night defence squadron based at Colerne in early 1942, No 264 received its first Mosquito (W4086) on 3 May, flew its first operational sorties on the type on 13 June, and registered its first Mosquito combat claim (a Do217 'damaged') on 27/28 - June. The next few months offered few combat opportunities and, exacerbated by various

'G-George' and 'D-Dog' of 264 Squadron, April 1943. *via RAF Museum*

technical problems with the aircraft, produced few successes. Thus, from December 1942 until the summer of 1943, the Squadron flew day sorties over the Biscay areas, claiming occasional victories over Luftwaffe aircraft in the process. These sorties were intermingled with night intruder sorties in early 1943, which role was intensified from August when the Squadron began re-equipping with Mosquito FBVIs. For a few months 264's crews undertook 'Flower' sorties against enemy airfields, etc in France, then commenced bomber support patrols mingling with main force bomber streams and hunting German interceptors. In December 1943 the first Mk XIIIs began arriving on the unit and continued the Squadron's night roles. Renewal of night bombing attacks on England by the Luftwaffe in early 1944 brought 264 back to its prime defensive function, and its crews claimed three victims over Hull on 19 March, but shortly after the Squadron moved south to assist the pre-invasion operations. Its contribution to the Allied invasion of Normandy commenced on 5/6 June, and during that month it claimed 13 German aircraft and a V1 bomb destroyed apart from other damage caused to the enemy. In July and August 264 Squadron joined other UK units in combating the V1 onslaught, then moved base to the Continent to continue support of the

Mosquitos of No 264 Squadron at Predannack, April 1943. *via RAF Museum*

invasion forces on 11 August, the second nightfighter unit on French soil (the first was 604 Squadron on 5 August). Inclement weather forced several moves of base in September 1944, and on the 24th the Squadron was sent home to Predannack, ostensibly for a 'rest' from its long operational activities. Moving to Colerne on 21 December, on 8 January it returned to the Continent to recommence operations. Appalling weather conditions in January and February precluded sustained sorties, but two victories were claimed in March 1945, while at least eight more claims were made in April; the ultimate victories were two aircraft destroyed on 25/26 April, though patrols continued until the end of hostilities. On 25 August 1945 the Squadron was disbanded at Twente, but was re-formed with Mosquito NF36s at Church Fenton on 20 November 1945 when No 125 Squadron was renumbered. As a component of No 12 Group's night defences, 264 Squadron retained its Mosquitos until December 1951 when they were replaced by Meteor NF11s.

Main bases

Colerne	May 1941
Predannack	April 1943

Fairwood Common	July 1943
Coleby Grange	November 1943
Church Fenton	December 1943
Hartford Bridge	May 1944
Hunsdon	July 1944
A8 (France)	August 1944
B17 (Caen/Carpiquet)	September 1944
Predannack	September 1944
Colerne	December 1944
Odiham	December 1944
B51 (Lille)	January 1945
B77 (Gilze/Rijen)	April 1945
Rheine	May 1945
Twente	June 1945
Church Fenton	November 1945
Wittering	December 1946
Coltishall	January 1948
Church Fenton	November 1949
Acklington	February 1950
Church Fenton	September 1950
Linton-on-Ouse	August 1951

Aircraft examples flown

W4053; W4080; W4081; W4083; DD605;
DD625; DD636, 'D'; DD639; DD642; DD643;
DD662; DD724, 'G'; DD750; DD780; DZ239;
DZ272; DZ298; DZ305, 'G'; DZ681; DZ727;
DZ750; HJ474; HJ652; HJ660; HJ714; HJ915;
HJ932; HK403; HK409; HK418, 'R'; HK466;
HK471, 'D'; HK479, 'F'; HK480; HK481, 'O';
HK502; HK506, 'G'; HK512; HK515, 'S';
HK528; HX834; HX852; KA290; MM455, 'Q';
MM467, 'J'; MM493, 'T'; MM521; MM559;
MM623; MT376; NT440; RK978; RK990, 'B';
RK997, 'L'; RL118, 'D'; RL129, 'G'; RL143;
RL152, 'J'; RL154, 'E'; RL177; RL195, 'A';
RL230, 'F'; RL250, 'H'; RL262, 'A'; TV968.

Commanding Officers

Wg Cdr H. M. Kerr DFC	May 1942
Wg Cdr W. J. Alington	March 1943
Wg Cdr E. S. Smith AFC	April 1944
Wg Cdr E.G. Barwell DFC	June 1945

No 268 Squadron

Although in *practice* No 268 Squadron became a Mosquito FBVI unit with effect from 16 October 1945, it was *officially* 're-formed' with effect from 19 September 1945 retrospectively. (See No 16 Squadron notes.) It was based at Cambrai/Epinoy at the time, with a detachment at Brussels from December 1945, but was disbanded again on 31 March 1946.

No 305 Squadron

No 305 (*Ziemia Wielkopolska*) Squadron was the fourth (last) Polish bomber squadron under RAF control when it initially formed at Bramcote on 29 August 1940. It flew Battles, Wellingtons and Mitchells until 3 December 1943 when it became temporarily non-operational to convert to Mosquito FBVIs, then recommenced operational sorties from 25 January 1944. Initially operating against V1 sites, the Squadron soon became almost exclusively engaged in night sorties against German airfields, gun sites, and other vital targets, commencing on 9 April with bomb raids on three airfields. From June it concentrated on enemy transportation systems, but from August was successfully destroying precision objectives — examples being an attack on Chateau Maulny (the German School of Sabotage) on 2 August and an accurate bombing of a petrol depot at Nomeny on 31 August. On 19/20 November the Squadron moved to France and immediately continued operations the next night (its 140th Mosquito sortie); it flew almost continuously during the nights of December, paying particular attentions to enemy trains, barges and road vehicles as its crews ranged far and wide. Throughout its service with the 2nd TAF, No 305 Squadron, with Nos 613 and, later, No 107 Squadrons, formed No 138 Wing, and these units often combined for specific bombing raids. Operations by this Wing ceased on the night of 25/26 April 1945 — a strafe of German troops and transport — after which No 305 Squadron remained on the Continent until October 1946, when it returned to England, and was ultimately disbanded at Faldingworth on 6 January 1947.

Main bases

Lasham	November 1943
Hartford Bridge	October 1944
Lasham	October 1944
Hartford Bridge	October 1944

A75 (Epinoy/Cambrai)	November 1944
Volkel	July 1945
Gilze-Rijen	September 1945
Melsbroek	November 1945
Wahn	March 1946
Faldingworth	October 1946

Top:

LR298 of 305 (Polish) Squadron at Lasham, March 1944. *J. Cynk*

Above:

Mosquito of 305 (Polish) Squadron at Lasham, March 1944; possibly LR262, 'Q'? *J. Cynk*

Aircraft examples flown

HP923; HR113; HR145; HR202; HR253; HR346, 'K'; HR360; HX908; HX980; LR261; LR262, 'Q'; LR289; LR295,'D'; LR300, 'P'; LR303, 'A'; LR313; LR328, 'G'; LR329; LR365, 'J'; NS923; NS824, 'Z' and 'P'; NS481; NS844, 'N'; NS846, 'B'; NS887, 'K'; NS888, 'M'; NS901; NS909, 'L'; NS913, 'W'; NS927, 'C'; NS929, 'V'; NT175, 'E';

NT193, 'F'; NT198, 'U'; NT227; NT233; NT234; NT236; NT299; PZ302; PZ335; PZ357; PZ371; PZ383; PZ391; PZ401; RS528; RS559; SZ978; ZS982; TA378.

Commanding Officers

Wg Cdr K. Konopasek	July 1943
Wg Cdr B. Orlinski	August 1944
Wg Cdr S. Grodzicki	February 1945

90

No 307 Squadron

As the first Polish nightfighter squadron, No 307 was originally formed at Kirton-in-Lindsey on 5 December 1940, and flew Defiants and Beaufighters until beginning re-equipment with Mosquito NFIIs in December 1942. The unit's first Mosquito sortie was flown on 14 January 1943, an eventful night defensive patrol by DZ271. From May to June that year the Squadron mounted a series of night 'Ranger' sweeps, then switched to daytime 'Instep' patrols over the Biscay waters and adding several combat victories to the unit tally. On 9 November it moved far north to Drem, and within five weeks had added three more enemy aircraft destroyed during patrols over the North Sea. Moving south again in March 1944, No 307 Squadron reverted to night patrols, then recommenced intrusion sweeps over France in preparation for D-Day. By September the Squadron became involved in tackling the V1 assaults on southern England by night, but by December had returned to its forte of night intruding over the Continent. In August 1943 it had re-equipped with Mosquito FBVIs, and with Mk XIIs and XIIIs in January 1944, but flew its last Mk XII sortie on 28 November as the Squadron had received its latest equipment, Mosquito NFXXXs in the previous month, these being fitted with *Monica* radar. With the XXXs No 307's crews continued their intruder sorties from December, varying these with bomber support high-level patrols, and flying a total of 132 sorties in February-March 1945,

NT333/G, 'EW-G', of 307 (Polish) Squadron at Castle Camps, 27 January 1945. *J. Cynk*

having moved base to Castle Camps on 27 January 1945. No 307 Squadron remained with Fighter Command until 2 January 1947 when it was disbanded at Horsham St Faiths.

Main bases

Exeter	April 1941
Fairwood Common	August 1943
Predannack	August 1943
Drem	November 1943
Coleby Grange	March 1944
Church Fenton	May 1944
Castle Camps	January 1945
Coltishall	May 1945
Horsham St Faiths	August 1945

Aircraft examples flown

DD304; DD618; DD644; DD569, DD717; DD724; DD729; DD780, 'S'; DZ260, 'B'; DZ261; DZ271; DZ291; DZ600; DZ698; DZ739; DZ749; DZ750; HJ648, 'X'; HJ651; HJ913, 'H'; HJ928, 'R'; HK108, 'N'; HK115, 'F'; HK119, 'J' and 'D'; HK129, 'Z'; HK139; HK141, 'P'; HK165, 'A'; HK168; HK176; HK179; HK180; HK199; HK201, 'Q'; H223, 'R'; HK228; HK231, 'O' and 'B'; HK234 'I'; HR141, 'P'; HX859; MT497, 'O'; MV533; MV539, 'M' MV542, 'Y'; MV595; NT259, 'W'; NT267, 'J'; NT303; NT333, 'G'; NT482, 'L'; NT565, 'A'; RK951, 'N'.

Commanding Officers

Wg Cdr J. Michalowski	July 1942
Wg Cdr J. Orzechowski	April 1943

Wg Cdr M. Lewandowski	November 1943
Wg Cdr G. Ranoszek	May 1944
Wg Cdr A. Andrzejewski	December 1944
Wg Cdr J. Damsz	March 1946

'EW-W', of 307 (Polish) Squadrons at Castle Camps, 28 January 1945. *J. Cynk*

No 333 Squadron

On 1 February 1943 a Flight of three Catalinas, manned by Norwegian crews and 'attached' to No 210 Squadron, was granted the title No 1477 (Norwegian) Flight, but on 10 May 1943 this Flight was retitled as No 333 Squadron at Leuchars, and a second ('B') flight was added comprising six Mosquito IIs. In August 1943 'B' Flight received its first FBVI as the start of re-equipment, but in the meantime had commenced Mosquito operations on 27 May and claimed its first enemy aircraft shot down on

13 June. The prime role for the Mosquito crews was daylight reconnaissance over Norwegian coastal waters, though additional tasks included convoy escort and anti-shipping patrols. In mid-September 1944 'B' Flight was transferred to Banff's Strike Wing and soon became regarded as virtually a separate unit, so much so that by May 1945 it had been decided to give the Mosquito Flight of No 333 Squadron a full, different squadron status. By then the European war had ended, and the Mosquito Flight's war tally stood at 18 enemy aircraft destroyed, three more probably destroyed, three U-boats claimed as sunk, and no small number of other vessels sunk or seriously damaged. The Norwegian Mosquitos

'B' Flight of 333 (Norwegian) Squadron at Banff. At right is NFII, DZ754, 'F'.

returned to Norway in May 1945, and on 21 November that year were officially transferred to the Royal Norwegian Air Force.

Aircraft examples flown
DZ705; DZ744; DZ752; HP858, 'K' and 'O'; HP859, 'M'; HP862, 'Q' and 'K'; HP864, 'H'; HP904, 'E'; HP910, 'L'; HR116, 'F'; HR118; HR126, 'S'; HR133; HR262, 'N'; HR569; LR560, 'C'; RF769, 'P'; RF827.

Commanding Officer
Cdr F. Lambrechts   May 1943

No 334 Squadron

As related in the history of No 333 Squadron, by May 1945 it had been decided to give the Squadron's 'B' (Mosquito) Flight at Banff separate squadron status, and this was accom-

DZ700, 'H' of 'B' Flight, 333 (Norwegian) Squadron, Banff.

plished on 22 June 1945 when the Flight was retitled as No 334 Squadron. By then it was based in Norway, and was re-equipped with 10 new Mosquito FBVIs, later supplemented by eight more VIs and three TIIIs. Despite severe reduction in strength for a period the Squadron continued operating Mosquitos until early 1952 when these were replaced by Republic F-84G Thunderjet aircraft.

Main bases
Gardermoen (Oslo)   May 1945
Stavanger/Sola   October 1949

Aircraft examples flown
RS690, 'F-AK'.

FBVI, RS650, 'AK-F', of 334 Squadron RNAF, June 1949. *C. E. Brown/RAF Museum*

Markings

Below:
Official war artist Capt D. Adams painting an aborigine insigne on Mosquito NT229; this was the aircraft usually flown by Wg Cdr G. Panitz DFC, OC 464 Squadron RAAF, and the one in which he was killed on 22 August 1944. *RAAF Official*

Below centre:
Wg Cdr J. de L. Wooldridge, DSO, DFC, DFM, OC 105 Squadron, and his Mosquito, June 1943. *Hawker Siddeley Aviation*

Below right:
Flg Off P. D. Wood DFC (left) of 605 Squadron AAF and the Mosquito which destroyed two enemy aircraft and four trains in a single night sortie. *IWM*

Right:
Mosquito PRIX, ML897, 'D' of No 1409 Met Flight. *Sqn Ldr H. Lees*

KNAVE OF DIAMONDS

Top:
Grim Reaper — the grisly insigne of DK333, 'F'
of 109 Squadron.   Wg Cdr F. Ruskell DFC

Above:
HK290, 'J' of 456 Squadron RAAF, July 1944.
The three 'bird' marks represented V1s
destroyed, while the two plain crosses
indicated enemy aircraft shot down.
W. A. Kellett via D. Vincent

Top right:
Left to right: Cpl J. Adamson, LACs A. C. H.
Mackay and S. Sawyer, and Cpl F. Nichols
admire the artwork on a Mosquito flown by
Flt Lt A. Torrance. Burma, 1945.   IWM

Bottom right:
Top Brass. Mosquito BIX used as a personal
'conveyance' by Air Marshal Sir Arthur
Coningham, and displaying his official rank
emblem insigne, 19 August 1944.
Hawker Siddeley Aviation

"Black Rufe"

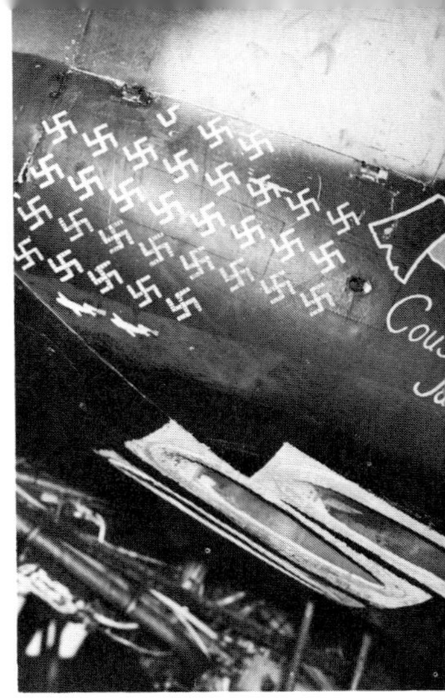

HAIRLESS JOE

LON'SOME

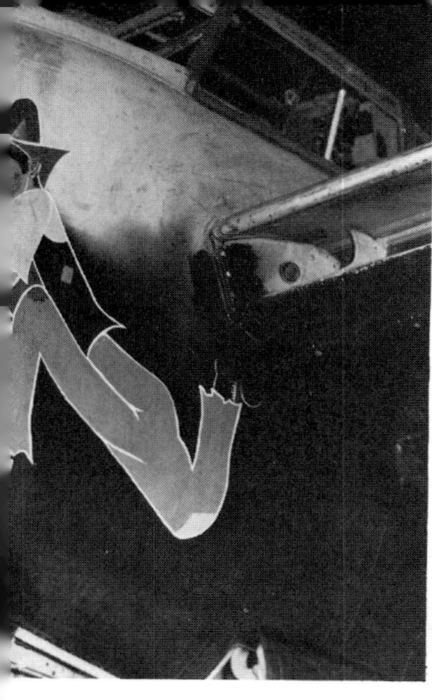

Above and above left:
Various insignia applied to the Mosquitos of No 418 Squadron RCAF. *Hairless Joe* **was HR147 'Z' flown by Wg Cdr Russ Bannock, DSO, DFC.** *all Public Archives of Canada*

Left:
'SM-C' of 305 (Polish) Squadron with Flg Off Wielgosz and Flt Sgt Perycz. The female names, *Janka* **and** *Kitus* **appear below the Polish national insigne.** *J. Cynk*

Far left:
HR352, 'S-Sugar', of 464 Squadron RAAF, March 1945 with its impressive war 'tally' at that time. The white bombs denoted daylight sorties, ie the Aarhus sortie and Operation 'Clarion' *D. R. Rutter via D. Vincent*

99

Left:
Flt Lt T. P. Lawrenson (Pilot) and Flt Lt D. W. Allen, DFC (Navigator) watch their recent sortie added to the bomb log of LR503, 'GB-F', 105 Squadron. This aircraft eventually completed 213 sorties, more than any other Mosquito. *Sqn Ldr H. Lees*

Below:
Two further views of LR503, which ended its unmatched career by crashing at Calgary airport on 10 May 1945.

No 400 Squadron

On 1 March 1941 No 110 (AC) Squadron (Auxiliary), RCAF was retitled No 400 Squadron RCAF, and flew army co-operation and reconnaissance duties with Tomahawks and Mustangs until February 1944. However, in December 1943 the Squadron began receiving Spitfire PRXIs and (in the event) a total of seven Mosquito PRXVIs for the unit's new role of photo-reconnaissance. It maintained this role when it moved base to the Continent on 1 July 1944 (though 'B' Flight remained at Odiham until 10 August 1944 before rejoining the Squadron in France), and continued to provide tactical photo-recce for the British 2nd Army until its disbandment at Luneberg on 7 August 1945.

Main bases

Redhill	October 1943
Kenley	December 1943
Odiham	February 1944
Sommervieu	July 1944
Ste Honorine-de-Ducy (B21)	August 1944
Avrilly (B34)	September 1944
Blakenburg (B66)	September 1944
Eindhoven (B78)	October 1944
Petit-Brogel (B90)	March 1945
Rheine (B108)	April 1945
Wunstorf (B116)	April 1945
Soltau (B154)	April 1945
Luneberg (B156)	May 1945
Copenhagen (B160)	July 1945
Luneberg (B156)	August 1945

Aircraft examples flown

MM275; MM277; MM284; MM306; MM307; MM353; MM356.

Commanding Officers

Wg Cdr R. A. Ellis DFC	September 1943
Sqn Ldr M. G. Brown DFC	November 1944
Sqn Ldr J. A. Morton DFC	July 1945

No 404 Squadron

Formed at Thorney Island on 15 April 1941 as the RCAF's second (first Coastal) squadron formed overseas, No 404 ('Buffalo') Squadron was a Coastal fighter unit flying Blenheim IVs and Beaufighters until the end of March 1945, then moved to Banff on 3 April to re-equip with Mosquito PRVICs. On 22 April the first Mosquito sortie was flown during which it strafed two German maritime aircraft at their moorings. Patrolling the Kattegat and Kiel Bay, the Squadron's last Mosquito sorties were flown on 4 May, when the OC Squadron led 55 Mosquitos on a strike against shipping in Kiel Bay, severely damaging eight ships. On 25 May 1945 No 404 Squadron was disbanded at Banff.

Aircraft examples flown

RF777, 'L'; RF838, 'A'; RF842, 'C'; RF844, 'D'; RF848, 'G'; RF849, 'J'; RF850, 'M'; RF851, 'H'; RF852, 'E'; RF853, 'N'; RF856, 'P'; RF857, 'Q' RF875, 'R'; RF879, 'S'; RF880, 'Y' and 'X'; RF882, 'Z'; RF895, 'R'.

Commanding Officer

Wg Cdr E. W. Pierce	August 1944

No 406 Squadron

No 406 ('Lynx') Squadron RCAF was the first nightfighter — and the RCAF's fifth — squadron to be formed overseas, at Acklington on 10 May 1941 as a nightfighter unit, initially equipped with Blenheims. Changing to Beaufighters from June 1941, the Squadron began re-equipment with Mosquito XIIs in April 1944, flying its first sorties in these on 4 July. In the latter month it replaced its XIIs with Mk XXXs — first Mk XXX sorties being flown on 10 August — while from 27 November

1944 the unit role was officially changed to intruders, flying the first such patrol on 5 December. As intruders the Squadron claimed 23 German aircraft destroyed and 14 others at least damaged. The final Mosquito sorties were flown on 9 May 1945 — six aircraft covering the liberation of the Channel Islands — and No 406 Squadron was disbanded at Predannack on 1 September 1945.

Main bases

Winkleigh	April 1944
Colerne	September 1944
Manston	November 1944
Predannack	June 1945

Aircraft examples flown

HK138; HK164, 'N'; HK180, 'A'; MM693; MM697; MM699, 'P'; MM708; MM709; MM727, 'B'; MM728; MM730; MM732; MM734, 'K'; MM739, 'D'; MM741, 'T'; MM744, 'G'; MM745, 'A'; MM747; MM751, 'S'; NS882; NT283, 'V'; NT312, 'M'; NT325, 'N'; NT423, 'O'; NT433, 'Y' and 'P'; NT453, 'E'; NT477, 'H'; NT478, 'R'; NT495, 'C'; NT498, 'P'; NT539, 'G'; NT544, 'Z'; NT549; RS525, 'F'; RS531, 'S'.

Commanding Officers

Wg Cdr R. C. Fumerton DFC	August 1943
Wg Cdr D. J. Williams DSO, DFC	July 1944
Wg Cdr R. Bannock DFC	November 1944
Wg Cdr R. G. Gray DFC	May 1945

No 409 Squadron

Formed on 7 June 1941 at Digby, No 409 ('Nighthawk') Squadron was the RCAF's seventh — and second nightfighter — squadron formed overseas. Initially flying Defiants, the Squadron replaced these in August 1941 with Beaufighters, then in March 1944 began re-equipment with Mosquito NFXIIIs. Its first Mosquito victory came on the night of 5/6 June 1944, but thereafter its crews increased their tally rapidly. Transferred to 2nd TAF from April 1944, No 409 Squadron's nightfighter role remained in support of the Allied invasion forces for the rest of the European war. On 24 August 1944 it moved base to France (by which time its crews had claimed some 30 combat victories in Mosquitos, apart from several V1 flying bombs), thus becoming the first nightfighter unit to be based on the Continent, and later the first to be based in Belgium and in Germany. During the winter months, despite several moves of airfield base, 409's crews found few victims, but resurged on 23/24 April 1945 when three crews destroyed six enemy aircraft between them, to bring the Mosquitos' tally to 56 destroyed since

NFXIII, MM466 of 409 Squadron RCAF on 31 January 1945, France. Also seeing service with 488 Squadron RNZAF, this was probably the highest-scoring Mosquito fighter, its crews claiming a total of at least 11 victories.
Public Archives of Canada

D-Day, plus 12 V1s destroyed; only to add three more victories on the following night. The final Mosquito war sorties were flown on 2 May 1945 — six aircraft on frontline patrols — before the Squadron was disbanded at Twente on 1 July 1945.

Main bases

Acklington	March 1944
West Malling	May 1944
Hunsdon	June 1944
Carpiquet (B17)	August 1944
St Andre (B24)	September 1944
Glisy (B48)	September 1944
Le Culot (B68)	October 1944
Vendeville (B51)	October 1944
Rheine (B108)	April 1945
Gilze-Rijen (B77)	May 1945
Twente (B106)	June 1945

Aircraft examples flown

HK366, 'U'; HK368, 'F'; HK381, 'C'; HK421, 'V'; HK425, 'D'; HK429, 'D'; JK430, 'P'; HK473, 'K'; HK506, 'H'; HK512, 'A'; HK566; MM437, 'W'; MM454, 'F'; MM456, 'M'; MM458, 'N'; MM459, 'Z'; MM466, 'G'; MM491; MM502, 'A'; MM508, 'K'; MM509, 'B'; MM513, 'J'; MM517, 'S'; MM518; MM522, 'S'; MM523' MM560, 'F'; MM563, 'S'; MM567, 'E'; MM573, 'P'; MM588, 'T'; MM589; MM590, 'H'.

Commanding Officers

Wg Cdr J. W. Reid	February 1943
Wg Cdr M. W. Beveridge DFC	August 1944
Wg Cdr J. D. Somerville DSO, DFC	October 1944
Wg Cdr R. F. Hatton	March 1945

No 410 Squadron

Formed at Ayr on 30 June 1941 as the RCAF's ninth — and third (last) nightfighter squadron overseas — No 410 ('Cougar') Squadron flew Defiants and Beaufighters until January 1943 but began re-equipment with Mosquito NFIIs at Acklington in November 1942, having received a TIII (HJ865) on 24 October for crew conversions. The first Mosquito sorties were then flown on 6/7 December, and the first confirmed Mosquito victory was claimed on 22 January 1943. On 21 February the Squadron moved south to Lincolnshire and more active operations, including 'Night Rangers'; in June-July four Mosquitos were detached to Predannack for Instep patrols. On 20 October the unit moved to West Malling to join No 11 Group and commenced regular night patrols, with increasing success in air combat,

NXXX of 410 Squadron RCAF taking off from Vendeville on 7 December 1944, and still retaining the 'invasion' markings on its rear fuselage. *Public Archives of Canada*

HK429, 'RA-N' of 410 Squadron RCAF.
Public Archives of Canada

exemplified on 10 December when DZ292 (Flg Off R. Schultz) destroyed three Do217s in a single patrol. That same month saw the arrival of Mosquito NFXIIIs fitted with Mk VIII AI radar, and on 13/14 February 1944 Sqn Ldr J. D. Somerville destroyed two Ju88s, while Schultz shot down a third; these were followed by a pair of Ju88s destroyed by Sqn Ldr C. Anderson on 22 February. Five more victims fell in March, but few contacts were made in April and May. Having moved to Castle Camps on 1 March, the Squadron moved again on 29 April to Hunsdon, then again to Zeals on 18 June. Flying support sorties over the Normandy beach-head it claimed 12 victories in June 1944, and three more in July, then began gradual conversion to Mosquito XXXs in August, claiming two Ju88s in these on 19/20 August. By the end of November the Squadron had claimed at least 38 victories since D-Day, but in the interim had crossed the Channel to a new base at Glisy (B48), on 22 September. Continuing its offensive against the Luftwaffe, the 'Cougars' tally rose to 46 destroyed by the end of the year. No 410 Squadron's final sorties were flown on 3 May 1945, by which time its war tally had risen to 75 destroyed, one 'shared' destroyed, two 'probables' and nine 'damaged' On 9 June 1945 the Squadron was disbanded at Gilze-Rijen.

Main bases

Acklington	October 1942
Coleby Grange	February 1943
West Malling	October 1943
Hunsdon	November 1943
Castle Camps	December 1943
Hunsdon	April 1944
Zeals	June 1944
Colerne	July 1944
Hunsdon	September 1944
Glisy (B48)	September 1944
Vendeville (B51)	November 1944
Glisy	January 1945
Gilze-Rijen (B77)	April 1945

Aircraft examples flown

DD608; DD720, 'G'; DD753; DD786; DZ246; DZ304; DZ305; DZ661; DZ757, 'Q'; HJ824; JH827; HJ913; HK919, 'B'; HJ928, 'R'; HJ929; HJ930; HJ936; HJ944; HK366, 'Q'; HK430, 'W'; HK431; HK432, 'F'; HK454; HK455, 'Q'; HK456, 'H'; HK458, 'S'; HK459, 'A'; HK462, 'E'; HK463, 'R'; HK465, 'P'; HK466, 'J'; HK467, 'T'; HK468; HK470, 'X'; HK476, 'O'; HK500, 'I'; HK521, 'L'; HK523, 'G'; MM456, 'D'; MM457, 'Z'; MM462, 'K'; MM477, 'U'; MM499, 'C'; MM501, 'V'; MM570, 'B'; MM571, 'Y'; MM702, 'H'; MM749, 'N'; MM755, 'W'; MM788, 'Q'; MT485, 'F'; MV527; NT255, 'G'; NT320, 'A'; NT485, 'F'; NT513; NT529.

Commanding Officers

Wg Cdr F. W. Hillock	August 1942
Wg Cdr G. H. Elms	May 1943
Wg Cdr G. A. Hiltz	February 1944
Wg Cdr E. P. Heybroek	April 1945

No 418 Squadron

No 418 ('City of Edmonton') Squadron was formed at Debden on 15 November 1941 as the RCAF's 14th — and only intruder — squadron overseas, and initially flew Boston IIIs. The first Boston sorties were flown on 27/28 March 1942, and the last in July 1943, but on 7/8 May 1943 the Squadron despatched its first Mosquito NFII patrol, during which a Ju88 was destroyed

NT137, 'H' of 418 Squadron RCAF.
Public Archives of Canada

near Nantes. At the end of May the Squadron had five Mosquitos on charge, but increased this total to 18 in June, and the final Boston sorties were flown on 8/9 July. The Squadron now concentrated on bomber support 'Flower' operations, with additional intrusion raids on German airfields and transport systems, but scoring few air combat victories until September 1943 when its tally began to mount steadily. In that month too three crews were 'detached' to No 617 Squadron RAF for a special raid by the 'Dam-Busters' against the Dortmund-Ems Canal on 15 September, with the Mosquitos attacking enemy defences in that area. Bad weather at the end of 1943 restricted the Squadron's operational activities, though six enemy aircraft were claimed as destroyed or damaged in December during a total of 37 sorties that month. From late January 1944, however, victories began to escalate again, when on 27 January four Mosquito crews on 'Day Rangers' claimed seven enemy aircraft

destroyed and an eighth damaged, all within 30 minutes of combat. Ten more were destroyed by night in the following month, but from March the Squadron was to fly mainly 'Day Ranger' sorties. One such sortie by two crews in March reaped a 'bag' of three destroyed in the air, plus four destroyed and 12 damaged on the ground. In April/May, during a six-weeks period alone, No 418 Squadron accounted for 30 enemy aircraft destroyed in the air, plus four 'probables', and a further 38 destroyed and 20 'damaged' on the ground. Intensive operations prior to and during the invasion of Normandy in mid-1944 added further victories, including many V1 flying bombs, 40 of these being destroyed in July, and a total of 83 V1s shot down by 21 August, the last anti-V1 sorties. In September the Squadron flew 36 sorties on reconnaissance to sight V2 rockets (operations coded 'Big Ben'), but also flew 100 intruder sorties over France, mainly attacking enemy transport targets. The Squadron's final official intruder

A trio from 418 Squadron RCAF crossing the Channel. *Public Archives of Canada*

sortie was flown on 18 November, and three days later the unit moved base to Hartford Bridge to join No 136 Wing, 2 Group, 2nd TAF, being declared 'non-operational' from 20 November while it worked up for its future role as low-level daylight raiders giving direct tactical support to the Allied armies. For these duties No 418 Squadron began converting to Mosquito FBVIs in November 1944, and operations were resumed on 31 December. For most of January 1945 weather conditions nullified operations, while Operation 'Clarion' on 22 February cost the Squadron four aircraft shot down. From 10 to 15 March it moved base to Belgium, becoming based at Coxyde (B71) from where it commenced intensive night sorties over Germany. April 1945 proved a busy month, during which No 418's crews flew 273 sorties, operating every night except two, while on the 25th base was moved to Volkel. The last sorties were flown on 2/3 May, by which time No 418's war tally had risen to 105 enemy aircraft destroyed, and nine probably destroyed in the air, plus 73 destroyed and 103 'damaged' on the ground, apart from 83 V1s destroyed. In addition many hundreds of trains, road vehicles, barges, etc had been destroyed. Its score of enemy aircraft — all but six of these in Mosquitos *not* fitted with AI radar — made No 418 Squadron the RCAF's highest-scoring nightfighter unit of the war. The Squadron was then disbanded at Volkel on 7 September 1945.

Main bases

Ford	March 1943
Holmsley South	April 1944
Hurn	July 1944
Middle Wallop	July 1944
Hunsdon	August 1944
Hartford Bridge	November 1944
Coxyde (B71)	March 1945
Volkel (B80)	April 1945

Aircraft examples flown

HJ715; HJ719; HJ733; HJ742; HJ763, 'V'; HJ772, 'H'; HJ821, 'S'; HJ823; HR148, 'B'; HR149, 'R'; HR184, 'Z'; HR195, 'P'; HR324, 'N'; HR358, 'K'; HX807; HX810; HX811, 'K'; HX819, 'J'; HX953, 'X; MM428, 'N; NS823, 'W'; NS830, 'G'; NS857, 'L'; NS906, 'W'; NS930, 'V'; NS939, 'V'; NT115, 'J'; NT137, 'H'; NT153, 'Y'; NT162, 'Y'; NT195, 'C'; PZ219, 'E'; PZ235, 'M'; PZ414, 'P'; PZ454, 'Y'; RS454, 'Y'; RS560, 'G'; RS561, 'F'; RS569, 'V'; RS594, 'L'; SZ962, 'U'; SZ964, 'X'; SZ965, 'T'; SZ967, 'V'; TA374, 'C'.

Commanding Officers

Wg Cdr J. H. Little	December 1942
Wg Cdr P. Y. Davoud DFC	June 1943
Wg Cdr D. C. S. MacDonald DFC	January 1944
Wg Cdr R. J. Bennell	February 1944
Wg Cdr A. Barker	March 1944
Wg Cdr R. Bannock DFC	October 1944
Wg Cdr J. C. Wickett	November 1944
Wg Cdr D. B. Annan	February 1945
Wg Cdr H. D. Cleveland, DFC	May 1945

No 456 Squadron

No 456 Squadron RAAF was formed at Valley on 30 June 1941, equipped initially with 18 Defiants, and was officially declared operational on 5 September 1941 (although the first operational sorties had been flown the previous night). At the end of September re-equipment with Beaufighters began, but these in turn began being replaced by Mosquito NFIIs in late December 1942; the first Mosquito patrol was flown on 22 January 1943. By the end of January the Squadron had 17 on strength, while at the end of February it was notified that its future roles would be 'Night Rangers' and intrusion, mixed with day sorties as long-range fighters. Though commencing 'Ranger' sorties while based at Valley, a move to Middle Wallop on 30 March brought the Squadron under the aegis of No 10 Group and full operational status. Over the following months many 'Ranger' and intruder sorties were flown mainly against enemy rail communications or airfields, while on 5 June three crews were detached to Predannack for 'Instep' patrols. In late July new Mosquito FBVIs began arriving on the Squadron, and were allotted to a special 'Ranger' Flight within the Squadron (six aircraft initially), which was soon detached to Predannack for two months, while on 17 August the main Squadron base was moved to Colerne. By October the Predannack

NT264, 'R' of 456 Squadron RAAF, being flown by Wg Cdr Basil Howard on 9 May 1945. Howard was killed in this aircraft in a crash on 29 May 1945.
R. W. Richardson via D. Vincent

Flight returned to the Squadron to join in the unit's 'Ranger' sorties, and on 17 November the whole unit moved again, this time to Fairwood Common. From 14 December No 456 Squadron was commanded by Wg Cdr K. M. Hampshire DSO (later DFC) whose driving energy and disciplined skills gave the unit fresh impetus over the ensuing months, and led to the Squadron's most successful operational efforts. On 29 January 1944 came the first example of a Mosquito XVII as the start of re-equipment, and on 29 February a total of 16 aircraft flew to the latest unit base at Ford, thereby coming under No 11 Group and in the front line of the UK's night defences. From then until D-Day, No 456 Squadron flew almost every night against a renewed Luftwaffe bombing assault against Britain, claiming 11 destroyed, plus two others as 'probables', during the first two months, adding several more in May. From 7 June the Squadron was fully employed in support of the Allied invasion of France, destroying four Heinkel He177s within the first 24 hours. The month of June saw the Squadron claim a total of 13 enemy aircraft destroyed (10 of these He177s) plus two 'probables', followed

by four more destroyed on 4 July, but from 24 June the crews also commenced anti-V1 ('Diver') patrols, destroying 10 by the end of July and 14 more in August 1944. From mid-September — using a forward airfield, Manston — the Squadron began deep penetration sorties over Europe, but in November the crews were again tasked with anti-V1 sorties, this time intercepting the Heinkel He111 'carriers' of the robot bombs. At the end of the year the unit moved from Ford to Church Fenton there to re-equip with Mosquito XXXs, and few sorties were despatched while training was undertaken for bomber escort duties, then; on 3 March 1945, the Squadron moved to Bradwell Bay, commencing operations from there on 17 March on bomber support duties, ranging far and wide over enemy territory. The unit's final sorties of April were flown on 26/27 April 1945 — four Mosquitos patrolling the Munich area — while the ultimate war sorties were flown on 2 May. On 15 June 1945 No 456 Squadron was disbanded at Bradwell Bay.

Main bases

Valley	June 1941
Middle Wallop	March 1943
Colerne	August 1943
Fairwood Common	November 1943
Ford	February 1944
Church Fenton	December 1944
Bradwell Bay	March 1945

FII, DD739, 'X' of 456 Squadron RAAF.

Aircraft examples flown

DD614; DD620; DD751, 'W'; DZ269, 'U';
DZ299, 'D'; DZ658; DZ681; DZ690; HJ702,
'X'; HJ817, 'E'; HJ818, 'H'; HJ925; HK249,
'B'; HK292, 'L'; HK286, 'A'; HK290, 'J';
HK295, 'X'; HK297, 'V'; HK312, 'G'; HK317,
'Y'; HK323, 'R'; HK353, 'M'; MM687, 'Z';
NT241, 'W'; NT264, 'R'; NT282, 'T'; NT295,
'P'; NT296, 'S'; NT299, 'D'; NT302, 'K';
NT307, 'Y'; NT328, 'H'; NT335, 'V';
NT363, 'U'; NT387, 'D'; NT545, 'Z'.

Commanding Officers

Wg Cdr E. C. Wolfe DFC	March 1942
Wg Cdr M. H. Dwyer	December 1942
Wg Cdr G. Howden DFC	June 1943
Wg Cdr K. M. Hampshire DSO	December 1943
Wg Cdr B. Howard DFC	November 1944
Sqn Ldr R. B. Cowper	May 1945

No 464 Squadron

Formed at Feltwell on 1 September 1942
officially (though unit records date from
27 August), No 464 Squadron RAAF first
equipped with Ventura bombers, commencing
operations with these on 6 December and flying
its last Ventura operations on 10 July 1943. On
21 July the Squadron moved base to Sculthorpe
to convert to Mosquito FBVIs, receiving its first
two aircraft on 21 August, increased to nine by
6 September, and on 3 October flew its first
Mosquito operations when 12 of its aircraft took
part in a bombing raid on a power station at
Mur-de-Bretagne. Its second operation was
mounted six days later, when two Mosquitos
failed to return. Operations were not resumed
until late November, due to bad weather, and on
31 December the Squadron moved base again,
to Hunsdon, along with Nos 21 and 487
(RNZAF) Squadrons, all three units comprising
No 140 Wing of 2nd TAF. January 1944 saw the
Squadron engaged in night intruder sorties, then
in February it changed (mainly) to day attacks
on V1 sites. On 18 February the Squadron contributed five crews to the now-legendary three-
squadron attack on Amiens Gaol, led by Gp
Capt P. C. Pickard DSO, DFC. From 1 March
the Squadron flew both anti-V1 site and night
intrusion sorties until D-Day, on the eve of
which it despatched 20 crews to strafe German
rail and road transport junctions in France. On
18 June the Squadron moved to Thorney Island
but was back on operations the same night, continuing its nightly attacks in support of the invasion forces in Normandy. The pace of operations for the Squadron remained intense for
several months, and included many sorties well
behind the beach-head battle zones, attacking
vital transportation centres, etc and on
31 October it contributed eight Mosquitos to a

precision raid on Aarhus University, Denmark, the local Gestapo HQ. The next two months saw appalling weather conditions which restricted operations, though 464 crews managed to fly 162 sorties throughout December. By 7 February 1945 the Squadron had completed a move to Rosierse-en-Santerre in France, resuming operations the same day, and contributed 16 Mosquitos to the massive Allied air assault on enemy transport facilities on 22 February, losing two crews which failed to return. On 21 March the Squadron provided six Mosquitos for another precision raid, this time on the Gestapo HQ house in the Shellhuset, Copenhagen, and lost two crews. In April 1945 the unit mounted a total of 257 sorties against widespread targets in Germany, including Berlin, Lübbecke and Hanover, and recorded its 2,000th sortie since D-Day on the night of 6/7 April while attacking the German capital city. On 17 April it was again involved in a precision raid, this time against the Gestapo HQ at Odense, Denmark, after which the Squadron took up new quarters at Melsbroek (B58) airfield and remained there until the end of hostilities; it flew its last war sorties on 2/3 May 1945. On 25 September 1945 the Squadron was officially disbanded.

No 464 Squadron RAAF at Thorney Island, cNovember 1944. For inexplicable reasons, each aircraft fin leading edge has been 'splodged' by some anonymous wartime censor. *Sport & General Agency*

Main bases

Sculthorpe	July 1943
Hunsdon	December 1943
Gravesend	April 1944
Thorney Island	June 1944
Rosieres-en-Santerre (B87)	February 1945
Melsbroek (B58)	April 1945

Aircraft examples flown

HJ772; HJ850, 'O'; HP934, 'X'; HP924, 'C'; HR175, 'L'; HR186, 'N'; HR337, 'D'; HR352, 'S'; HX858; HX866; HX910; HX912, 'F'; HX914, 'O'; HX919, 'P'; HX921, 'Y', 'X' and 'P'; HX948; HX964; HX977, 'K' and 'T'; LR256; LR332; LR334, 'F', 'E' and 'B'; LR362, 'Z'; MM400, 'J'; MM402, 'A'; MM403, 'V'; MM404, 'T'; MM407, 'Y'; MM410, 'U'; MM427, 'J'; MM482, 'A'; NS884; NS890, 'B'; NS896, 'D'; NS926; NS937; NS943, 'N'; NS966, 'D'; NS994, 'F'; NS999; NT129; NT143; NT144, 'A'; NT177, 'O'; NT189, 'O'; NT229; NT231; NT236, 'K'; PZ259, 'X'; PZ309; PZ350; PZ353, 'G'; PZ378, 'U'; PZ452, 'Y'; PZ463; RS609, 'V'; RS617; SZ958, 'C'; SZ966; SZ999; TA120, 'E'; TA372, 'Y'; TA475, 'Y'.

Commanding Officers

Wg Cdr J. Meakin DFC	April 1943
Wg Cdr R. W. Iredale DFC	December 1943
Wg Cdr G. Panitz DFC	June 1944
Wg Cdr A. W. Langton DFC	August 1944
Wg Cdr N. Vincent DFC	January 1945

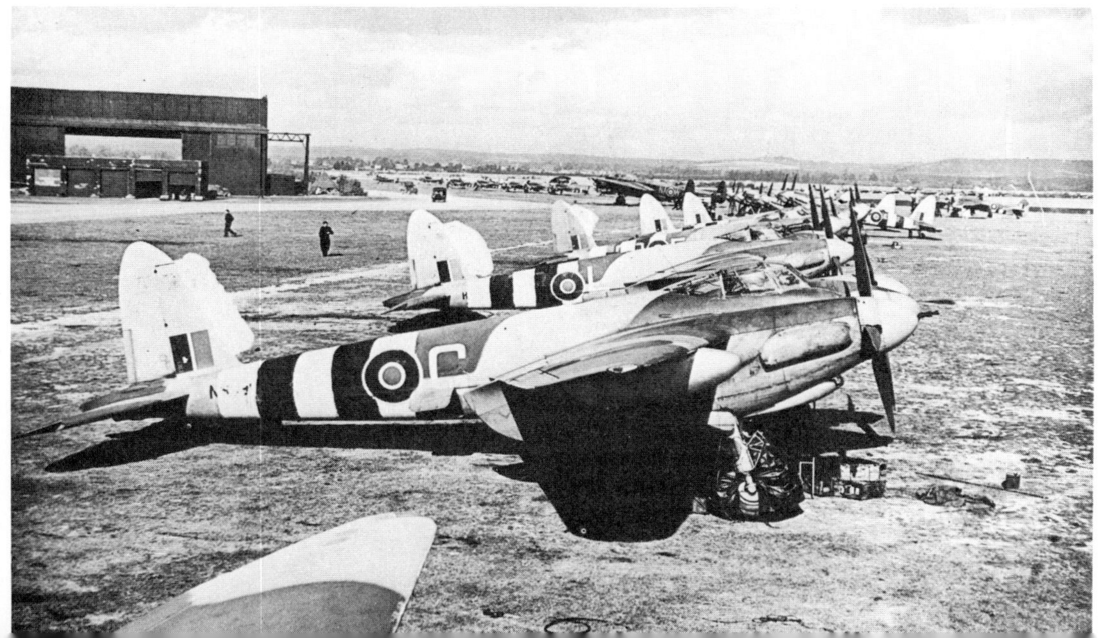

Top:
MM403, 'V' of 464 Squadron RAAF, late 1944. A veteran of the legendary Amiens Gaol raid, this Mosquito was lost on the night of 17 January 1945. *RAAF Official*

Above:
NT144, 'A-Able' (of 464 Squadron RAAF) at Thorney Island, January 1945, which completed 86 operational sorties with the Squadron
N. J. Willoughby via D. Vincent

Left:
Mosquitos of No 464 Squadron RAAF, believed at Hunsdon. 'SB-Y' was HX921, which later served as 'SB-P' with the Squadron.
Odlum Collection via D. Vincent

No 487 Squadron

No 487 Squadron RNZAF was formed at Feltwell on 15 August 1942, and flew Ventura bombers from 6 December 1942 until re-equipment with Mosquito FBVIs commenced from 21 August 1943 at Sculthorpe. Mosquito operations were begun on 3 October, alongside Nos 21 RAF and 464 RAAF Squadrons, all three units forming No 140 Wing. Henceforth No 487's main role was night bombing, though it was also to take part in various outstanding daylight precision attacks and other forms of operation. From December 1943 it participated in attacking V1 sites, but also despatched six crews on the Amiens Gaol raid of 18 February 1944, and took part in a low-level daylight raid on 18 March against an electrics factory at Hengelo. Continuing to operate both by day and by night, No 487 Squadron next took part in several high-level bomb attacks on French objectives, then played a significant part in the post-invasion raids on enemy transport systems in France during June-July 1944. On 14 July No 487 Squadron took part in a raid on Gestapo barracks at Bonneuil Matours, while on 1 August 12 of its crews flew alongside 12 Mosquitos from No 21 Squadron to bomb German barracks at Poitiers in a low-level attack. On 31 August six of No 487's Mosquitos destroyed an SS HQ at Vincey, near Metz. The last day of October saw the Squadron provide eight Mosquitos for the Wing attack on the Gestapo HQ at Aarhus, but increasingly bad weather prevented several operations in the following weeks. For Operation 'Clarion' on 22 February 1945 No 487 Squadron despatched 18 aircraft, five of which failed to return (the unit was by then based at Rosieres-en-Santerre, France). On 21 March 1945 it despatched seven Mosquitos for No 140 Wing's attack on the Shellhuset Gestapo HQ in Copenhagen, and also took part in a similar daylight precision raid against the Gestapo HQ at Odense on 17 April. The Squadron's final war sorties were flown on 3/4 May when a dozen Mosquitos bombed and strafed enemy trains. In July 1945 the unit base was moved to Epinoy, where on 19 September 1945 the Squadron was renumbered officially as

Tight trio from 487 Squadron RNZAF, led by FBVI, MM417, 'T', each carrying two 500lb HE bombs on underwing carriers. Photo taken on 29 February 1944. *IWM*

No 16 RAF, only to be retrospectively numbered No 268 Squadron RAF with effect from October.

Main bases

Sculthorpe	July 1943
Hunsdon	December 1943
Gravesend	April 1944
Thorney Island	June 1944
Rosieres-en-Santerre	February 1945
Melsbroek	April 1945
Epinoy (Cambrai)	July 1945

Aircraft examples flown

HP924, 'T'; HP933, 'A'; HR182, 'O'; HR197, 'T'; HX831; HX855, 'Q'; HX856, 'H' and 'N'; HX909, 'C'; HX915; HX922, 'F'; HX962, 'C'; HX974, 'J'; HX982, 'T'; LR333, 'R'; MM417, 'T'; MM419, 'N'; NS838, 'A'; NS840, 'X'; NS981, 'B'; NS999, 'C'; NT135, 'A'; NT144, 'A'; NT171, 'F'; PZ164, 'K'; PZ195, 'L'; PZ330, 'V'; PZ332, 'A'; PZ339, 'T'; PZ449, 'R'; RS570, 'X'; SZ985, 'M'; TA119, 'A'.

Commanding Officers

Wg Cdr A. G. Wilson	May 1943
Wg Cdr I. S. Smith DFC	February 1944
Wg Cdr R. C. Porteus	August 1944
Wg Cdr R. W. Baker	January 1945
Wg Cdr F. H. Denton DFC	February 1945
Wg Cdr W. P. Kemp	August 1945

No 488 Squadron

Re-formed at Church Fenton on 25 June 1942 as a future nightfighter unit, No 488 Squadron was first equipped with Beaufighters for this role, but commenced re-equipment with Mosquitos from 30 June 1943 when its first example arrived for crew conversion training. By August 1943 the Squadron had become based at Drem to complete its change to Mosquitos and, on 3 September, it began its move south to Bradwell Bay for active operations. The first two Mosquito operational sorties were flown on 15 September, each of which claimed a victim (a Heinkel He111 and a Do217), but one crew failed to return. The following weeks brought few opportunities for contact with the Luftwaffe, but on 8 November an Me410 was destroyed, followed by other Me410s on 26 November and 20 December. The 1944 'scoreboard' was 'opened' on the night of 2/3 January when an Me410 was shot down, while on 21 January one crew claimed two more victories, these being the virtual start of a run of successes, with four 'kills' in February, six in March, and two more in April. In May No 488 Squadron shifted base to Zeals, and continued to claim victories during May and June 1944, destroying nine in the latter month over France, while in July at least eight more fell to 488's guns. In the same month the unit moved base to Colerne, then moved again to Hunsdon on 9 October, where it began replacing its Mosquito XIIs and XIIIs with Mk XXXs, but in the interim kept up its scoring rate with 12 victories in August; its leading scorer was the New Zealander, Flt Lt G. Jameson, DSO, DFC. The re-equipment with Mosquito XXXs had commenced from 3 September (the first arrival) and virtually took the Squadron off operations for several weeks while crews 'converted' to the new radar techniques required; in November the unit crossed the Channel to become based at Glisy, Amiens from the 15th, and after settling in claimed four more victories in December. 1945 brought relatively few opportunities for combat though operational patrols were maintained, with some 'gaps' due to weather conditions. On 4 April the Squadron moved to Gilze-Rijen to join Nos 219 and 410 Squadrons, and made its ultimate victory claim from here on the night of 25 April. This claim completed the Squadron's war tally of 67 destroyed, three 'probables', and 11 'damaged'. No 488 Squadron was then officially disbanded at Gilze-Rijen on 26 April 1945, though most crews actually left in early May.

Main bases

Ayr	September 1942
Drem	August 1943
Bradwell Bay	September 1943
Zeals	May 1944
Colerne	July 1944
Hunsdon	October 1944
Glisy (B48)	November 1944
Gilze-Rijen (B77)	April 1945

Aircraft examples flown

HK121; HK186; HK197, 'F'; HK203; HK204; HK208; HK227; HK228; HK235; HK363; HK365; HK367; HK368; HK377; HK380; HK381; HK420; HK423; HK427; HK457; HK461; HK504; HK532; HK534; MM439; MM466, 'R'; MM476; MM502; MM513, 'D'; MM532, 'U'; MM551; MM556, 'B'; MM566; MM622; MM809, 'H'; MM813; MM820; MM822; MT456; MT458; MT477; MT570; NT260, 'F'; NT263; NT314; NT327; NT372, 'B'; NT512; NT527.

Commanding Officers

Wg Cdr J. Nesbitt-Dufort DSO	March 1943
Wg Cdr A. R. Burton-Gyles DFC	July 1943
Wg Cdr P. H. Hamley	September 1943
Wg Cdr R. C. Haine DFC	January 1944
Wg Cdr R. G. Watts	October 1944

No 489 Squadron

Serving from 1941 to 1945 as a torpedo-strike unit of Coastal Command, No 489 Squadron RNZAF flew Beauforts, Hampdens and Beaufighters successively until June 1945 when, based then at Banff, it began re-equipment with Mosquito FBVIs. Before reaching full strength and operational status, however, the Squadron was disbanded, at Banff, on 1 August 1945.

Commanding Officers

Wg Cdr D. H. Hammond	February 1945

No 500 Squadron

No 500 Squadron was reformed at West Malling from 10 May 1946 as a nightfighter unit of the Auxiliary Air Force, equipped with Mosquito NFXXXs. In 1948, following an Air Ministry policy decision to convert all AAF squadrons to day fighter roles, this Squadron became the first AAF unit to commence re-equipment with Meteor F3s; its first example arrived on the Squadron on 14 August 1948.

Aircraft examples flown

MV557; NT279; NT450; NT603; NT606, 'H'; NT619.

Commanding Officers

Sqn Ldr P. Green OBE, AFC	August 1946
Sqn Ldr M. C. Kennard DFC	February 1949

No 502 Squadron

On 17 July 1946 No 502 Squadron AAF was reformed at Aldergrove as a light bomber unit, equipped with Mosquito BXXVs, but this role was changed by the end of 1947 and the Squadron received its first NFXXX on

No 515 Squadron line-up at Little Snoring, near Norwich, 1945. *via T. Cushing*

17 December 1947 as the beginning of that role changed to nightfighters. In the following year, however, an Air Ministry policy decision for all AAF squadrons to become day fighter units resulted in these Mosquitos being replaced by Spitfire F22s.

Aircraft examples flown
KB565; MV524; NT242; NT282; RR306; TV982; VP349

Commanding Officers
Sqn Ldr W. H. McGiffin — July 1946

No 504 Squadron

Re-formed at Syerston on 10 May 1946 as a Mosquito light bomber unit, No 504 Squadron AAF received no Mosquito bombers but was 'changed' to a nightfighter Squadron and received Mosquito NFXXXs instead, starting in May 1947, and moving to Hucknall in November 1946. Here, in 1948, the Squadron again changed role and aircraft, being designated as a day fighter unit and receiving Spitfire F22s.

Aircraft examples flown
NT334; NT426, 'O'; NT450; NT561; NT562, 'M'; NT566; RK933, 'L'; VP345.

Commanding Officer
Sqn Ldr A H. Rook DFC, AFC — May 1946

No 515 Squadron

No 515 Squadron, flying Beaufighters on non-operational duties from Hunsdon in late 1943, was transferred from No 11 Group, Fighter Command to No 100 (SD) Group, Bomber Command on 15 December 1943 for bomber support duties, and began re-equipment with Mosquitos when four Mk IIs arrived on the unit, by then based at Little Snoring, on 29 February 1944; these Mk IIs were interim trainers until the issue of FBVIs. The Squadron's first sortie on 5 March was flown by the Squadron Commander, Wg Cdr F. F. Lambert, DSO, DFC in a borrowed No 605 Squadron Mosquito FBVI, and claimed a Heinkel He177 near Bretigny. The unit's prime role henceforth was night intrusion over German airfields, though on several occasions it also provided daytime escorts for Lancasters of No 5 Group raiding Germany, and from D-Day also supplied day support over the Normandy battle areas. By December 1944 the Squadron's aircraft had been fitted with *Ash* radar and continued its night intruder sorties. In April 1945 the unit added a fresh role to its activities by acting as Markers for other bombing squadrons, and flew its first Master Bomber sortie on 134 April, but intrusion sorties in the same month reaped several victims from Luftwaffe aircraft. The Squadron was disbanded on 10 June 1945, still based at Little Snoring.

Aircraft examples flown
DD666; DD756; HJ654; NS933, 'G'; NS944; NS957, 'V'; NS961, 'H'; NS992, 'S'; NS993, 'S'; PZ184; PZ188, 'W' & 'J'; PZ203, 'X';

PZ217, 'K'; PZ337, 'D'; PZ338, 'A'; PZ398; PZ440; PZ457, 'P'; PZ459, 'D'; RS513; RS518, 'L'; RS548, 'H'; RS566, 'F'; RS575.

Commanding Officers

Wg Cdr F. F. Lambert DSO, DFC	January 1944
Wg Cdr H. C. Kelsey DFC	December 1944

No 521 Squadron

Formed originally for meteorological duties on 1 August 1942 at Bircham Newton, No 521 Squadron was, in effect, a renumbered No 1401 Flight, and initially flew a complement of four Hudson IIIs, three Gladiators, two Spitfire Vs and two Mosquito IVs; the latter flying 'Pampa' reconnaissances over Europe. On 19 March 1943 the 'Pampa' Flight Mosquitos were transferred to RAF Oakington, and the remaining Flights (by then Gladiators, Spitfires and Hampdens) were collectively downgraded to become No 1401 Flight again, thus effectively 'disbanding' No 521 Squadron on 31 March 1943.

Aircraft examples flown

W4051; DK328; DK329; DZ316; DZ359; DZ362; DZ406; DZ475.

No 527 Squadron

On 1 August 1952 the 'N' and 'R' Calibration Squadrons of the Watton Central Signals Establishment were amalgamated to re-form No 527 Squadron, and employed a variety of aircraft types, including a few Mosquito B35s. On 21 August 1958 the Squadron was renumbered as No 245 Squadron.

No 540 Squadron

On 19 October 1942 the two Mosquito Flights, 'H' and 'L', of No 1 Photo Reconnaissance Unit (PRU) — a total of 12 Mosquitos — combined to form No 540 Squadron; the six Spitfire Flights became, in pairs, the nucleii of Nos 541, 542 and 543 Squadrons. Initially No 540 Squadron flew Mosquito IVs, but in June 1943 exchanged these for Mk IXs, and later (from June 1944) flew Mosquito XVIs and PR32s. Primarily tasked with constant photo coverage of shipping of the German, Italian and Vichy French navies, the Squadron's crews, like all PRU units, flew over most areas of Europe and the Mediterranean zones. On 8 March 1943 the Squadron Commander, Wg Cdr M. Young, became the first Mosquito pilot to photograph Berlin; while in November that year No 540 Squadron's crews were first to photograph V1s. By October 1943 the Squadron had 20 Mosquitos on strength, and was regularly covering enemy territories as far afield as Norway, Germany, Austria, Italy and Yugoslavia, and utilising airfields on Malta, in Tunisia, Gibraltar, etc for refuelling. In the preamble to D-Day in early 1944 the Squadron concentrated particularly on watching enemy rail systems in Northern Europe and France, then by Septem-

Above:
DZ383, a PRIV of 540 Squadron, May 1943.
Crown Copyright

Left:
PR34, PF662, 'DH-T' of 540 Squadron, viewed in July 1950.

ber spread its workload again, with a watching brief on the German battleship *Tirpitz* at Tromso until this was put out of action by RAF bombers. In March 1945 the Squadron moved to France for operations on a general photo survey of that country, then returned to England in November 1945 to continue aerial survey duties until it was disbanded at Benson on 30 September 1946. Some 15 months later, on 1 December 1947, the Squadron was re-formed at Benson, equipped with Mosquito PR34s and continued flying these until March 1953, but it had begun to replace the Mosquitos with Canberra PR3s from December 1952.

Main bases

Leuchars	October 1942
Benson	February 1944
Coulommiers	March 1945
Benson	November 1945
Benson	December 1947

Aircraft examples flown

W4051; W4059; W4061; DD615; DD659; DK284; DK311; DK315; DK319; DK320; DZ342; DZ364; DZ368; DZ383; DZ404; DZ419; DZ424; DZ438; DZ473; DZ480; DZ517; DZ592; LR405; LR406; LR407; LR408; LR412, 'A'; LR415; LR416; LR422, 'O'; LR426; LR432; LR435; LR467; MM276, 'N'; MM299; MM300; MM351; MM355; MM358; MM397; NS525; NS571; NS580; NS588; NS640; NS643; NS693; NS800; NS814; PF662, 'T'; PF679, 'A'; PZ345; RF970; RF980; RG128; RG139; RG158; RG181, 'F'; RG215, 'S'; RG228; RG236, 'C'; RG241; RG245, 'S'; RG290, 'N'; RG302, 'B'; RG303; RG311; RS502, 'Y'; RS512, 'H'; VL613, 'X'; VL624; VL625, 'D'.

Commanding Officers

Wg Cdr M. J. B. Young DFC	October 1942
Wg Cdr Lord Douglas-Hamilton OBE	May 1943
Wg Cdr J. R. H. Merifield DSO, DFC	March 1944
Wg Cdr A. H. W. Ball DSO, DFC	September 1944

No 544 Squadron

When, on 19 October 1942, No 1 PRU's various Flights provided the foundations of Nos 540, 541, 542 and 543 Squadrons, the remaining elements of the 'parent' unit — a Spitfire flight at Gibraltar and the Benson Night Photography Flight flying Wellingtons and Ansons — were 'united' under the new title No 544 Squadron. In April 1943 the Benson-based Wellingtons were replaced by Mosquito IVs, which in turn gave way to Mosquito IXs in October 1943, Mk XVIs from March 1944, and finally PR34s from June 1945. Throughout 1943 the unit carried out photo-recce sorties over (mainly) northwest Europe, but from early 1944 extended its fields of operations to France, southern Germany and Italy, and maintained a regular watch along Norway's coastline. After several weeks of photo-cover for the D-Day landings

PRXVI NS502, 'M' of 544 Squadron. *IWM*

and subsequent fighting in Normandy in June-August 1944, the Squadron restarted its longer-range sorties and was soon including trips to Russia, Poland, Egypt and Italy. By early 1945 its main work load was northern Europe, particularly Germany, despite increasing air opposition by Luftwaffe jet fighters and consequent losses. The first few months of peace saw No 544 Squadron engaged in fast courier flights, but on 13 October 1945 it was disbanded at Benson.

Aircraft examples flown
DZ494; DZ538; DZ596; DZ600; LR411;
LR417; LR419; LR423; LR425; LR431,
LR432 'L1'; LR436; LR478; MM231; MM239;
MM240; MM242; MM246; MM247; MM272;
MM273; MM283; MM307; MM352; MM396;
NS500; NS502, 'M'; NS525; NS587; NS633;
NS652, 'O'; NS682, 'K'; NS795; NS803;
RF981; RG115; RG133; RG195; RG196;
RG197; RG198.

Commanding Officers
Sqn Ldr W. R. Acott	October 1942
Sqn Ldr J. R. H. Merifield DFC	July 1943
Wg Cdr D. C. B. Walker	October 1943
Wg Cdr D. W. Steventon DSO, DFC	November 1943
Sqn Ldr F. L. Dodd DSO, DFC, AFC	September 1945

No 571 Squadron

Formed at Downham Market on 7 April 1944, No 571 Squadron was one of several units created during the latter years of World War 2 for the expansion of RAF Bomber Command's assault on Germany; in this case as a new squadron for No 8 (PFF) Group's Light Night Striking Force. Intended for equipment with Mosquito XVIs, the initial Flight formed was detached to Graveley for working-up experience and from there flew the Flight's first sorties on 12/13 April — two aircraft to Osnabruck — and operated from Graveley for eight more nights before the Flight rejoined the main unit, by then based at Oakington from 24 April. By 20 May Squadron strength comprised two Flights, and sorties against German cities and industrial centres occupied its crews for the

BXVI, ML963, '8K-K' of 571 Squadron, late 1944.
C. E. Brown/RAF Museum

remainder of the war. From June 1944 the Squadron's Mosquitos often carried 4,000lb HC 'Cookie' blast bombs as their load; the aircraft's enlarged bomb bays leading to the nickname 'Fat-Belly' for such modified Mosquitos. On 3 October the unit despatched its 1,000th operational sortie — to Kassel — by which time its aircraft were also dropping mines on Germany's vital waterways, apart from attacking 'favourite' objectives like Berlin. In November it participated in several major daylight operations by No 8 Group's Mosquito force, bombing Duisburg and nearby industrial sites, while in December other targets included low-level precision raids against key railway tunnels and depots. In January 1945 the overall Mosquito force concentrated primarily on bombing Berlin, visiting the German capital no less than 61 nights during the final months of the war, of which No 571 Squadron took part on 22 nights. By March 1945 the Squadron was also contributing to several Mosquito day raids on Germany, and its last war sorties were flown on 26/27 April 1945 when 11 Mosquitos bombed Grosenbrode. On 20 July 1945 No 571 Squadron moved from Oakington to Warboys, where it was disbanded on 20 September 1945. Its final tally of operational sorties flown amounted to 2,546 despatched.

Aircraft examples flown
ML935; ML942, 'D'; ML963, 'K'; ML963; ML972; ML988; MM113; MM115; ML116, 'M'; MM119; MM124; MM145; MM148; MM156; MM169; MM179; PF379; PF383; PF387; PF389; PF394; PF395; PF433; PF438; PF500; RV305; RV315; RV323; RV325; RV355; RV357.

Commanding Officers

Wg Cdr J. M. Birkin DSO, DFC, AFC	April 1944
Wg Cdr R. J. Gosnell DSO, DFC	November 1944
Wg Cdr R. W. Bray DFC	March 1945

No 600 Squadron

A successful nightfighting unit which had seen operational service from the outbreak of war in

England, North Africa, Malta and Sicily, No 600 Squadron AAF was based at Cesenatico, Italy, in December 1944 when its crews began conversion from Beaufighters to Mosquito XIXs, being detached to Foggia for this training. First Mosquito operational sorties were flown beginning on 22 January 1945, but by that stage of the Italian campaign little Luftwaffe opposition was being met by night, and the Squadron added only three victories to its war tally in Mosquitos, all in April 1945. Moving base to Campoformido in May 1945, the Squadron was disbanded there on 21 August that year.

Aircraft examples flown
TA123, 'H'; TA133, 'X'; TKA406; TA425; TA426, 'G'; TA429; TA448.

Commanding Officers
Wg Cdr L. H. Styles DFC	March 1944
Wg Cdr A. H. Drummond	December 1944

No 604 Squadron

In December 1943 No 604 Squadron AAF, based at Scorton and flying Beaufighter VIFs as nightfighters, was transferred to No 85 (Base)

Mk XIII of 604 Squadron AAF at Hurn, June 1944. In the background are Typhoons of No 183 Squadron. *Keystone Agency*

Group, 2nd TAF, and on 26 April 1944 moved base to Church Fenton, where it commenced conversion to Mosquito XIIs. A further move to Hurn on 2 May to Hurn saw the Squadron ready for operations again, and the first two Mosquito 'kills' were claimed on the night of 14 May 1944, followed by a third victory the next night. In June at least nine more German aircraft were shot down as the Squadron flew in support of the Allied invasion forces in Normandy, while July brought a further 12 victories, including the unit's 100th victory of the war scored by Wg Cdr M. C. Maxwell DFC on 8/9 July. August 1944's tally then added 16 more 'kills'. In the meantime the Squadron had been on the move again, to Colerne on 13 July, from where six of its Mosquitos flew to France (Maupertus, A15) on 24 July, to act as a forward detachment, while the rest moved to Zeals to 'guard' the concentration of personnel and stores being sent to France at that period. On 5 August, however, the whole Squadron moved to Picauville (A8), being joined there on 26 August by No 264 Squadron. On 9 September No 604 Squadron moved base again, this time to Carpiquet (B17), but on 24 September

flew back to Predannack for rest and refurbishment and re-equipment with Mosquito XIIIs. In December 1944 the Squadron returned to France, taking up 'residence' at Vendeville (Lille) (B51), and claiming four victories on 1/2 January, followed by another 'kill' three nights later. By the end of April 1945 at least four more victories had been claimed, the last victim for the Squadron being 'chalked up' on 26/27 March. On 18 April 1945 the Squadron was disbanded at Vendeville.

Main bases
Church Fenton	April 1944
Hurn	May 1944
Colerne	July 1944
Zeals	July 1944
Picauville (A8)	August 1944
Carpiquet (B17)	September 1944
Predannack	September 1944
Odiham	December 1944
Vendeville (B51)	December 1944

Aircraft examples flown
HK181, 'J'; HK183, 'L'; HK457, 'K'; HK525; HK526, 'U'; HK527; HK529; HK533; MM429; MM449, 'R'; MM459; MM461; MM462, 'T'; MM465; MM496,'T'; MM497; MM500; MM503, 'B'; MM514, 'R'; MM517; MM525, 'P'; MM526; MM527; MM528, 'H';

FII, DZ716, 'UP-L' of 605 Squadron AAF.
IWM

MM552; MM563; MM569, 'J'; MM621; TA122.

Commanding Officers
Wg Cdr M. Constable Maxwell DFC	April 1944
Wg Cdr F. D. Hughes DFC	July 1944

No 605 Squadron

Based at Ford and flying Boston III intruders, in late 1942 No 605 Squadron AAF had been patiently awaiting re-equipment with Mosquitos for several weeks, but the first example actually arrived on the Squadron on 3 February 1943. Little time was lost 'converting' and the first Mosquito sorties were despatched on 10 March; and the next two operational sorties reaped victories. Equipped initially with Mosquito NFIIs, the Squadron began operating Mk VIs from July 1943 and added rapidly to the unit's 'bag', claiming 10 destroyed and two more 'damaged' in September alone. In that month Wg Cdr B. R. O'B. Hoare DSO, DFC succeeded to command of the Squadron and promptly added a victory on his first sortie with No 605. On 19 January 1944 Hoare claimed the unit's 100th victory of the war, while in March 1944 the Squadron claimed 17 victories, including four on 5 March. By D-Day the crews had added at least 11 more 'kills'. On 14/15 June a No 605 Squadron Mosquito made the first V1 'kill', and by the end of that month had accounted for 36 V1s, followed by the destruction of a further 29 V1s in July; these sorties were additional to the Squadron's normal intruding patrols over German airfields, etc. Based at Manston, the Squadron detached aircraft to St Dizier, France, from 20 September 1944, from where Flg Off R. Lelong took-off on 2 October for a daylight 'Ranger' to the Baltic, and his combat report claimed six enemy aircraft destroyed plus one 'probable' and five 'damaged' — a unit record for a single sortie, and made more remarkable by the Mosquito's return flight from Germany to base on one engine. Five nights later two Mosquitos flew to Vienna and left 10 enemy aircraft destroyed and six more damaged behind them. In November 1944 the Squadron was transferred to No 136 Wing, 2nd TAF; and on 15 March 1945 it moved base to Coxyde, Belgium, and on 28 April to Volkel. When the European war ended No 605 Squadron's war tally included 98 enemy aircraft destroyed, eight probably destroyed, 79 'damaged', 75 V1s destroyed, and almost 500 trains and barges, etc, destroyed or disabled. On 31 August 1945 the Squadron was retitled No 4 Squadron at Volkel, but re-formed as No 605 Squadron AAF again on 10 May 1946, equipped with Mosquito NFXXXs ostensibly, though for the first year most of its aircraft were in fact Mosquito T3 trainers. In July 1948 the Mosquitos were replaced by DH Vampire F1s, the unit thereby becoming the first AAF squadron to operate this type of jet fighter.

Main bases

Ford	June 1942
Castle Camps	March 1943
Bradwell Bay	October 1943
Manston	April 1944
Hartford Bridge	November 1944
Coxyde (B71)	March 1945
Volkel (B80)	April 1945
Honiley	May 1946

Aircraft examples flown

DZ657; DZ684; DZ714; DZ716, 'L'; DZ717, 'O'; DZ723; DZ724, 'S'; DZ760, 'K'; HJ761, 'P'; HJ768; HJ775, 'U'; HJ778, 'A'; HJ784, 'F'; HJ790, 'R'; HJ809, 'D'; HR203; HR205; HR338; HR349; HX823, 'B'; HX953; MM415; MM790, 'F'; NS876; NS880; NS892; NS936; NT114; NT153; NT155; NT186; NT291; NT479; NT590; PZ312; PZ355; PZ373; PZ377; PZ453; RS678, 'T'; RS557; SZ967; SZ980; SZ984; TA122; TA381; TA383; TE809.

Commanding Officers

Wg Cdr G. Denholm DFC	August 1942
Wg Cdr C. D. Tomalin DFC AFC	May 1943
Wg Cdr B. R. O'B. Hoare DSO, DFC	September 1943
Wg Cdr N. J. Starr DFC	April 1944
Wg Cdr R. A. Mitchell DFC	September 1944
Wg Cdr A. W. Horne DFC, AFC	March 1945
Sqn Ldr R. J. Walker	June 1946

No 608 Squadron

Re-formed at Downham Market on 1 August 1944 as the latest addition to No 8 (PFF) Group's Light Night Striking Force, No 608 Squadron AAF was equipped with Mosquito BXXs initially, then BXXVs in October 1944, and BXVIs from 26 March 1945. The Squadron's first Mosquito sortie was flown on 5/6 August 1944 when KB242 raided Wanne Eickel, the first of 78 sorties that month. Flying the unit's first Mosquito BXXV sorties on 6 October — to Berlin — 608 Squadron participated in most of the LNSF's night and day operations during the winter of 1944-45, usually carrying 4,000lb HC 'Cookie' bombs to such targets as Cologne, Dusseldorf, Bremen, Brunswick and Berlin. The Squadron's final war sorties were despatched to Kiel with 'Cookies' (16 aircraft) on 2/3 May 1945, thereby concluding a gross total of 1,726 operational sorties since August 1944. Disbanded on 24 August 1945, the unit's Mosquitos were delivered to Upper Heyford four days later for 'disposal'. On 31 July 1946 No 608 Squadron AAF was re-formed at Thornaby-on-Tees, Nominally to be equipped with Mosquito bombers, but in the event its role was changed before receiving any aircraft; Mosquito NFXXXs were delivered in 1947 for nightfighter duties. These were replaced by Spitfire F22s in August 1948.

Main bases

Downham Market	August 1944
Thornaby-on-Tees	July 1946
Middleton St George	1947

Aircraft examples flown

KB146; KB189; KB212, 'F'; KB231; KB242, 'B'; KB261; KB265, 'F'; KB356; KB358, 'L'; KB360; KB364; KB388; KB400, 'U'; KB404; KB413, 'V'; KB438, 'F'; KB441, 'Q'; LR555, 'R'; NT373, 'A'; NT471, 'D'; NT548, 'B'; NT609, 'C'; PF483, 'V'; PF487; PF496; PF502; PF505, 'D'; RV358; RV360, 'F'; VA866, 'K'; VA876; VA888, 'L'; VP351, 'P'.

Commanding Officers

Wg Cdr W. W. G. Scott	August 1944
Wg Cdr R. C. Alabaster DSO, DFC	November 1944
Wg Cdr K. Gray	April 1945
Sqn Ldr W. A. Brown DFC	July 1946

No 609 Squadron

A fighter unit throughout 1939-45, during which it flew Spitfires and Typhoons, No 609 Squadron AAF was disbanded at Wunstorf officially on 15 September 1945 and its Typhoons were flown back to Lasham five days later for 'disposal'. On 10 May 1946 the Squadron was re-formed at Church Fenton, designated as a nightfighter unit, then moved shortly after to Yeadon to receive Mosquito NFXXXs, though most crew training took place at Linton-on-Ouse due to Yeadon's short runways. By 1947 the Squadron was considered 'operational' on Mosquitos, but in April 1948 these were replaced by Spitfire LFXVIes.

Aircraft examples flown

NT283; NT334; NT422, 'D'; NT449; NT568, 'B'; NT615; TA341; VA883; VA926.

Commanding Officer

Sqn Ldr P. A. Womersley DFC	May 1946

No 613 Squadron

From 1939 to 1943 No 613 Squadron AAF was an Army co-operation unit, flying Hectors, Lysanders and Mustangs, but on 11 October 1943 it moved base from Snailwell to Lasham, and was officially transferred to No 2 Group, 2nd TAF with effect from 15 October. Conversion to Mosquito FBVIs commenced at Sculthorpe from that date, and next day the first Mosquito T3 trainer was delivered to Lasham. Training continued as Mosquito FBVIs began arriving, and on 19 December the Squadron's first operational sortie was flown in LR271 — a met recce. Its first bombing sorties followed on 31 December when six Mosquitos bombed a rocket site at Maintenay. Thereafter the unit began night intrusion sorties mainly, though its crews occasionally took part in daylight precision attacks. One example of the latter was an attack by six Squadron Mosquitos, led by Wg Cdr R. Bateson, on the Dutch Central Population Registry building housing Gestapo records on 11 April 1944. In the following month sorties were flown against radio stations, gun sites and V-sites, while in June 1944 most objectives were German communication systems, the Squadron continuing these sorties through July and early August. On 18 August the Squadron despatched 14 Mosquitos to bomb SS barracks at Egletons, obtaining at least 20 direct hits and virtually destroying the target, while during the Arnhem operations in September No 613's crews attacked German barracks in that zone. In October 1944 No 613 Squadron moved to Hartford Bridge, then in November crossed to France to be based at Epinoy (Cambrai), arriving there on 19/20 November and resuming operations within 24 hours. The pace of operations during the next three months was intense, often entailing crews flying two sorties per night, and losses were incurred, but the Squadron continued its assaults on enemy targets until late April 1945, flying its final operations on 26/27 April with a Strafe of German rail junctions and trains. On 8 August 1945 the Squadron was renumbered as No 69 Squadron at Epinoy.

Main bases

Lasham	October 1943

| Hartford Bridge | October 1944 |
| Epinoy (A75) | November 1944 |

Aircraft examples flown
HJ666; HJ771; HP927, 'B'; HP928; HP930,
'D'; HR182; HX828; LR260; LR269; LR271;
LR272; LR275; LR297; LR350; LR355, 'H';
LR364, 'E'; LR366, 'L'; LR370, 'Y'; LR375;
LR376, 'Q'; MM408, 'F'; NS844, 'A'; NS845,
'E'; NS859, 'P'; NS898, 'E'; NS987; NT134;
PZ194; PZ222; RS600.

Commanding Officers

Wg Cdr K. H. Blair DFC	October 1943
Wg Cdr R. N. Bateson DFC	February 1944
Wg Cdr C. Newman	June 1944
Wg Cdr P. B. Lucas DSO, DFC	December 1944

Above:
An FBVI of 613 Squadron AAF.
R. C. B. Ashworth

Below:
**NFXXX, NT508, 'RAW-E' of 616 Squadron
RAuxAF at Finningley, c1947-48.**
via A. Thomas

No 616 Squadron

No 616 Squadron AAF's unique claim to fame
in RAF annals was its selection as the Service's
first-ever jet fighter unit, when it began receiving Gloster Meteor Is in July 1944, and became
fully operational on these from August that year.
Disbanded at Lubeck on 29 August 1945, the
Squadron was re-formed as a nightfighter unit
at Finningley on 10 May 1946 officially (though
crews, etc only began assembling from 31 July),
and began equipping with Mosquito NFXXXs
from November 1946. In December 1948 the
unit role was changed to day fighter and its

Mosquitos were replaced by Meteor F3 jets.

Aircraft examples flown
NT283; NT311; NT423, 'J'; NT508, 'E';
NT536, 'F'; NT590, 'G'; RK936, 'H'.

Commanding Officer
Sqn Ldr K. Holden DFC   June 1946

No 617 Squadron

Although primarily an all-Lancaster unit, No 617 ('Dambusters') Squadron first received a Mosquito on strength on 30 August 1943, while in September 1943 three Mosquito crews from 418 Squadron RCAF were temporarily attached for 'liaison' training with 617's Lancasters as a portent of future Mosquito use. The first actual Mosquito operations by 617 Squadron came on 5 April 1944, when Wg Cdr G. L. Cheshire DSO, DFC (later VC) flew ML976, 'N' to mark Toulouse. Thereafter several of 617's crews flew Mosquitos to mark targets for the Squadron's Lancasters.

Aircraft examples flown
DZ415; ML975; ML976, 'N'; NS992; NS993, 'N'; NT202; NT205, 'L'; NT423.

No 618 Squadron

In early 1943 two squadrons were specifically formed to use the special weapons devised by Barnes Wallis for attacks on German dams and/or shipping. Of these two units, No 617 Squadron carried the *Upkeep* 'bouncing bomb' and destroyed the Möhne and Eder dams in May 1943, while No 618 Squadron was formed at Skitten, under the aegis of No 18 Group, Coastal Command, on 1 April 1943, with the intention of using a 'naval version' of *Upkeep*, known as *Highball*, against the German capital

ship *Tirpitz*. In the event No 618 Squadron was never to fly actual operations throughout the war, but spent two years in frustrating 'trials' of *Highball* and other projected innovations. Mosquito IVs began arriving on the Squadron from 3 April, though these had yet to be modified to carry *Highball*, with the intention of attacking the *Tirpitz* on 15 May 1943 (the day *before* 617's legendary dam-busting operation), under the code-name Operation 'Servant', but by 14 May the Squadron had only seven fully modified Mosquitos ready, and 'Servant' was cancelled. For the remainder of 1943 the Squadron continued its trials, was nearly disbanded in September, but remained in being in early 1944, and in July 1944 was earmarked for aircraft carrier-borne operations in the Pacific theatre against Japanese shipping as a special 'mine-laying' unit under the auspices of Operation 'Oxtail'. On 28 October the Squadron's total of 28 Mosquitos was loaded aboard two 'Woolworth' carriers, *Fencer* and *Striker*, and three days later these sailed for their ultimate destination — Melbourne, Australia — arriving there on 23 December. By early February 1945 the Squadron was based at Narromine, New South Wales, but procrastination by 'higher authority' in deciding the unit's future operational employment meant that No 618 Squadron flew no operations in the Pacific theatre. Even the Squadron's subsequent disbandment was confused. Officially, it was intended to be disbanded on 21 July 1945 at Narromine, yet subsequent records indicate some aircraft and personnel still being referred

Above:
HR609, 'S1' of 618 Squadron RAF which crashed near Narromine, Australia on 12 June 1945, its crew escaping with minor injuries.
E. Knight via D. Vincent
99

Below:
KB416, 'AZ-P', of 'B' Flight, 627 Squadron
D. Garton via P. H. T. Green

to as No 618 Squadron at least until August 1945.

Main bases

Skitten	April 1943
Benson	September 1943
Wick	June 1944
Fishermans Bend	December 1944
Narromine	February 1945

Aircraft examples flown

DK293; DZ355; DZ423; DZ468; DZ486; DZ489; DZ493; DZ520, 'A'; DZ533; DZ537; DZ543; DZ545; DZ546, 'G'; DZ547, 'VY'; DZ558, 'G'; DZ579, 'M'; DZ582, 'U'; DZ639, 'P'; DZ652, 'O'; HR373; HR580, 'T1'; HR609, 'S1'; HR614; HR621; HR623, 'C1'; HX903; MM424; NS572; NS577; NS729; NS732; NS735; PZ274, 'S'; PZ276; PZ282, 'H1'; PZ295, 'G1'; PZ297, 'R1'; PZ303, 'Q1'.

Commanding Officer

Wg Cdr G. H. B. Hutchinson
  DFC   April 1943

No 627 Squadron

Formed officially on 12 November 1943, No 627 Squadron actually came into being on 24 November when 'C' Flight of No 139 Squadron at Wyton was moved to Oakington and retitled with 627's 'numberplate'. Equipped with Mosquito BIVs, the new squadron was part of No 8 (PFF) Group, and commenced operations that night (24/25 November) when DZ615 flew to Berlin on an uneventful sortie. For the following six months 627's crews flew as part of the PFF's Light Night Striking Force, despatching almost 400 sorties by early April 1944, but on 13 April 1944 the Squadron was officially 'detached' from No 8 Group to No 5 Group, with which it was to remain for the rest of the war. As No 5 Group's sole Mosquito squadron, No 627 henceforth operated primarily as a marker unit for the many Lancaster attacks mounted by the Group against Germany. The Squadron's first marking sorties were flown by four aircraft on 1 May against Tours. Newer versions of Mosquito reached No 627 Squadron from then on, with the first Mk XX sorties being flown on

BIV, DZ518, 'AZ-F' of 627 Squadron at Oakington, January 1944.
D. Garton via P. H. T. Green

7 July 1944, the first Mk XXV sorties on 11 November 1944, and the initial Mk XVI trips on 21 March 1945. From June 1944 the Squadron also flew day sorties, marking V1 sites, while in late 1944 some mine-laying runs were added to the prime tasks, and occasionally the Squadron mounted its own bombing raids against specific targets. During the latter months of the European conflict No 627's Mosquitos continued to provide precise marking, by day and by night, for 5 Group's 'heavies', ensuring maximum destruction of key objectives, and its final operations were flown on 25/26 April 1945 when 10 aircraft were despatched to attack oil targets at Tonsberg (Vallo). On 1 October 1945 the Squadron was, in effect, 'disbanded' at Woodhall Spa when it was renumbered as No 109 Squadron.

Main bases

Oakington	November 1943
Woodhall Spa	April 1944

Aircraft examples flown

W4072, 'Q'; DK313, 'A'; DZ353, 'B'; DZ412, 'Q'; DZ418, 'B'; DZ420, 'P'; DZ421; DZ422; DZ461, 'U'; DZ462, 'N'; DZ477, 'K'; DZ478; DZ479, 'F'; DZ482, 'P'; DZ484, 'G'; DZ516, 'O'; DZ518, 'F'; DZ525, 'B'; DZ530, 'N'; DZ594, 'X'; DZ601; DZ606, 'H' & 'M'; DZ611, 'G'; DZ615; DZ617; DZ632; DZ633, 'D'; DZ637, 'X'; DZ641, 'C'; DZ642; DZ643, 'O' and 'P'; DZ646; DZ650, 'Q'; KB122, 'T'; KB195, 'B'; KB215, 'H'; KB267, 'E'; KB329; KB345, 'J'; KB362, 'K'; KB416, 'P'; KB490, 'Q'; KB533, 'N'; ML906; NS536; PF444, 'N'.

Commanding Officers

Wg Cdr R. P. Elliott DSO, DFC	November 1942
Wg Cdr G. W. Curry DFC	June 1944
Wg Cdr B. R. W. Hallows DFC	January 1945
Wg Cdr R. Kingsford-Smith DSO, DFC	April 1945

No 680 Squadron

On 1 February 1943 three former PRU units in the Mediterranean zone of operations were retitled as full squadrons when 'B' Flight of 69 Squadron on Malta became No 683 Squadron, No 4 PRU became No 682 Squadron, and No 2 PRU, based at LG219, was renumbered as

Left:
MM335 of 680 Squadron.   *via S. Howe*

Left:
MM335 and (behind) RG138 of 680 Squadron.
via S. Howe

No 680 Squadron. At that time No 680 Squadron was operating Spitfire IXs and XIs, plus a few Beaufighters, on photo-recce sorties across southern Italy and the eastern Mediterranean territories in general, but on 24 February 1943 a North African Central Intelligence Unit (CIU) was formed to co-ordinate all PR work, and thereafter 680 Squadron's area of operations was defined as the eastern Mediterranean and Greece (except Corfu); from the beginning of 1944 No 336 PR Wing was established to co-ordinate the work of Nos 680, 682, 683 and 60 (SAAF) Squadrons. Of these, Nos 682 and 683 were allotted 10 Spitfires each, while No 680 Squadron was promised six Mosquitos; No 60 Squadron SAAF had two flights each of seven Mosquitos. On 16 February No 680 Squadron received its first Mosquito, a PRIX, LR444, while next day a PRXVI (MM297) arrived, and by May the unit possessed one PRIX and nine PRXVIs. By June 1944 the unit's Spitfires were gradually being phased out, leaving the unit predominantly Mosquito-equipped, and in the latter months of the year the Mosquito crews had extended their 'hunting grounds' as far afield as Austria, Bavaria, Czechoslovakia and Germany. By December the Squadron had 11 Mosquitos and a few Spitfires on strength — the latter for short-range work only — by which time the unit was based in Italy, but in February 1945 it was moved back to Egypt where it undertook aerial survey flights over Egypt, Palestine and neighbouring territories. The Squadron was then renumbered as No 13 Squadron on 1 September 1946 at Ein Shemer, Palestine.

Main bases

Matariya	December 1943
San Severo	August 1944
Deversoir	February 1945
Aqir	February 1946
Ein Shemer	August 1946

Aircraft examples flown
LG219; LR444; MM287; MM289; MM291; MM297; MM330; MM333; MM335; MM347, 'N'; MM348; NS496; NS530; NS534; NS683; NS705; RF987, 'O'; RG117; RG316.

Commanding Officers

Wg Cdr J. R. Whelan DFC	February 1943
Wg Cdr J. C. Paish	October 1944

No 681 Squadron

Formed on 2 January 1943 at Dum Dum, Calcutta by the renumbering of No 3 PRU, No 681 Squadron was equipped with Spitfire IVs and controlled by No 171 PR Wing. In August 1943 two Mosquito IIs arrived at Dum Dum (on the 9th), while in September Mosquito PRIVs also began arriving, totalling five by November. Though No 681 Squadron flew several sorties with these Mosquitos, in November these were taken off strength to form the nucleus of No 684 Squadron.

Aircraft examples flown
DZ696, 'S'; DZ697, 'J'; HJ730, 'Y'; HJ759, 'W'; LR440, 'V'; LR441.

No 683 Squadron

Formed at Luqa, Malta on 1 February 1943 (official date) by retitling 'B' Flight of No 69 Squadron, No 683 Squadron was primarily a

Spitfire PR unit, but received at least two Mosquitos in March 1943, and flew some 20 PR sorties in these before the aircraft were transferred to other units.

Aircraft examples flown
DZ553; HJ672, 'A'.

No 684 Squadron

On 29 September 1943 a mixed 'bag' of two Mosquito IIs, three Mosquito VIs — ex-No 681 Squadron — together with four Mitchells was entitled No 684 Squadron at Dum Dum. Two Mosquito PRIXs were added in October, and Mosquito operations commenced on 1 November, the first of 38 lone-range PR recces that month. On 9 December the Squadron moved base to Comilla, and by the end of February 1944 had on strength 20 assorted Mosquito VIs, IXs, and XVIs. Moving back to Dum Dum on 31 January 1944, then to Alipore on 6 May, the Squadron flew deep penetration reconnaissance sorties over Burma and Siam throughout that year, with some flights lasting from six to eight

PRXVI, NS787, 'M' of 684 Squadron. *IWM*

hours. By January 1945 Squadron aircraft strength was 12 Mosquitos and, by using forward airfields at Akyab and Cox's Bazaar for refuelling, these extended their operational range further south and east, with the notorious Burma-Siam railway as one of the unit's constant priority 'targets'. By March 1945 the Squadron's constant aerial survey had covered some 75% of the survey work required by the Allied armies mustering for an advance on Malaya; while — combined with No 681 Squadron — the unit had mapped almost 60% of Burma (roughly) three times the area of all England). By June 1945 the Squadron was maintaining a detachment of minimum three Mosquito crews on the Cocos Islands, where the first long-range Mosquito PR34s entered Squadron service in that month, and commenced PR34 sorties from 3 July. By September 1945 this detachment had seven PR34s on strength. Postwar duties for No 684 Squadron included complete aerial surveys of Indo-China, Cambodia and Siam, later extended to India, but on 1 September 1946 the unit was renumbered as No 81 Squadron at Bangkok.

Main bases

Dum Dum	September 1943
Comilla	December 1943
Dum Dum	January 1944
Alipore	May 1944
Saigon	October 1945
Don Muang (Bangkok)	January 1946

Aircraft examples flown

DZ697; LR443; LR464; NS479; NS622; NS657; NS688; NS787, 'M'; RG185, 'Z'; RG186, 'G'; RG203, 'E'; RG210, 'J'; RG213, 'O'; RG249, 'U'; RG254, 'M'; RG263, 'P'.

Commanding Officers

Sqn Ldr B. S. Jones	September 1943
Wg Cdr W. B. Murray	December 1943
Wg Cdr W. E. M. Lowry DFC	November 1944
Wg Cdr K. J. Newman DFC	November 1945
Wg Cdr J. R. H. Merifield DSO, DFC	April 1946

No 692 Squadron

Formed at Graveley on 1 January 1944, No 692 ('Fellowship of the Bellows') Squadron was initially equipped with Mosquito BIVs as part of No 8 (PFF) Group's Light Night Striking Force, and shortly after was 'adopted' by an association in Buenos Aires which called itself 'The Fellowship of the Bellows', hence the name incorporated in the unit title. Operations commenced on the night of 1/2 February when a lone Mosquito (of three despatched) bombed Berlin. On 23 February 1944 a modified Mosquito IV, DZ647, 'B' became the first Mosquito to drop a 4,000lb HC 'Cookie' bomb on Germany, in this case Düsseldorf. Another Mosquito 'first' fell to the Squadron on 12/13 May 1944 when its crews laid mines in the Kiel Canal. In the interim No 692 Squadron began operating Mosquito XVIs, the first sortie in this

DZ637 of 692 Squadron about to 'digest' a 4,000lb HC 'Cookie' at Gravel, spring 1944. This Mosquito was the third RAF Mosquito to drop a 'Cookie' 'in anger'. *Keystone Agency*

134

version being a raid on Duisburg on 5 March, while on 13/14 April the Squadron dropped its 'Cookies' on Berlin for the first time. It participated in the intense operations flown by the PFF in support of the D-Day invasion of Normandy, bombing rail marshalling yards at Osnabruck on 5/6 June with 10 'Cookies', and thereafter began concentrating on oil targets in Germany as part of the 'Transportation Plan'. On 29/30 June the unit flew its final Mosquito IV sorties, becoming an all-Mk XVI squadron for the remainder of its Service life. On 12 September 1944 the No 692 flew its first daylight sorties, bombing Gelsenkirchen and Wanne Eickel with 'Cookies' — six aircraft in total — and repeated such daylight raids over the following months, intermixed with its more usual nightly forays. A further innovation for No 692's crews came in January 1945 when low-level sorties were flown dropping 'Cookies' on enemy railway tunnels, after which the principal night target became Berlin to which No 692 despatched 20 Mosquitos on the night of 21/22 March 1945 — its greatest single effort in one night. The final weeks of war saw No 692's crews attacking German airfields and harbours, and on 2/3 May 1945 they made the Squadron's last war effort by sending a total of 23 Mosquitos (in two separate strikes) to bomb Kiel, the last of 1,457 sorties despatched since the unit first formed. On 20 September 1945 the Squadron was disbanded at Gransden Lodge.

Main bases

Graveley	January 1944
Gransden Lodge	June 1945

Aircraft examples flown

DZ478, 'L'; DZ534, 'M'; DZ547; DZ611; DZ637, 'C'; DZ647, 'B'; DZ650, 'L'; ML940; ML942; ML959, 'G'; ML963; ML966, '?'; ML969; ML970, 'O'; ML971; ML977; MM118; MM128; MM129; MM133, 'D'; MM135; MM141; MM143; MM149; MM150; MM172, 'V'; MM183, 'A'; MM224; PF383; PF384; PF388, 'C'; PF392, 'R'; PF397, '?'; PF400, 'M'; PF414, 'P'; PF430, 'T'; PF441, 'B'; PF445, 'A'; PF448, 'F'; PF450; PF455, '?'; PF456, 'J'; RV310, 'S'; RV311, 'Q'; RV312, 'X'; RV318, 'H'; RV320.

Commanding Officers

Wg Cdr W. G. Lockhart DSO, DFC	January 1944
Wg Cdr S. D. Watts DFC	March 1944
Wg Cdr J. Northrop DFC, AFC	July 1944

Left:
MM133, 'D' (Flt Lt J. A. R. Leask) on its return from Berlin on 24 March 1945 — Leask's first operational sortie with 692 Squadron.
J. A. R. Leask, DFC

Above:
MM133, 'D' of 692 Squadron before the Berlin sortie, March 1945. This aircraft later went to the Netherlands. *J. A. R. Leask, DFC*

Mozzie Miscellany

Above:
W4051, 'LY-U', of No 1 PRU, which was the prototype PR version of the Mosquito.

Below:
NFXVII, DZ659, 'ZQ-H' of the Fighter Interception Unit (FIU), in October 1944.
via RAF Museum

Above:
FBVI, HR242, 'FMO-W' of No 204 AFS, Driffield. *via R. C. Sturtivant*

Below:
TT35, TJ154 at the Sylt Armament Practice Station (APS). *via R. C. Sturtivant*

Above:
Mosquitos of No 1655 MTU (part of 16 OTU), Cottesmore. 'GA-F' at right was RR292.

Below:
TA634 of No 3 CAACU, Exeter.

Above right:
FBVI, NT206, '9Y-AX' of 132 OTU, East Fortune. *R. C. B. Ashworth*

Below right:
TT35, RV365 of No 233 OCU. *J. D. R. Rawlings*

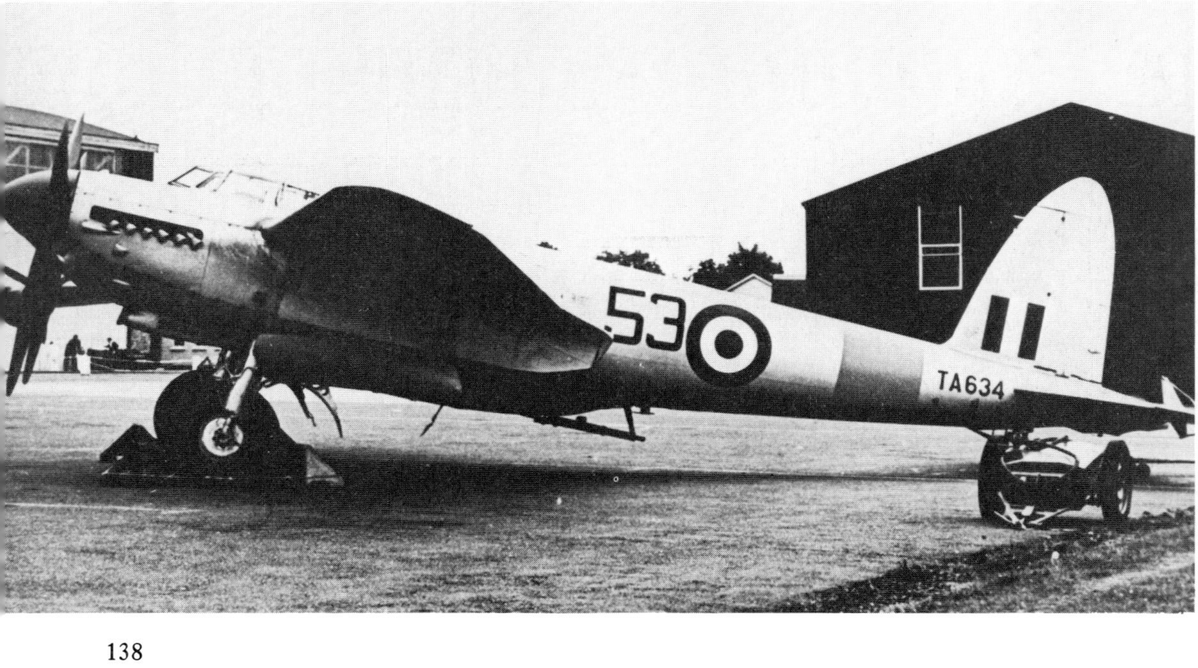

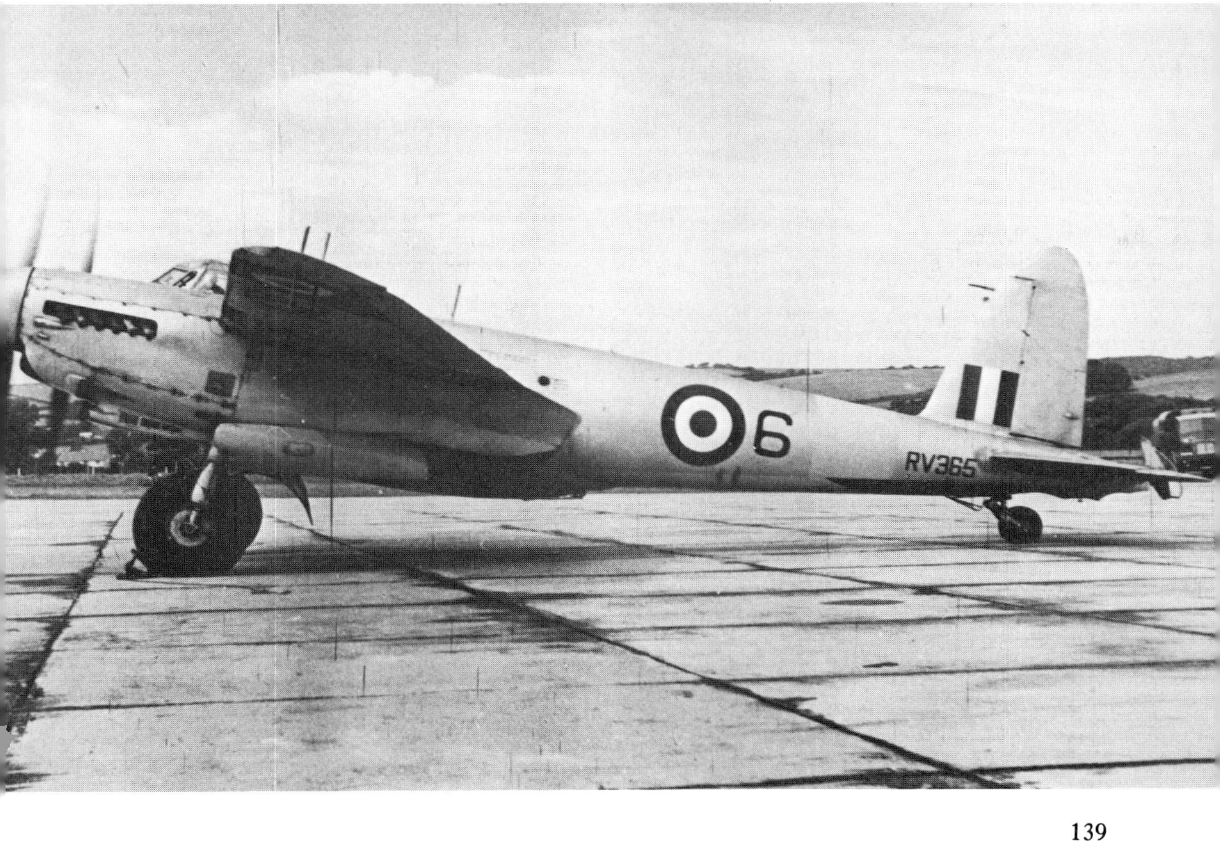

Above:
One of BOAC's converted (unarmed) FBVIs, G-AGGD (ex-HJ681), which was delivered to the airline in April 1943.

Below:
ATA pilots waiting to ferry production nightfighters on 12 February 1942. From left: Cdr F. Francis, Capt F. White, Cdr 'Doc' Whitehurst, Flt Capt Dlugaszewski, Flt Capt Jim Mollison (the prewar record flier), and Flt Capt Bill Harben (ranks given being those eventually achieved).   *Hawker Siddeley Aviation*

Appendix 1 — Service Use

Mosquito Squadrons under RAF Control
Nos 4, 8, 13, 14, 16, 18, 21, 22, 23, 25, 27, 29, 36, 39, 45, 46, 47, 55, 58, 68, 69, 81, 82, 84, 85, 89, 96, 98, 105, 107, 108, 109, 110, 114, 125, 128, 139, 140, 141, 142, 143, 151, 157, 162, 163, 169, 176, 180, 192, 199, 211, 219, 235, 239, 248, 249, 254, 255, 256, 264, 268, 305 (Polish), 307 (Polish), 333 (Norwegian), 334 (Norwegian), 400 RCAF, 404 RCAF, 406 RCAF, 409 RCAF, 410 RCAF, 418 RCAF, 456 RAAF, 464 RAAF, 487 RNZAF, 488 RNZAF, 489 RNZAF, 500 RAuxAF, 502 RAuxAF, 504 RAuxAF, 515, 521, 527, 540, 543, 544, 571, 578, 600 AAF, 604 AAF, 605 RAuxAF, 608 RAuxAF, 609 RAuxAF, 613 AAF, 616 RAuxAF, 617, 618, 627, 680, 681, 683, 684 and 692.

Principal Mosquito Training and Miscellaneous Units (RAF)
Operational Training Units (OTUs): Nos 6, 8, 13, 16, 51, 54, 60 and 132
Operational Conversion Units (OCUs): Nos 226, 228, 229, 231 and 237
Flights: Nos 1300, 1317, 1401, 1409, 1474 and 1692 (BST)
No 1672 Mosquito Conversion Unit (MCU)
No 1655 Mosquito Training Unit (MTU)
No 1660 Conversion Unit (CU)
No 204 Advanced Flying School (AFS)
Bomber Support Development Unit (BSDU)
Bombing Trials Unit
Central Bomber Establishment

Armament Practice School (APS)
Path Finder Navigation Training Unit (PFFNTU)
Central Gunnery School
Central Fighter Establishment
Fighter Interception Unit (FIU)
Air Torpedo Development Unit (ATDU)
Empire Air Armament School (EAAS)
Bomber Development Unit
Central Signals Establishment
Signals Flying Unit
Special Installation Unit
Photographic Development Unit
No 1 Photographic Reconnaissance Unit (PRU)
Empire Test Pilots School

RN Squadrons
Nos 728, 762, 771, 790 and 811

RAAF Squadrons (Australia)
Nos 1, 87 and 94; No 5 OTU

SAAF (under RAF Control)
No 60 Squadron

RCAF (in Canada)
No 13 Squadron

Foreign Air Forces (Postwar)
Belgium; China; Czechoslovakia; Dominican Republic; France; Israel; New Zealand; Norway; Sweden; Turkey; Yugoslavia.

Appendix 2 — Squadron Codes

Squadron	Codes	Squadron	Codes	Squadron	Codes
4	NC:UP	125	VA	410	RA
8	HV	128	M5	418	TH
11	OM	139	XD	456	RX
13	—	140	—	464	SB
14	CX	141	TW	487	EG
16	EG	142	4H	488	ME
18	WV	143	NE	489	P6
21	YH	151	DZ	500	RAA
22	—	157	RS	502	RAC
23	YP	162	CR	504	RAD
25	ZK	163	—	515	3P
27	—	169	VI	521	—
29	RO	176	—	527	WN
36	—	180	EV	540	DH
39	—	192	DT	543	—
45	OB	199	—	544	—
46	—	211	—	571	8K
47	KU	219	FK	578	—
55	—	235	LA	600	BQ
58	OT	239	HB	604	NG
68	WM	248	DM:WR	605	UP:RAL
69	WI	249	GN	608	6T:RAO
81	—	254	QM	609	RAP
82	UX	255	YD	613	SY
84	PY	256	JT	616	RAW
85	VY	264	PS	617	—
89	—	268	EG	618	—
96	ZJ	305	SM	627	AZ
98	VO	307	EW	680	—
105	GB	333	KK	681	—
107	OM	334	VB	683	—
108	—	400	—	684	—
109	HS	404	EO	692	P3
110	VE	406	HU	60 SAAF	—
114	RT	409	KP		

Appendix 3 — RAF Mosquito Operations — Miscellaneous Statistics

Certain figures quoted below should not be regarded as complete, due simply to the fact that many contemporary official records are either incomplete, semi-ambiguous in interpretation, and/or seldom related in conclusions. Cases in point are the figures for bomb tonnages dropped which, for obvious reasons, can only apply to Mosquitos which returned from operations; there being no way that accurate figures can be ascertained for the fate of bomb loads carried by aircraft which failed to return. Thus such figures quoted here must be regarded as minimums only.

Bomber Command

Total sorties flown	39,795
Total casualties (aircraft) to enemy action	289
Bomb tonnage dropped	26,867*

*This gross tonnage exceeded the *total* bomb tonnage dropped in Bomber Command by Blenheims, Battles, Bostons, Mitchells, Venturas, Hampdens, Whitleys, Manchesters, and B-17 Fortresses collectively throughout the entire war. Moreover, this Mosquito tonnage was under 1,000 tons less than the equivalent figure for Stirlings.

Within the aegis of Bomber Command, the following figures are inclusive.

No 8 (PFF) Group

Sorties flown	26,255
Losses (aircraft) to enemy action	108
Total 4,000lb HC 'Cookie' bombs dropped	approx 10,000

No 100 Group

Sorties flown	7,884
Losses (aircraft) to enemy action	69
Enemy aircraft shot down	249
Enemy aircraft destroyed on ground	18

In addition to Bomber Command

No 2 Group

Sorties flown	18,975
Losses (aircraft) to enemy action	at least 237

Selected 'Veteran' Mosquitos

Aircraft	Total Sorties	Units
LR503	213	109 and 105 Sqns
LR504	200	109 Sqn
ML897	161	1409 Flt
LR507	148	105 Sqn
ML914	148	105 Sqn
ML922	111	105 Sqn
LR385	104	21 and 487 Sqns
DZ319	102	109 Sqn
DK331	100	109 Sqn
LR508	96	105 Sqn
LR422	69	540 Sqn

Principal Mosquito Marks

Mk	First Deliveries	Unit	First Operations
PR1	13 July 1941	1 PRU, Benson	17 September 1941
FII	9 March 1942	157 Sqn	27 April 1942
BIV	11 April 1942	1 PRU, Benson	31 May 1942 (by No 105 Sqn)
FBVI	18 February 1943	418 Sqn RCAF	7 May 1943
BIX	21 April 1943	109 Sqn	11/12 June 1943
PRIX	29 May 1943	540 Sqn	20 June 1943
NFXII	28 February 1943	85 Sqn	24 March 1943
BXVI	10 December 1943	109 Sqn	5 March 1944 (by No 692 Sqn)
PRXVI	December 1943	140 and 400 Sqns	4 February 1944 (by No 140 Sqn)
FBXVIII	22 October 1943	248 Sqn	24 October 1943
NFXIX	21 April 1944	85 Sqn	5/6 June 1944
BXX	11 November 1943	139 Sqn	2 December 1943
NFXXX	13 June 1944	219 Sqn	21 June 1944

Appendix 4 — Select Mosquito Bibliography

The international fame and prowess of the Mosquito is reflected in the continuing publication of books, features, etc, even today. The following published references therefore must be regarded as a personal selection by this author only, and in no way any comprehensive listing.

De Havilland Aircraft Since 1909: A. J. Jackson; Putnam, 1978

Mosquito: Sharp/Bowyer; Faber, 1967

Mosquito: P. Birtles; Jane's, 1980

Mosquito Monograph: D. Vincent; Private, 1982

DH Mosquito: M. Hardy; David & Charles, 1977

Mosquito at War: C. Bowyer; Ian Allan, 1973

The Wooden Wonder: E. Bishop; Parrish, 1959

Aircraft of the RAF since 1918: O. Thetford; Putnam, 1976

Famous Bombers of the WW2: W. Green, Macdonalds, 1959

DH Mosquito: Aircam No 28; Osprey, 1972

DH Mosquito Mks I-IV: Profile No 52

DH Mosquito Fighters: R. C. Jones; Ducimus

DH Mosquito Crash Log: D. J. Smith; MC Pubs, 1980

'The Wooden Wonder': *Wings*, Pt 39; Orbis, 1977

'Mosquito Genetics': *Flight*, 20 April 1944

'Mosquito Fighter-bombers': *Flight*, 7 September 1944

'Mosquitos of the 8th USAAF': *Flight*, 22 February 1945

'The Mosquito': *Flight*, 6 May 1943

'The De Havilland Mosquito': *Aeroplane*, 7 May 1943

'A Fighting Mosquito Squadron': *Aeroplane*, 21 May 1943

'Mosquito IV Details': *Aeroplane*, 2 July 1943

'Mosquito Versatility': *Flight*, 11 November 1943

'Mosquito Squadron': *Flight*, 9 December 1943

'Mosquito Squadron': *Flight*, 14 January 1943

RAF Bombers of WW2, Vol 1: P. Moyes; Hylton Lacy, 1968

Low Attack: J. Wooldridge; Sampson Low, 1944

Defence Until Dawn: L. Hunt; Private, 1949

2nd Tactical Air Force: C. Shores; Osprey, 1970

2 Group, RAF: M. J. F. Bowyer; Faber, 1974

Bomber Squadrons of the RAF: P. Moyes; Macdonalds, 1964

Fighter Squadrons of the RAF: J. Rawlings; Macdonalds, 1969

Coastal & Support Squadrons of the RAF: J. Rawlings; Jane's, 1982

RCAF Squadrons: Kostenuk/Griffith; Canada, 1977

Pathfinder Force: G. Musgrove; Macdonald & Jane's, 1976

Path Finders at War: C. Bowyer; Ian Allan, 1977

Coastal Command at War: C. Bowyer; Ian Allan, 1979

Bomber Group at War: C. Bowyer; Ian Allan, 1981

Photo-Reconnaissance: A. Brookes; Ian Allan, 1975

Fighter Squadron at War: A. Brookes; Ian Allan, 1980

Scramble: J. Braham; Muller, 1961

Night Flyer: L. Brandon; Kimber, 1961

Night Fighter: Rawnsley/Wright; Collins, 1957

Night Intruder: J. Howard-Williams; David & Charles, 1976

Wings of Night: A. Hamilton; Kimber, 1977

The Gates Burst Open: Livry-Lemel/Remy; Arco, 1955

The Sixth Floor: R. Reilly; Frewin, 1969

Mission Completed: Sir B. Embry; Methuen, 1957

Battle-Axe: D. Ransom; Air Britain, 1968